THE HERB-LOVER'S
RECIPE BOOK

THE HERB-LOVER'S RECIPE BOOK

150 delectable ideas for cooking with herbs,
shown in over 500 photographs

JOANNA FARROW

greene&golden

This edition is published by greene&golden, an imprint of Anness Publishing Ltd, Blaby Road, Wigston, Leicestershire LE18 4SE; info@anness.com

www.annesspublishing.com

If you like the images in this book and would like to investigate using them for publishing, promotions or advertising, please visit our website www.practicalpictures.com for more information.

Publisher: Joanna Lorenz
Managing Editor: Helen Sudell
Project Editor: Simona Hill
Copy Editor: Jan Cutler
Designer: Nigel Partridge
Production Controller: Wendy Lawson

PUBLISHER'S NOTE
Although the advice and information in this book are believed to be accurate and true at the time of going to press, neither the authors nor the publisher can accept any legal responsibility or liability for any errors or omissions that may have been made nor for any inaccuracies nor for any loss, harm or injury that comes about from following instructions or advice in this book.

ACKNOWLEDGEMENTS

Photographers: Karl Adamson, Edward Allwright, Steve Baxter, Nicki Dowey, James Duncan, Gus Filgate, John Freeman, Ian Garlick, Michelle Garrett, Peter Henley, John Heseltine, Amanda Heywood, Janine Hosegood, Andrea Jones, Dave Jordan, Dave King, Don Last, William Lingwood, Patrick McLeavey, Michael Michaels, Steve Moss, Thomas Odulate, Debbie Patterson, Craig Robertson, Sam Stowell, Polly Wreford.

Recipes: Catherine Atkinson, Alex Barker, Angela Boggiano, Ruby Le Bois, Carla Capalbo, Lesley Chamberlain, Kit Chan, Jacqueline Clarke, Maxine Clark Cleary, Frances Cleary, Carole Clements, Andi Clevely, Trish Davies, Roz Denny, Patrizia Diemling, Stephanie Donaldson, Matthew Drennan, Joanna Farrow, Rafi Fernandez, Christine France, Silvano Franco, Sarah Gates, Shirley Gill, Brian Glover, Nicola Graimes, Rosamund Grant, Juliet Harbutt, Jessica Houdret, Deh-Ta Hsiung, Shehzad Hussain, Christine Ingram, Judy Jackson, Peter Jordan, Manisha Kanini, Soheila Kimberley, Lucy Knox, Masaki Ko, Sara Lewis, Patricia Lousada, Gilly Love, Norma MacMillan,Sue Maggs, Sally Mansfield, Maggie Mayhew, Norma Miller, Sallie Morris, Janice Murfitt, Annie Nichols, Elizabeth Lambert Oritz, Katherine Richmond, Anne Sheasby, Jenni Shapter, Liz Trigg, Hilaire Walden, Laura Washburn, Stuart Walton, Steven Wheeler, Kate Whiteman, Elizabeth Wolf-Cohen, Jenni Wright.

Stylists: Alison Austin, Shannon Beare, Madeleine Brehaut, Frances Cleary, Tessa Evelegh, Marilyn Forbes, Annabel Ford, Nicola Fowler, Michelle Garrett, Carole Handslip, Cara Hobday, Kate Jay, Maria Kelly, Lucy McKelvie, Marion McLornan, Marion Price, Jane Stevenson, Helen Trent, Sophie Wheeler, Judy Williams, Elizabeth Wolf-Cohen.

Home Economists: Eliza Baird, Alex Barker, Julie Beresford, Sascha Brodie, Stephanie England, Annabel Ford, Christine France, Carole Handslip, Kate Jay, Jill Jones, Clare Lewis, Sara Lewis, Bridget Sargeson, Joy Skipper, Jenni Shapter, Carole Tennant.

NOTES

For all recipes, quantities are given in both metric and imperial measures and, where appropriate, measures are also given in standard cups and spoons. Follow one set, but not a mixture because they are not interchangeable.

Standard spoon and cup measures are level.
1 tsp = 5ml, 1 tbsp = 15ml, 1 cup = 250ml/8fl oz

Australian standard tablespoons are 20ml. Australian readers should use 3 tsp in place of 1 tbsp for measuring small quantities of gelatine, cornflour, salt etc.

Medium (US large) eggs are used unless otherwise stated

CONTENTS

INTRODUCTION

For centuries, herbs have been prized all over the world for their remarkable seasoning qualities. This book celebrates those special characteristics, which can transform a collection of foods into something quite delicious and irresistible.

In addition to being a veritable cornucopia of enticing recipes that encompass every type of dish, this book reveals how herbs can be used to flavour oils, teas, drinks, pickles, sauces, dips, butters, cheeses, condiments and sugars. It also includes information on growing, harvesting and preparing herbs as well as a directory of some of the most popular.

GROWING AND USING HERBS

With a little careful planning, starting a herb garden is well within the capability of even inexperienced gardeners, and once established, herbs are fairly undemanding plants to grow. They are generally not too fussy as to soil type, and require little special treatment or heavy digging, yet the pleasure that is derived from them is enormous. Visually, the muted, dusky colours and pretty, delicate flowers create a hazy, romantic atmosphere that provides so much pleasure for the gardener, particularly towards the end of a warm summer's day when their aromatic scents waft through the air. Then there is the pleasure of cooking with herbs to enhance the taste of your everyday cuisine. Whatever you choose to serve, be it fish or meat dishes, salads and soups, even desserts and ice creams — all can be improved with the addition of a generous sprinkling of herbs.

HERB GARDENS

Whatever the size and site of your garden, if you love cooking you will always be able to find a small corner of the garden near the kitchen in which to grow a ready supply of favourite herbs for use in the cooking pot.

PLANNING A HERB GARDEN

Before planting out, it's worth spending a little time planning the herb garden. There are no fixed rules as to what to start with and how much to grow. As with any gardening there is a certain amount of trial and error. Not every herb will grow well in every garden and it may well take a couple of seasons to determine which grow most successfully. You will also need to consider the type of garden you want

Below: Formal herb gardens contained within clipped borders require careful planning and cultivation.

to develop. A formal garden that uses plants as edging takes a few years to mature whereas a brick or gravel-surrounded bed will look pretty within a season, and herbs grown in containers look effective within weeks. There is no correct time of year to start the garden, although planting the herbs out in the spring allows plenty of time for them to develop.

Many herbs such as rosemary, marjoram, oregano, sage and thyme enjoy maximum sunshine, while others, like mint, chervil and chives, prefer partial shade. Generally they all need protection from the wind and this can be provided by low hedges, walls, fences and taller bushes and shrubs. Most herbs prefer a well-drained soil,

Right: Herb gardens cultivated for culinary use can be laid out in an attractive, colourful and formal design.

particularly those of Mediterranean origin. To lighten a heavy clay soil, work in some sand and/or grit from a garden centre (not builder's sand) before planting out.

Below: A clipped bay surrounded by colourful lavender makes a glorious, scented centrepiece for this garden. Both plants have many uses in the kitchen.

Leafy herbs grown solely for culinary use can be successfully grown in surprisingly little space, such as a small bed, container, hanging basket or, if space is really at a premium, indoors on a window sill. Alternatively, grow them in amongst other border plants.

Remember that accessibility is very important. You do not want to go traipsing through wet grass or soil to gather herbs for cooking, so plant them in the most convenient spot nearest to the kitchen. The more common, most frequently used herbs can be planted near the front of the plot while those rarely used can flourish in a more out-of-the-way spot. Stepping stones and small brick or gravel paths can be laid so that you can easily get to less accessible herbs.

Annual herbs like chervil, coriander (cilantro), basil and dill will die down at the end of the season and need replanting the following spring. It is worth distributing these amongst perennial herbs like chives, marjoram, oregano, sage, thyme, rosemary, fennel and parsley, which start to thrive very early in the spring following mild winters.

Some herbs like mint, borage and chives have a tendency to spread

Above: Herbs planted in-between paving stones and along paths make good use of limited space.

vigorously. These are best planted in separate containers so they don't monopolize the whole plot. If you want to grow mint with the other herbs, use a bucket with holes in the base and submerge it in the plot as a way of containing the mint's growth. Do not be tempted to grow too many different types of herbs to start with. You can always add more the following season.

Herb Borders

When space is limited, a small border or bed of herbs meets most culinary requirements, even if interspersed with other non-herbal plants. If there is simply insufficient space, supplement it with additional tubs or containers on the patio or near the kitchen door.

Plant taller herbs such as lovage, bay, fennel and angelica at the back of the plot with smaller herbs at the front, to create an interesting height graduation. If the plot is wide, disperse stepping stones or bricks into the soil to make the herbs at the back more accessible.

Another idea is to create a graduated rockery which also provides easy access to all the herbs. This looks particularly attractive for sun-loving herbs that thrive in hot climates. Once planted amongst the rocks, the soil can be scattered with scree (small irregular rocks of about 2–5cm/¾–2in).

Above: This herb wheel makes a splendid focal point for a large garden.

Herb Wheels

These were a popular feature in Victorian gardens when large wooden cartwheels were widely available. They provide a great way of containing a small selection of leafy culinary herbs. Before use, the wheel must be treated with a plant-friendly preservative to stop the wood from rotting. It is then set down on the prepared plot so the spaces between the spokes can be filled with different herbs. Simply saw off some of the spokes if they are too close together.

The same idea can be created using bricks. This has the added advantage that the herb garden can be designed to a size that suits the garden space and culinary requirements. The choice of herbs is entirely dependent upon individual preference, but aesthetically a selection of low-growing herbs of similar heights looks very effective around the edges, perhaps with a taller plant in the centre.

Island Beds

Planting herbs in a round or rectangular island bed provides easy access and can be designed to fit any available space. In larger beds lay narrow paths through the plot to separate the different herbs and prevent invasive herbs growing into the others. A wide brick or gravel path makes an attractive, practical surround. As with all herb gardens, plant the taller herbs to create a backdrop against the others. A bay tree makes an impressive focal point in the centre of the bed. Alternatively, use a large and attractive urn or garden pot, planted with a small bay, lavender or rose bush.

Right: Elizabethan knot gardens, made up of perfectly manicured box hedging, help keep herbs and flowers neatly compartmentalized in the garden.

Formal Box-edged Garden

This is the most ambitious type of herb garden. You will need at least a 4m/13ft-square area of flat space, and the garden will take several years for the box edging to mature. A simple box-edged garden can be divided into four small beds, separated by two paths which cross over in the centre. The corners of the beds can be cut away in the centre to allow for a large potted centrepiece such as a small bay or lavender bush. Plant the young box plants fairly closely together around the edges of the beds so they grow together for trimming into a tightly clipped "wall".

Raised Herb Bed

These are ideal for small gardens where there is little or no planting area, such as in a small courtyard, or where the soil is unsuitable. This is often the case with gardens on heavy clay that many herbs dislike. A raised herb bed can be built to any shape or size in timber or stone, or, more formally, using a brickwork frame. Raised garden beds can also make gardening easier for the disabled or elderly, as the planting, tending and gathering becomes so much more manageable and easily contained. The height of a raised bed is a matter of personal preference; they can be any height from about 30–45cm/12–18in.

Timber Beds

These can be built to any height, and composed of flat planks or narrow, halved tree trunks, secured into box shapes at the corners. Before using any timber, treat with a wood preservative that is suitable for plants.

Stone Beds

Beds walled with two or three layers of rustic stone look really effective and make a simple way of containing herbs in a small or narrow bed.

Brick Beds

These are both durable and attractive, particularly if made using old bricks. Check they are frostproof as ordinary house bricks might not be suitable. Thoroughly consider the site, shape and size of the bed before starting work. They can be laid out as functional squares or rectangles, in decorative shapes, or made to fit a corner of the garden.

Left: This island bed has paths through the centre to ensure easy access to all the herbs.

MAKING A RAISED BED

Raised beds can be laid out as functional squares and rectangles or made to fit a corner of the garden.

YOU WILL NEED
>   dowel, string, fine sand and builder's
>   set square
>   concrete made of one part cement to
>   four parts ballast
>   bricks
>   mortar made of one part cement
>   to four parts of sharp or
>   builder's sand
>   waterproof paint
>   rubble
>   gravel or pea shingle (pea stone)
>   topsoil
>   potting compost (soil mix)

1 Mark out the shape of the bed on the ground, using dowel and string. Use a builder's set square to mark the right angles. Define the lines with a dribble of fine sand.

2 Dig out the soil along the markings to a depth and width of 15cm/6in. Fill in with concrete to within 5cm/2in of the top. Firm down, level and leave for 24 hours to set.

3 Build up four or five courses of bricks and set into mortar, checking frequently with a spirit level.

4 Tidy up the mortar around the edges while still wet, using a pointing trowel. Leave to harden.

5 Coat the inside wall with waterproof paint. Put in a layer of rubble, then gravel or pea shingle for drainage.

6 Fill in with topsoil and add a top layer of a potting compost. Plant up the bed with your chosen herbs.

GROWING LEAFY HERBS IN CONTAINERS

Most herbs grow very well in containers, and there is a wide variety to choose from. A collection of several containers of different materials and shapes makes an attractive display on the patio. Do not choose anything too large if you want to be able to move pots around, for example, when you want to bring them into a sheltered position during the winter.

For convenience, several different herbs can be grown in one container, but bear in mind that they are not all compatible. Mint and parsley do not grow well together and fennel does not mix with caraway, dill or coriander (cilantro). Mint, tarragon and chives are best grown in separate containers as they will stifle any other herbs they are mixed with. Some herbs, like rosemary, thyme, marjoram and sage, like a sunny spot, while mint, chervil and chives prefer a more filtered light.

During the spring and summer months all container-grown herbs need daily watering, particularly those grown in very small pots, as they can dry out in a matter of hours. However, do not be tempted to overwater any herbs. The soil should never become waterlogged.

Growing Herbs in Pots

Whatever type of pot you choose make sure there is a hole in the base for drainage. Fill the base with a layer of broken terracotta or stones and then a layer of grit or sand before filling with potting compost (soil mix). Once the herbs have been planted and watered, raise the container off the ground using wooden battens or clay pot supports to free the drainage holes and prevent clogging.

Hanging Baskets

These look lovely filled with a mixture of upright and trailing herbs. Go for sturdy herbs such as sage, thyme, curled parsley and rosemary. Before filling with compost (soil mix), line the basket with moss to stop the compost falling through. Soak the moss and compost well before planting by standing the basket in a large container of water. Avoid hanging the basket in a very exposed area.

Above: Herbs are ideal plants to grow on the kitchen windowsill.

Growing Herbs Indoors

Most culinary herbs will thrive indoors provided they are sited in a light and sunny position and enjoy a fairly humid environment, away from central heating and severe temperature extremes. Indoor herbs benefit from being grown collectively because of the massed humidity.

Indoor herbs are less likely to grow into bushy, thriving plants because they are growing in a less natural environment. One way to overcome this problem is to alternate pots grown on the windowsill with some kept outside. Choose as large a pot as you can to fit the space available. Basil is one of the most successful herbs to grow indoors

as it is protected from garden pests which often decimate it outside. Care must be taken not to overuse indoor herbs, otherwise the plant will die from loss of foliage.

Below: Herbs in pots add immediate colour and impact to the garden.

HARVESTING, DRYING AND STORING HERBS

In summer when herbs are plentiful, harvest them for using fresh, but also consider picking a supply to preserve for use later in the year. Not all herbs are worth drying though, since some flavours deteriorate with storage.

HARVESTING HERBS

Whatever time of the day you manage to pick herbs for cooking or preserving, their wonderful, aromatic flavour will be sure to enhance the simplest of dishes. Ideally however, herbs are best harvested during the morning, after the dew has evaporated but before the heat of the sun has warmed them. Until then their volatile oils, which provide maximum flavour, are at their most concentrated. As the day progresses the oils start to evaporate into the atmosphere, giving the herb garden such a wonderful fragrance later in the day. Unless you are going to use them immediately, avoid harvesting herbs while it is raining or while they are still wet.

Herb leaves have their most pronounced flavour just before they start to flower, as both the flowers and seeds gradually drain the flavour from the leaves. When picking, try to chop the ends from the straggly stems to keep the plant pruned into a compact, bushy shape. For perennials, particularly young ones or any that have recently been planted, do not pick more than about 10 per cent of the growth so the plants can quickly re-establish themselves.

Below: Twist the leaves of the garlic around string and store in bunches.

Above: Dried bay leaves can be attractively displayed as a wreath.

HARVESTING FLOWERS

Most herb flowers used for cooking or garnishing should be picked when fully opened. Lavender flowers, however, are best picked just as they start to bloom. With all herb flowers, harvest just before they are needed as they tend to wilt quickly, particularly on a warm day and when they are dry.

HARVESTING SEEDS

Seeds from herbs can be harvested for cooking, preserving or replanting. Choose a dry day and snip the entire seed-head into a paper bag. Put in a warm place so that the seeds drop into the bag as they dry. Transfer to a small jar, or, if they are for next season's crop, label the bag and store in a dark, dry place until the spring.

If you have a large herb garden and can afford to gather generous bunches for a constant supply, keep them indoors in a jug (pitcher) or bowl of cold water until you are ready to use them. Replace them as soon as they start to look limp and bedraggled.

DRYING HERBS

Although we tend to consider fresh herbs have a far superior flavour to dried, properly preserved dried herbs

Above: Pick herbs in the morning to help retain the best flavour, tie in bunches and hang up to dry in a warm, dry place out of the sun.

make an excellent substitute for fresh once the plants have died down. Indeed, dried mint is a popular ingredient in some Middle Eastern recipes and dried Greek oregano is often preferred to the fresh for many dishes. Bear in mind when cooking with dried herbs that the flavour is much more concentrated. You will only need about a third of the quantity of dried when substituting for fresh.

Traditionally, herbs for drying were tied in large bunches and left to hang upside-down in the warmth of the kitchen. While this looks attractive and certainly works for short-term use, the herbs will gradually gather dust and moisture from the atmosphere. A very hot kitchen will also destroy the flavour. Better results are achieved by drying herbs on trays or wire racks in a warm place such as an airing cupboard or the oven plate-warming drawer, but definitely not in the sun! Robust herbs

like sage, bay, thyme, oregano, marjoram, mint and rosemary are particularly suited to drying. After a day or two the leaves should be brittle and dry enough to crumble into jars. Cover with lids or cork stoppers and store in a cool, dark place.

FREEZING HERBS

Delicate herbs like basil, parsley, chervil, dill and tarragon are best preserved by freezing. Chop the freshly picked herbs, pack measured quantities in tiny plastic bags and freeze immediately, to preserve maximum flavour. If preferred, basil leaves can be picked from their stems and frozen in a thin layer in a larger bag. You can also make up little bouquet garnis of mixed herbs combining sprigs of bay, parsley and thyme or mixtures of herbs suitable for tomato sauce and pasta dishes. A *fines herbes* blend of parsley, chives, tarragon and chervil is ideal for egg, fish and chicken dishes.

Store all the little bags in a suitable container so that they do not slip to the bottom of the freezer.

SALTED HERBS

Before freezing became popular, herbs were often layered in salt, both to preserve the flavour of the herbs and to flavour the salt. If you would like to do this, use a wide-necked, lidded glass jar and layer the fresh herbs, chopped, or in sprigs, with coarse salt.

COOK'S TIP

Bottles and their lids must be washed and sterilized before using to avoid contaminating the contents. Put dry bottles in the oven set at 150°C/300°F/ Gas 2 for 15 minutes. Sterilize the tops by placing the whole bottle in a pan of water. Bring to the boil and boil for 15 minutes.

PREPARING LEAFY HERBS

There are several different ways of preparing leafy herbs. The technique used depends on the individual characteristic of the herb, its culinary use and whether it is fresh or dried.

Washing and Drying

Leafy herbs must be carefully washed and dried before use. Wash them under cold running water to dislodge any dirt or insects then shake them as dry as possible. To dry them completely place the leaves flat on a paper towel, cover with another one, then press gently. Alternatively leave them to dry on a wire rack.

Stripping Herbs from their Stems

For woody-stemmed herbs, the leaves can be stripped from the stems before use. Hold the sprig at the tip and strip off the leaves with a fork. This technique can also be used to remove the leaves from dried herb sprigs. Strip large leaves from the stems using your fingers. Discard the stems.

COOK'S TIP
If you are not ready to use a freshly picked herb immediately, submerge the cut ends in cold water and store in a cool place. Alternatively, you can wrap the leaves loosely in a plastic bag and chill in the refrigerator.

Above: A mezzaluna is useful for chopping large quantities of herbs.

Snipping

To prepare chives snip (chop) them directly into a container. Hold the stems in one hand and, using kitchen scissors, snip the chives into pieces.

Tearing

Soft, fragrant leaves like basil should be removed from the stalks and torn directly into the dish when used for salads, dressings and sauces. Basil should never be chopped with a knife or cut with scissors – this will bruise the leaves, removing the essential oils and will make the flavour of the herb bitter. Tearing will maintain the beautiful colour of the leaves, whereas chopping will blacken them. Pick the leaves from the plant at the last minute and add to the dish just before serving so that none of the delicious flavour is lost.

Chopping

Herbs can be chopped coarsely or finely depending on personal preference, and according to the dish they are to be used in. Remove any coarse stalks and gather the herbs into a tight clump with one hand while you chop with the other. Then chop with both hands on the knife until they are sufficiently fine.

Slicing

Large, soft-leafed herbs like lovage, sorrel, basil and rocket (arugula) can be finely sliced, either for garnishing or so that their flavours can be readily released into dishes such as salads, soups and sauces. Wash the leaves if necessary, pat them dry and remove the stalks. Stack them on top of one another and roll up tightly. Slice finely using a chopping knife.

Crumbling Dried Leaves

Once thoroughly dried and ready for storing, herbs should crumble readily between the fingers. Work over a sheet of paper or a small bowl. If the herbs are coarse, use a food processor, or put them in a small plastic bag and crush them with a rolling pin. Store the crumbled herbs in a dark container with a sealed lid. Keep in a cool place away from moisture.

Bruising

To release the flavour of any herbs into dishes that are cooked quickly, the herbs can be bruised first. Use a mortar and pestle to lightly crush the whole leaves or sprigs just before adding them to a dish.

Making a Bouquet Garni

A bouquet garni is useful when you want the flavour of the herbs but do not want them to show in the finished dish. A classic bouquet garni comprises parsley stalks, a sprig of thyme and a bay leaf tied together with string, although you can tailor the contents to suit your personal preference or the dish you are cooking, omitting some ingredients and adding more of others. Other vegetables or herbs you may like to include are a piece of celery stick for poultry dishes; a rosemary sprig for beef or lamb; or a piece of fennel or leek, or a strip of lemon zest, to flavour fish dishes.

1 Bundle the selection together and tie firmly with string.

Garnishing

Small sprigs, cut at the last minute from the tips of the herbs make pretty garnishes. Alternatively, pick the small whole leaves from herbs such as mint, basil and parsley and scatter over the dish just before serving, handling them as little as possible.

Once it has been used to flavour a soup, stew or casserole, fish it out with a spoon.

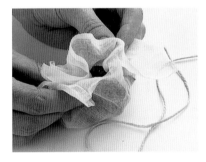

2 Another way to make a bouquet garni is to wrap the herbs in squares of muslin. This is a good choice where the herbs may be dried or crumble easily. Break or tear the herbs into small pieces and place in the centre of a 10–13cm/4–5in square of clean muslin. Bring the edges of the muslin up over the herbs and tie firmly into a bag with a length of string.

3 Use the string to tie the bundle to the pan handle, making it easy to remove. Make muslin bundles in batches so that they are readily at hand for cooking.

PREPARING VEGETABLE HERBS AND BULBS

The definition of what constitutes a herb is broad and wide-ranging. It is not just green leafy herbs such as parsley, rosemary, bay and thyme that we readily acknowledge as being herbs that fit the definition. It may be surprising to know that many vegetables such as cucumbers, peppers and artichokes, bulbs such as onions and garlic, flowers like marigolds, cowslip and lavender, seeds such as sunflower and poppy, and fruits such as fig and lemon, also fit under the broad umbrella of a herb. Paramount among these are members of the allium family – onions, shallots, garlic, spring onions (scallions) – and the capsicum family, notably (bell) peppers and chillies. Knowing how to prepare these commonly used ingredients will ensure the best results.

Seeding Chillies

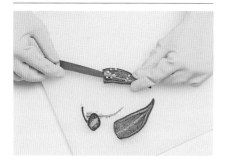

Slit the chilli lengthways, open it out then scoop out and discard the seeds. Raw chillies contain volatile oils which irritate sensitive skin such as lips and the area around the eyes, so take care when handling them. Either use protective gloves or make sure you wash your hands thoroughly afterwards. Alternatively, slice the chilli into fine rings and scatter over the dish.

Roasting Peppers

Peppers are such a versatile vegetable. They can be eaten raw in salads (washed, sliced and with the seeds removed), or cooked in many different ways, such as stuffed with a delicious filling of rice and vegetables. Roasting (broiling) peppers under the grill (broiler) brings out their natural sweet flavour more than any other method of cooking.

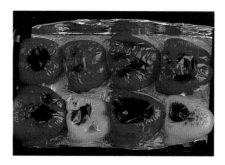

Cut the bell peppers in half and remove the seeds, membrane and stalk. Place on a baking sheet skin-side up and either cook under a hot grill, or in the oven until the skins are blackened. Remove from the heat.

USING GARLIC

Part of the allium family, garlic adds an unmistakable and delicious, pungent flavour to foods. It can also be eaten cooked or raw, although a little goes a long way. Most recipes call for just one or two cloves from the bulb to be used.

To break up the bulb, push the tip of a knife through the outer papery layer of the bulb between two cloves. Use the opening to lever the bulb apart. The cloves will come away easily.

Peeling Garlic Cloves

Each clove of garlic has a fine skin that must be removed. The easiest way to peel garlic is to place it on a chopping board and use the flat side of a wide-bladed knife to crush the clove. Place the blade flat on the clove and press it down firmly with your fist or the heel of your hand, breaking the skin of the garlic. The skin will then peel off easily. This also bruises the garlic, which allows the flavour to come out.

Chopping and Crushing Garlic

1 For a mild flavour, cut the garlic into thin slices, across the clove, or chop the clove roughly.

2 For a stronger flavour, crush the garlic rather than chop it. To make a paste you can use a mortar and pestle or a garlic press, or you can simply crush the garlic with the flat blade of a knife.

Roasting Garlic

Garlic can be roasted in much the same way as peppers, either by placing the whole bulb under a heat source or by placing the individual cloves under the heat. Roasting reduces the strength of flavour of the herb, leaving a sweetly aromatic herb. Once roasted, squeeze the garlic out of the skins for a delicious purée to add to salsas, dressings and dips.

Peeling Shallots

If you are peeling a lot of shallots, it is easier if you blanch them first in boiling water. Cut off the neck of each shallot and cut a thin slice off the bottom, but leave the root base intact. Place in a bowl and add enough boiling water to cover. Leave for about 3 minutes, drain, then slip the shallots out of their skins.

Peeling Onions

The easiest way to peel an onion is to cut off the top and bottom. Slit the skin and peel it off with your fingers.

Chopping Onions

Onions can be tricky to cut as they can slip about if you are not careful. First, slice the onion in half from top to bottom and place it cut-side down. Slice across the onion, leaving a small section uncut at the root end, then slice down through the onion at right angles to these cuts from neck to root.

Minty Fresh Breath
To stop your breath smelling after eating onions, try rubbing the soles of your feet with pure peppermint oil. Within 30 minutes the smell on your breath should be mint.

Above: To remove the smell of garlic from your hands, sprinkle them with salt, then rinse in cold water before washing them with hot water and soap.

Leave the root end uncut to prevent the onion falling apart. Slice across the onion at right angles to the second set of cuts.

Watering Eyes
Chopping onions makes you cry because this action releases the volatile chemicals that give onions their strength. An old wives' tale suggests that if you bite on a crust of bread while preparing onions, then you won't cry. Perhaps the crust forms a barrier to prevent the onion's water vapour from reaching your nose and eyes.

COOK'S TIP

It is unwise to prepare any members of the onion family too far in advance. Raw alliums can develop "off-flavours" due to sulphur compounds that are released when their cell walls are broken.

PREPARING AROMATIC INGREDIENTS

Aromatic spices, leafy herbs, seeds, flower petals, fruits and nuts all have their own distinct flavours that will add colour, texture, and vital flavour to food.

PREPARING SEEDS, SPICES AND NUTS

The seeds of many herbs are used in food preparation either whole, lightly crushed or ground into powder. They can also be gently roasted or dry-fried to enhance their flavour. Similarly, most nuts are available whole, chopped or ground, or, in the case of almonds, flaked (sliced), and they too can be roasted to emphasize their flavours.

Roasting Seeds

Seeds like coriander, mustard, fennel, cumin and caraway can be lightly roasted before crushing and using, to bring out their flavours. Heat a small, heavy pan over a moderate heat for about 1 minute. Add the seeds and dry-fry them, shaking the pan constantly for a couple of minutes until the aroma starts to rise. Watch the pan, as the seeds will soon start to burn.

Grinding Seeds and Nuts

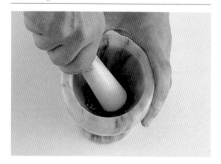

Although most herb and spice seeds can be purchased ready ground as powder, there is nothing quite so fragrant as the aroma of freshly ground

seeds. Small, easily ground seeds such as cumin, fennel and caraway can be crushed using a pestle and mortar. Place a small amount, about a tablespoon or two, in the mortar and grind in a circular motion. Some harder seeds, such as coriander, can be ground in a spice or pepper mill. Some people prefer to use a coffee grinder; grind the seeds in short bursts.

Grating Nutmeg

Nutmeg is widely available, both whole and ground, but as the flavour of the powder deteriorates quickly, it is worth buying a whole one and storing it in an airtight container. Grate (shred) the amount needed using a fine grater.

Chopping Nuts

Nuts are widely sold whole, chopped or ground and there is probably not much need to process them yourself. But if you do have a fresh supply and want to chop or grind them, do this in a food processor. The flavour will be so much better than commercially packed ones.

Roasting Nuts

Nuts, like seeds, can be roasted to accentuate their flavour. Place them in a pan over a moderate heat until lightly browned.

Infusing Saffron

Saffron threads are always infused in warm water before use to release their wonderful aroma and yellow colour. Warm a little water, add the saffron and leave to infuse (steep) for about 5 minutes. You can use both the strands and the liquid in the recipe.

Infusing Vanilla

Vanilla pods (beans) impart a sweet aromatic flavour to foods. They are generally used whole and most commonly in milk or sugar. To flavour sugar for use in custards and desserts, simply pour sugar into a clean, dry screwtop jar. Add a whole pod, then seal the jar. Leave for a few weeks before using.

To flavour milk and cream for use in ice creams and custards, add a whole vanilla pod to a pan of milk. Heat the milk with the vanilla pod until just boiling, then remove from the heat. (To intensify the flavour split the pod lengthways.) Cover and infuse for 10 minutes. Remove and discard the pod.

Savoury sauces can be infused in the same way, using herbs that complement the main ingredient – parsley sauce is the best known, although the herb remains in the sauce.

Preparing Fresh Root Ginger

This spice is one of the oldest cultivated and most popular medicinal herbs. Its unmistakable hot, fragrant and peppery taste is used in a huge variety of sweet and savoury dishes, such as tisanes, soups, stir-fries, curries, grains, desserts and cakes. More often than not it is ground ginger that is used in recipes, but finely grated (shredded) ginger can also be used.

1 Fresh root ginger is most easily peeled using a vegetable peeler or a small, sharp paring knife.

2 Chop ginger using a sharp knife to the size specified in the recipe.

3 Grate ginger finely – a box grater works well. Freshly grated ginger can also be squeezed to release the juice.

Above: Lavender flowers are one of the most versatile herbs.

FLOWERS

Many flowers add delicate flavour and beautiful colour to summer salads, desserts and cakes. Harvest herb flowers carefully as they tend to be delicate and only pick when dry or they will collapse. Gently pull the flowers from the stems.

Infusing Floral Herbs

Lavender flowers can be added to sugar in the same way as vanilla pods, or heated with liquid to impart their essential aroma.

HERB OILS AND VINEGARS

Flavouring culinary oils and vinegars with fresh herbs is an easy yet wonderful way to enjoy their flavours right through the winter months. They also make perfect gifts, presented in attractive bottles or jars. After making up bottles of oil, store in a cool place for at least a couple of weeks before use so that the herby flavours are absorbed, after which the flowers should be removed. Drain the oil through muslin, and pour the liquid into clean bottles, after which it will be good for three to six months. Herb oils are delicious for cooking chicken and fish, flavouring soups and breads and drizzling on to pizzas and roasted vegetables, while the vinegars add a refreshing tang to sauces and salad dressings and are great for zipping up syrupy desserts.

VARIATIONS

Mixed Herb Oils Try combining several herbs in one bottle. Rosemary, bay, thyme, marjoram and oregano are delicious together. Lemon, orange or lime slices add a refreshing tang to any of the combinations.

Spiced Herb Oils For a spicy flavour, add any of the following – cinnamon sticks, dried chillies, whole cloves, mace blades, cardamom pods, coriander seeds or peppercorns.

Garlic-infused Herb Oils Used sparingly, garlic adds a delicious flavour to oil. Peel several cloves, put in a small pan and just cover with the oil you are using for bottling. Poach very gently for about 25 minutes. Leave to cool then drain the garlic. Fill clean, dry bottles with the infused oil.

WARNING

There is some evidence that oils containing fresh herbs and spices can grow harmful moulds, especially once the bottle has been opened and the contents are not fully covered by the oil. To protect against this, it is recommended that the herbs and spices are removed once their flavour has passed to the oil.

HERB OILS

Strongly flavoured herbs such as thyme, bay, basil, rosemary, marjoram, oregano, sage and tarragon are particularly suited to flavouring oils, and in some cases the flowers work well too. Use a single herb or a mixture of two or more and add additional ingredients like garlic and chilli for a more robust flavour. Choose oils, like light olive oils, sunflower oil and grapeseed oil, that will not overpower the herbs. The paler the colour of the oil, the more the herbs will show through – worth bearing in mind if giving as presents. Once made for a couple of weeks, check the intensity of the flavour. If too indistinct (remember it will be further diluted once used in cooking) remove the sprigs and add fresh ones to the jar.

Aromatic Herb Oil

Use your favourite herb to flavour this delicious oil for use in salad dressings or for cooking.

MAKES ABOUT 600ML/1 PINT/2½ CUPS

INGREDIENTS
   Several large sprigs of rosemary, thyme, oregano, tarragon or sage
   4 bay leaves
   about 600ml/1 pint/2½ cups light olive oil or sunflower oil, or a mixture of the two

1 Wash the herbs and pat dry, discarding any damaged parts. Push the herbs down into clean, dry bottles so the tips face upwards. Don't cram too many into a small space.

2 Fill the bottles up to the necks with the oil and cover with the cork.

Basil Oil

When making basil oil the leaves can be lightly bruised to bring out the flavour. If you like, use garlic-infused (steeped) oil instead of natural olive oil for a delicious Mediterranean flavour.

MAKES 450ML/¾ PINT/ SCANT 2 CUPS

INGREDIENTS
   handful of basil leaves, about 15g/½ oz/½ cup
   450ml/¾ pint/scant 2 cups olive oil

1 Bruise the basil leaves lightly using a mortar and pestle, then stir in a little of the oil.

2 Transfer the mixture to a clean, dry bottle and pour over the remaining oil. Cover with a lid or cork and store in a cool place for 2–3 weeks.

3 To remove the basil leaves and replace with fresh sprigs for decoration, line a sieve with muslin and drain the oil into a jug (pitcher). Allow all the oil to soak through before removing the leaves from the sieve.

4 Discard and pour the oil back into the jar. Add fresh leaves. Cover with a lid or cork and store in a cool place.

Marjoram Flower Oil

Use this fragrant oil to cook an aromatic, vegetable-filled omelette or mix with breadcrumbs and garlic to top baked vegetables.

MAKES 450ML/¾ PINT/SCANT 2 CUPS

INGREDIENTS
30–40 marjoram flower clusters, clean, dry and free of insects
450ml/¾ pint/scant 2 cups olive oil

1 Fill a large, clean, dry jam jar with the flower clusters (do not worry about removing any small leaves).

2 Cover with the olive oil, making sure the flowers are submerged. Cover with a lid and leave in a warm place for two weeks, shaking the jar occasionally.

3 Line a small sieve with clean muslin or a coffee filter bag and position over a jug (pitcher). Use to strain the oil.

4 Pour the oil into a cleaned, attractive bottle with a 450ml/¾ pint/ scant 2 cups capacity. Cover with a lid or cork and store in a cool, dry place for 3–6 months.

Above: For very strong herbs such as chillies and garlic, use rich nut oils. For more delicate ones use light olive oil.

Below: Try any flowers that you have an abundance of. Thyme, rosemary, lavender, mint and basil are all delicious.

HERB VINEGARS

Many herbs and their flowers make delicious vinegars as their flavours are very readily absorbed. Basil, rosemary, thyme, bay, tarragon, dill, mint and even rose petals give good results. Red or white wine vinegar, sherry or cider vinegars all work equally well although a richly coloured, red wine vinegar might obscure the sprigs of herbs in the bottles. Do not use an untreated aluminium pan for heating the vinegar as it might impart a metallic taste.

Aromatic Vinegar

Garlic, lemon, bay and a good-quality vinegar provide a well-flavoured base for your choice of herb.

MAKES 600ML/1 PINT/2½ CUPS

INGREDIENTS
15ml/1 tbsp mixed peppercorns
2 lemon slices
4 garlic cloves, peeled
small handful of basil, rosemary, thyme or tarragon sprigs
3 bay leaves
600ml/1 pint/2½ cups good-quality vinegar

1 Put the peppercorns, lemon slices and garlic cloves into a clean, dry bottle with a capacity of about 600ml/1 pint/2½ cups. (Alternatively use two smaller bottles.)

2 Push herb sprigs into the bottles with the tips facing upwards. Add the bay leaves.

3 Fill the bottles up to the necks with the vinegar. Cover with a lid or cork and store in a cool place for 2 weeks, then remove the herbs.

Rosemary-infused Vinegar

Heating the vinegar for infusing (steeping) the herbs makes a strong-flavoured herb vinegar that is ready for almost immediate use.

MAKES 600ML/1 PINT/2½ CUPS

INGREDIENTS
600ml/1pint/2½ cups white wine or cider vinegar
90ml/6 tbsp chopped fresh rosemary, plus several whole sprigs

1 Bring the vinegar just to the boil in a large pan. Pour over the chopped rosemary in a bowl. Cover and leave to infuse (steep) for 3 days.

2 Strain the vinegar through a muslin-lined sieve into a large jug (pitcher). Pour into a 600ml/1 pint/2½ cup clean, dry bottle or two smaller bottles. Push several sprigs of rosemary, tips facing uppermost, into the bottle for decoration. Fit with a stopper or cork. Use immediately if you keep the herbs in the vinegar or store for up to 6 months without the herbs.

Below: Rosemary is one of the most useful culinary herbs.

Mint Flower Vinegar

This makes a lovely vinegar for a summery salad dressing.

MAKES 450ML/¾ PINT/SCANT 2 CUPS

INGREDIENTS
large handful of mint flowers with stems and leaves attached
450ml/¾pint/scant 2 cups white wine or cider vinegar
extra mint flowers for decoration

1 Put the flowers in a large, clean jar or a wide-necked bottle. Bring the vinegar to the boil, then pour over the flowers.

2 Cover and leave for 3 to 4 weeks. Remove the flowers and pour the vinegar into a clean 450ml/¾pint/scant 2 cup jar or bottle. (An empty vinegar bottle or pickle jar can also be used.) Fit with a lid or stopper and store in a cool place.

VARIATION
Spiced Herb Vinegar
Use a mixture of spices like cinnamon sticks, allspice berries, mace blades, cardamom pods and coriander or cumin seeds.

Thyme and Raspberry Vinegar

Fruit and herbs always make a delicious
marriage of flavours. This rich, sweet
and fragrant vinegar gives a summery
freshness to fruity salads and can be
used to deglaze the pan when making
game and poultry dishes.

MAKES 750ML/1¼ PINTS/3 CUPS

INGREDIENTS
  600ml/1 pint/2½ cups red wine
    vinegar
  15ml/1 tbsp pickling spice
  450g/1lb/2⅔ cups fresh raspberries
  small handful of fresh thyme sprigs,
    preferably lemon thyme

1 Put the vinegar and pickling spice into
a pan and heat gently for 5 minutes.
Put the raspberries in a bowl.

2 Pour the vinegar over the raspberries.
Stir in the thyme, then cover and leave
in a cool place to infuse (steep) for
2 days, stirring occasionally.

3 Remove the thyme sprigs and strain
the vinegar through a large plastic sieve
into a large jug (pitcher). Pour into
clean, dry bottles and seal with a
stopper or cork.

Rose-petal Vinegar

Use this delicately rose-flavoured
vinegar in a dressing for light
summer salads.

MAKES 300ML/½ PINT/1¼ CUPS

INGREDIENTS
  4 large red or pink unsprayed roses
  300ml/½ pint/1¼ cups white wine or
    cider vinegar
  rose petals, for decoration (optional)

1 Choose an unblemished rose, then
gently pull the rose petals from the
flower-heads. Scald the vinegar by
bringing it almost to boiling point. Allow
to cool.

Below: Rose-petal vinegar.

2 Chop off any damaged parts of the
petals and put the petals in a large,
clean, dry glass jar or bottle. Add
the cooled vinegar, cover with a stopper
or cork and store in a sunny position for
about three weeks before using.

3 Strain the vinegar into a clean jar and
discard the petals.

HERB TEAS AND TISANES

Well before the arrival of tea from China, people had discovered that infusing (steeping) the leaves, fruit and flowers of almost any edible plant in boiling water produced a refreshing, flavoursome drink which was easy, quick, free and in most cases beneficial to their health. These herbal drinks, or "tisanes", have enjoyed a remarkable revival as both supermarkets and tea specialists cater to our desire to experiment with an ever-increasing range of healthy alternatives to coffee and traditional tea.

Almost any herbs and herb flowers can be used, and the technique is generally the same. Several sprigs of the freshly picked herb are steeped in a cup of hot, but not boiling water, and left for several minutes to infuse. Remove the leaves by straining through a sieve. Serve hot or cold with honey, lemon or sugar, if you like.

MEDICINAL TISANES

Many tisanes are used as much for their therapeutic qualities as they are for their refreshing flavour. Rosemary is said to stimulate the circulation and alleviate migraine. Lavender, hyssop, thyme and marjoram infused together in a pot are taken as a remedy for cold symptoms, and hops, chamomile and lime flower are used to help beat insomnia. Peppermint is an excellent aid to digestion.

Above: Lavender tisane has an uplifting, sweet scent.

Left: Lime-blossom tisane will ensure a good night's sleep.

Lavender Tisanes

Put three sprigs of lavender flower-heads in a heatproof glass cup or mug and pour boiling water over. Leave to infuse (steep) for about 4 minutes, stirring the sprigs frequently, then remove them and serve warm or cold, sweetened with a little honey, if you like.

To make a soothing brew to relieve a headache, mix 2.5ml/½ tsp of dried lavender with 5ml/1 tsp of wood betony. Top up with hot water and leave to infuse for 10 minutes. Strain and drink.

Rose-petal Tea

A mixture of dried rose petals and China tea makes a highly scented and refreshing drink. It looks lovely served unstrained in small glasses so the petals can be seen in the base.

MAKES 130G/4½OZ

INGREDIENTS
15g/½ oz dried, scented red or pink unsprayed rose petals
115g/4oz oolong or other mild- to medium-strength China tea

1 Mix the rose petals with the tea and store in an airtight container.

2 Make as for ordinary tea, and serve without milk.

Below: Mix dried rose petals with oolong tea and store in an airtight container in a dark place.

Left: Rose petals add a distinctive scent to tea.

Iced Apple-mint Tea

A jug (pitcher) of iced tea can be stored overnight in the refrigerator for a refreshing, summery thirst quencher.

MAKES 900ML/1½ PINTS/3¾ CUPS

INGREDIENTS
15ml/1 tbsp Indian tea
60ml/4 tbsp chopped fresh mint
15ml/1 tbsp caster (superfine) sugar
300ml/½ pint/1¼ cups clear apple juice
ice cubes and sprigs of mint to serve

1 Put the tea and chopped mint in a pot or large jug and add 750ml/1½ pints/3 cups boiling water. Leave to infuse (steep) for 5 minutes.

2 Strain into a jug and stir in the sugar. Leave to cool. Add the apple juice and chill until ready to serve.

3 Serve in tall glasses with ice cubes and sprigs of mint.

Below: Chamomile, with its pretty, daisy-like flowers, is one of the better-known herbs. Taken in tea, it helps to assist digestion and settle nerves and anxiety leading to peaceful sleep.

VARIATIONS

Chamomile Tisane Infuse (steep) three or four flower-heads in hot but not boiling water as for Lavender Tisane. Do not infuse them for too long as the drink might become bitter.

Hyssop Tisane Make as above, using one sprig of flowering hyssop.

Lemon Verbena Tisane Take a flowering spray of lemon verbena and a couple of leaves and infuse.

Lime-blossom Tisane Use lime flowers as they begin to open. Steep five or six flowers for each cup and add hot, but not boiling water.

Peppermint Tisane Make as above, infusing one large sprig of peppermint leaves and flowers.

Chamomile and Peppermint Tisane Mix together 75g/3oz dried chamomile flowers and 25g/1oz dried peppermint leaves. Store and use as Rose-petal Tea.

Lemon Balm and Ceylon Tea Mix together 25g/1oz dried lemon balm and 115g/4oz Ceylon tea. Store and use as for Rose-petal Tea.

Marigold and Verbena Tisane Mix together 50g/2oz dried marigold petals and 25g/1oz dried lemon verbena leaves. Store and use as for Rose-petal Tea.

HERB CORDIALS AND DRINKS

From fragrant and Sparkling Elderflower Drink to smooth, tangy Rosehip Cordial, herbs and flowers can be used as a base for an interesting assortment of drinks, and as a lively addition to various fruit, vegetable and dairy-based drinks. Fruit and herbs can be infused (steeped) in alcohol to create an irresistibly punchy tipple, or steeped in syrups to make fresh-tasting, vibrant cordials that keep for months. Many herbs, particularly those in flower, make stunning additions to fruit punches, for summer parties and barbecues.

CORDIALS

Home-made cordials have a fresh, intense flavour that can rarely be bought in a shop. They can be lavished on to scoops of fruit or vanilla ice cream, swirled into fruit compotes or salads or simply served topped up with ice-cold water or lemonade as a thirst-quenching drink.

Rosehip Cordial

Collect rosehips from the hedgerows for this delightful cordial. It makes a wonderful autumn and winter drink.

MAKES 1.75 LITRES/3 PINTS/7½ CUPS

INGREDIENTS
   1kg/2¼lb rosehips
   granulated sugar

1 Put 1.75 litres/3 pints/7½ cups water in a large, heavy pan and bring to the boil. Meanwhile blend the rosehips in a food processor until finely chopped. Add to the boiling water and return to the boil. Cover with a lid and simmer very gently for 10 minutes. Turn off the heat and leave for 15 minutes.

2 Sterilize a jelly bag by immersing it in boiling water for 2 minutes. Drain and suspend the jelly bag over a large bowl. Strain the rosehips through the jelly bag and leave overnight until the juices stop dripping through.

COOK'S TIP
Cordials can be stored, chilled in the refrigerator, for 3 weeks. Sterilize bottles before use.

3 Measure the juice and return to the pan. Add 350g/12oz/1¾ cups sugar for every 600ml/1 pint/2½ cups syrup. Heat gently, stirring until the sugar has dissolved. Bring to the boil and boil for 5 minutes, or until syrupy. Pour into thoroughly cleaned bottles and cover with stoppers or corks. Store in the refrigerator.

Below: Rosehip cordial is a healthy drink, high in vitamin C.

Rosemary, Redcurrant and Orange Cordial

Redcurrants and oranges combine with a subtle hint of rosemary to make a tangy, summery cordial.

MAKES ABOUT 900ML/1½ PINTS/3¾ CUPS

INGREDIENTS
900g/2lb/8 cups fresh redcurrants
8 large sprigs of rosemary
finely grated rind and juice of
2 oranges
granulated sugar

1 Strip the redcurrants from their stems, put in a pan and mash lightly using a potato masher. Add the rosemary, orange rind and 300ml/½ pint/1¼ cups water. Bring just to the boil, then remove from the heat and leave to cool. Stir in the orange juice.

2 Sterilize a jelly bag by immersing it in boiling water for 2 minutes. Suspend the jelly bag over a large bowl. Strain the fruit and juices through the bag overnight until the mixture is dry.

3 Put the juice in a pan adding 350g/12oz/1¾ cups sugar for every 600ml/1 pint/2½ cups syrup. Heat gently until the sugar has dissolved then bring to the boil and boil for 5 minutes, or until syrupy. Pour into thoroughly cleaned bottles and cover with stoppers or corks. Store in the refrigerator.

Lemon Barley and Bay Syrup

Despite its image as a remedy for minor ailments, chilled lemon barley juice is both delicious and invigorating. The gentle earthiness of the bay leaves blend perfectly with the tangy flavour of the lemons.

MAKES 750ML/1¼ PINTS/3 CUPS

INGREDIENTS
75g/3oz/½ cup pearl barley
3 lemons
4 bay leaves
75g/3oz/6 tbsp granulated sugar
ice cubes, lemon slices and sprigs of lemon balm, to decorate

Above: Fragrant herbal cordials are cool and refreshing in summer. Serve with decorative, floral ice cubes.

1 Put the pearl barley in a bowl and cover with boiling water. Stir well then rinse thoroughly until the water runs clear. Put in a pan with 1 litre/1¾ pints/4 cups boiling water. Bring to the boil, cover with a lid and simmer gently for 45 minutes.

2 Scrub the lemons and pare off the rind with a sharp knife. Squeeze the juice and reserve. Put the pared rind in a bowl with the bay leaves and sugar.

3 Strain the hot barley water over the sugar mixture and stir until the sugar has dissolved. Cover and leave overnight.

4 Add the lemon juice and transfer to a jug (pitcher). Chill for up to two weeks. Serve undiluted with ice, lemon slices and sprigs of lemon balm to decorate.

Basil, Tabasco and Tomato Juice

Drinks that combine herbs, fruit and vegetables are renowned for boosting health and vitality. Serve any time.

MAKES ONE GLASS

INGREDIENTS
small handful fresh basil leaves
5cm/2in length cucumber, roughly chopped
3 vine-ripened tomatoes, roughly chopped
½ red (bell) pepper, deseeded and roughly chopped
60ml/4 tbsp freshly squeezed orange juice
few drops Tabasco sauce, to taste

1 Put all the ingredients, except the Tabasco in a food processor or blender and process until smooth, scraping the mixture from around the sides of the bowl.

2 Pour into a tall glass and add Tabasco to taste. Serve with ice cubes if you like.

Mint Cup

Sweet, tangy and irresistibly minty, this summer cup is perfect for *al fresco* eating and drinking.

SERVES FOUR TO SIX

INGREDIENTS
large handful fresh mint leaves
30ml/2 tbsp caster (superfine) sugar
plenty of crushed ice
30ml/2 tbsp freshly squeezed
  lemon juice
175ml/6fl oz/¾ cup freshly squeezed
  grapefruit juice
600ml/1 pint/2½ cups tonic
  water, chilled
mint sprigs and lemon slices,
  to decorate

1 Crush the mint leaves with the sugar using a mortar and pestle, or a small bowl and the back of a spoon.

2 Transfer the mixture to a serving jug (pitcher) and fill with crushed ice.

3 Add the lemon juice, grapefruit juice and tonic water.

4 Stir gently and serve decorated with sprigs of mint and lemon slices.

VARIATION
Lemon Balm, Chilli and Lime Crush
For an evening dinner party, substitute lemon balm instead of the mint leaves and use lime juice instead of the lemon. Add a few drops of chilli oil with the grape-fruit juice. A splash of Tequila can be added for extra kick!

Summer Punch

Borage, cucumber and mint give a subtle but essential fragrance to a classic Pimm's drink. Let all the ingredients chill together in the jug before topping up with the alcohol at the last minute, if you have time.

SERVES FOUR TO SIX

INGREDIENTS
several sprigs of borage flowers
¼ cucumber
1 orange, scrubbed
ice cubes
¼ bottle Pimm's, chilled
several sprigs of mint or lemon balm
chilled lemonade for topping up
extra borage flowers, to decorate

1 Remove each of the borage flower-heads from the green calyx by gently easing it out. Halve the cucumber lengthways and cut into thin slices. Chop the orange into small chunks leaving the skin on.

Above: It would not be summer without a jug (pitcher) of refreshing punch, topped with fruit and chilled with ice.

2 Put the cucumber and orange in a large jug and add the ice cubes, Pimm's, mint or lemon balm and borage. Top up with lemonade and serve decorated with extra borage flowers.

Above: Sparkling elderflower drink is light and refreshing, just perfect for summer, and will make an unusual addition to a special occasion.

Sparkling Elderflower Drink

Made simply from elderflowers, sugar, lemons and white wine vinegar, this sparkling drink is surprisingly potent, perfect for country weddings and other summer celebrations.

MAKES 4.5 LITRES/8 PINTS/20 CUPS

INGREDIENTS
    12 elderflower heads
    juice and finely grated (shredded)
        rind of 1 lemon
    30ml/2 tbsp white wine vinegar
    700g/1½lb/3½ cups caster
        (superfine) sugar

1 Strip the elderflower heads from the stalks and put in a very large bowl with the lemon rind, juice, vinegar, sugar and 4.5 litres/8 pints/20 cups water. Cover with muslin and leave for 24 hours.

2 Strain the mixture through a fresh piece of muslin into sterilized bottles, using a funnel. Cork the bottles and leave in a cool place for 2 weeks before drinking undiluted.

Strawberry and Lavender Gin

Flavouring gin with fruits is an ancient tradition. Lavender makes a delicate, fragrant addition.

MAKES ABOUT 750ML/1¼ PINTS/3 CUPS

INGREDIENTS
    400g/14oz/3½ cups ripe but still
        firm strawberries, thickly sliced
    175g/6oz/scant 1 cup caster
        (superfine) sugar
    8 large lavender flowers
    750ml/1¼ pints/3 cups gin

1 Place all the ingredients in a large, wide-necked jar. Cover with the lid. Leave in a cool place for one week, shaking the jar gently each day.

2 Strain the gin and return to the bottle. Chill for up to 4 months. Serve over ice or with chilled tonic water.

Mint Flower Yogurt Drink

The familiar combination of yogurt and mint are blended here with beautifully scented raspberries. Enjoy this cooling drink on a hot summer's day.

SERVES TWO

INGREDIENTS
    250ml/8fl oz/1 cup natural (plain)
        yogurt
    75g/3oz/½ cup fresh raspberries
    50g/2oz/¼ cup caster (superfine) sugar
    2 sprigs flowering mint, plus extra,
        to decorate

Put all the ingredients in a food processor or blender with 120ml/4fl oz/½ cup chilled water. Blend until smooth. Pour into glasses and serve decorated with sprigs of flowering mint.

Above: Enjoy mint flower yogurt drink on a hot summer day, or for a refreshingly fruity breakfast drink, substitute a fresh ripe peach instead of the raspberries.

HERB PICKLES AND PRESERVES

Above: Fruits and vegetables made into savoury preserves taste better if they are left to mature.

From bottled fruits and vegetables to sweet jellies and jams, most preserves benefit from the feast of flavours provided by the herb garden. Presentation plays an important role in the making of pickles and preserves as they are frequently given as gifts. An assortment of different bottles and jars is worth collecting and saves you rooting around at the last minute looking for suitable containers.

COOK'S TIPS

• All jars and bottles should be thoroughly sterilized before using for preserves. Wash in soapy water and remove any old labels. Dry them and put in the oven set at 150°C/300°C/Gas 2 for 15 minutes before filling.
• Cellophane jam-pot covers are ideal for all preserves except pickles as the vinegar will gradually evaporate through them and spoil the top of the pickle.
• Many preserving bottles and jars have attached lids with rubber seals. Remove the seals before sterilizing.

Spiced Pears with Ginger

Use any firm pears for this tangy, spiced preserve. It is particularly good with cold meats such as ham, gammon or smoked chicken or turkey.

MAKES 1KG/2¼LB

INGREDIENTS
  600ml/1 pint/2½ cups red wine vinegar
  rind of 1 lemon
  4cm/1½in length fresh root ginger,
    peeled and sliced
  1 cinnamon stick
  10ml/2 tsp whole allspice berries
  2 bay leaves
  450g/1lb/2¼ cups granulated sugar
  1kg/2¼lb pears
  cloves

1 Put all the ingredients except the pears and cloves in a large pan and heat gently until the sugar dissolves, stirring frequently.

2 Peel the pears, leaving them whole, and stud a clove into each one. Add to the vinegar and simmer very gently, covered with a lid, until the pears are very tender, about 25–30 minutes. Lift out the pears and transfer them to hot jars. Boil the syrup until slightly thickened and pour over the pears. Seal the jars immediately.

Bottled Cherry Tomatoes with Basil

Other small, well-flavoured tomatoes can be used instead of cherry tomatoes but these look particularly pretty.

MAKES 1KG/2¼LB

INGREDIENTS
  1kg/2¼lb cherry tomatoes
  5ml/1 tsp salt per 1 litre/1¾ pint/
    4 cup jar
  5ml/1 tsp sugar per 1 litre/1¾ pint/
    4 cup jar
  handful of fresh basil
  4 garlic cloves per jar

1 Preheat the oven to 120°C/250°F/Gas ½. Prick each tomato with a wooden cocktail stick, then pack them tightly into sterilized jars with heatproof lids, adding salt and sugar as you go.

2 Fill the jars to within 2cm/¾in of the tops, tucking the basil and garlic in among the tomatoes. Rest the lids on the jars but do not seal. Stand the jars on a baking sheet lined with newspaper.

3 Place the filled jars in the oven and cook for about 45 minutes, or until the juices start simmering. Remove from the oven and seal immediately. Store and use within 6 months.

Dill Pickle

Use a glut supply of dill to make this classic preserve, delicious with both cheese and cold meats.

MAKES 3 LITRES/5¼ PINTS/12 CUPS

INGREDIENTS
675g/1½lb ridge cucumbers
large bunch fresh dill
5 garlic cloves, peeled and sliced
900ml/1½ pints/3¾ cups white
    wine vinegar
45ml/3 tbsp coarse salt
10ml/2 tsp mixed peppercorns
3 bay leaves
2 star anise

1 Trim the ends off the cucumbers and cut into 5cm/2in pieces. Place in a bowl of cold water and chill for 24 hours.

2 Drain and pierce the cucumber pieces in several places with a wooden cocktail stick.

COOK'S TIP
Add 45ml/3 tbsp sugar to the vinegar for a sweeter flavour.

3 Pack into sterilized jars with plenty of dill and the garlic. Put the vinegar in a pan with 375ml/13fl oz/scant 1⅔ cups water. Add the salt, peppercorns, bay leaves and star anise. Bring to the boil and boil for 5 minutes. Pour over the cucumbers and seal immediately.

Kashmir Chutney

Ginger, cayenne, coriander and garlic are used to flavour this traditional family recipe for chutney. Enjoy it with a cheese ploughman's or hot or cold grilled (broiled) sausages and meats.

MAKES ABOUT 2.75KG/6LB

INGREDIENTS
1kg/2¼lb green apples
15g/½ oz garlic cloves
1 litre/1¾ pints/4 cups malt vinegar
450g/1lb/3¼ cups fresh or semi-
    dried dates
115g/4oz stem ginger
450g/1lb/3¼ cups seedless raisins
450g/1lb/2 cups light muscovado
    (molasses) sugar
2.5ml/½ tsp cayenne pepper
20g/¾ oz salt
large handful fresh coriander (cilantro)

1 Core and coarsely chop the apples.

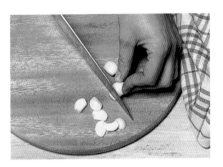

2 Peel and chop the garlic. Put the apples and garlic in a large, heavy pan with enough vinegar to cover them.

3 Boil until the apples are softened. Add the remaining ingredients, except the coriander, to the pan. Cook for 45 minutes, stirring frequently, until thickened and pulpy. Chop the coriander, stir in and cook for 2 minutes. Spoon into sterilized jars and seal immediately.

Left: Pickles add flavour to plain food.

VARIATION
Dry-fry 30ml/2 tbsp mustard seeds in a small pan until they start to pop. Use instead of the star anise.

Tomato Ketchup

Use really ripe tomatoes to give maximum flavour to this spicy sauce.

MAKES 2.75KG/6LB

INGREDIENTS
    2.25kg/5lb ripe tomatoes
    1 onion, peeled
    8 cloves
    6 allspice berries
    6 black peppercorns
    several sprigs fresh rosemary
    3 bay leaves
    25g/1oz fresh root ginger, peeled
        and sliced
    1 celery heart
    30ml/2 tbsp dark brown sugar
    65ml/4½ tbsp raspberry or red
        wine vinegar
    3 garlic cloves, peeled
    15ml/1 tbsp salt

1 Peel and halve the tomatoes and scoop out the seeds. Place the flesh in a large, heavy pan. Stud the onion with cloves and tie in a double-thickness layer of muslin with the allspice, peppercorns, rosemary, bay and ginger.

2 Chop the celery and add to the pan with the bag of spices, sugar, vinegar, garlic and salt. Bring to the boil, reduce the heat and simmer, uncovered, stirring frequently for about 1½ hours.

3 Remove the muslin bag, squeezing out the juices, and blend the tomato mixture in a food processor or blender until smooth.

4 Return to the pan and simmer for 5 minutes. Transfer to jars and store in the refrigerator for up to 2 weeks.

Mint Sauce

Home-made mint sauce is far superior to shop-bought and keeps for several months in the refrigerator. To make a 250ml/8fl oz/1 cup quantity, finely chop 1 large bunch fresh mint and put in a large bowl. Add 105ml/7 tbsp boiling water and leave to infuse (steep). When cooled to lukewarm, add 150ml/¼ pint/⅔ cup white wine vinegar and 30–45ml/2–3 tbsp caster (superfine) sugar to taste. Pour into a clean bottle or jar and store in the refrigerator.

Papaya and Lemon Relish

Although this relish makes a small quantity, its flavour is strong and a little goes a long way.

MAKES ABOUT 450G/1LB

INGREDIENTS
    1 large unripe papaya
    1 onion, thinly sliced
    40g/1½ oz/⅓ cup raisins
    250ml/8fl oz/1 cup red wine vinegar
    juice of 2 lemons
    150ml/¼ pint/⅔ cup elderflower
        cordial
    165g/5½ oz/generous ¾ cup golden
        granulated sugar
    1 cinnamon stick
    2 bay leaves
    5ml/1 tsp paprika
    2.5ml/½ tsp salt

Left: Tomato Ketchup and Mint Sauce.

1 Peel the papaya, halve lengthways and scoop out the seeds. Roughly chop the flesh and put in a heavy pan.

2 Add the onion, raisins and vinegar. Bring to the boil and simmer gently for 10 minutes. Add the remaining ingredients and bring to the boil, stirring. Reduce the heat and simmer gently for 50–60 minutes.

3 Transfer to sterilized jars, cover and store for at least 1 week before using. Chill once opened.

VARIATION
Mango and Lemon Relish Use one large, firm mango instead of the papaya.

Lavender Jelly

This pretty jelly really captures the essence of summer. Serve it with roast lamb, chicken or duck, or even with warmed scones (US biscuits) or croissants. Do not worry about peeling and coring the apples as the mixture is strained through a jelly bag.

MAKES ABOUT 1.8KG/4LB

INGREDIENTS
 1.8kg/4lb cooking apples, washed
  and roughly chopped
 105ml/7 tbsp lavender flowers,
  chopped
 about 1.3kg/3lb/6¾ cups sugar

1 Put the apples in a pan with 75ml/ 5 tbsp of the lavender flowers and 1.75 litres/3 pints/7½ cups water. Simmer gently for about 25 minutes, or until the apples are soft and mushy.

2 Sterilize a jelly bag by immersing it in boiling water for 2 minutes. Drain and suspend the jelly bag securely over a large bowl.

3 Strain the apple mixture through the bag and leave overnight until the juices stop dripping through.

4 Measure the juice and return to the pan, adding 450g/1lb/2¼ cups sugar for every 600ml/1 pint/2½ cups juice. Heat gently, stirring until the sugar has dissolved. Bring to the boil and boil until setting point is reached (see Cook's Tip).

5 Leave to cool for 15 minutes then stir in the remaining lavender flowers. Transfer to dry, sterilized jars and cover with a lid. Store in a cool place for up to 6 months.

VARIATION
Apple, Strawberry and Rosemary Jelly
Use chopped rosemary instead of the lavender and substitute 900g/ 2lb/8 cups whole strawberries for half the apples, adding them for the final 5 minutes' cooking time.

Pickled Plums de Provence

These savoury plums are transformed into an unusual accompaniment for cold roast meats by adding aromatic herbs, including rosemary, garlic and sweet lavender.

MAKES ABOUT 1.3KG/3LB

INGREDIENTS
 1.3kg/3lb firm plums
 4 sprigs rosemary
 4 bay leaves
 4 lavender flowers
 2 thyme sprigs
 4 unpeeled garlic cloves
 900ml/1½ pints/3¾ cups white
  wine vinegar
 500g/1¼ lb/2¾ cups granulated sugar

1 Prick over the plums with a wooden cocktail stick and pack them into 1 medium and 1 small Kilner jar, tucking in the herb sprigs and garlic.

2 Put the vinegar and sugar in a pan and heat gently until the sugar dissolves. Bring to the boil and boil for 5 minutes, or until syrupy. Allow to cool, then remove the herb sprigs.

3 Pour over the plums, making sure they are completely covered. Seal tightly and store in a cool place for at least 1 month before using.

COOK'S TIP
To check if jelly or jam is at setting point, put a small amount on a saucer – if it holds its shape it is ready.

Left: Lavender jelly is an unusual addition to the store cupboard (pantry).

HERB SAUCES

A well-flavoured sauce, mayonnaise or dip makes an imaginative accompaniment to serve with a variety of dishes. Tasty combinations of herbs, such as dill and capers, rosemary and onion; parsley and bay, or garlic and mixed herbs, are ideal additions to sauces to serve with plain foods.

White Sauce

This classic white sauce is an essential part of many savoury dishes. A good sauce, which is smooth, glossy and buttery, makes the perfect base to which herbs, spices and other flavours can be added (see variations).

MAKES ABOUT 600ML/1 PINT/2½ CUPS

INGREDIENTS
 40g/1½ oz/3 tbsp butter
 40g/1½ oz/⅓ cup plain (all-purpose)
  flour
 600ml/1pint/2½ cups milk
 good pinch of freshly grated nutmeg
 30–45ml/2–3 tbsp double (heavy)
  cream (optional)
 salt and ground black pepper

1 Melt the butter in a heavy pan over a moderate heat. Remove from the heat and stir in the flour.

2 Gradually whisk in about a quarter of the milk until completely smooth, then whisk in the remainder. Set the pan over a moderate heat and bring to the boil, whisking continuously.

3 When the sauce starts to thicken, reduce the heat to its lowest setting and cook gently, stirring frequently until smooth and glossy. Stir in the nutmeg, cream, if using, and seasoning to taste.

VARIATIONS

Cheese Sauce Add 50g/2oz/½ cup finely grated (shredded) Cheddar cheese, 5ml/1 tsp finely chopped fresh thyme and 2.5ml/½ tsp Dijon mustard at step 3 of the White Sauce recipe.

Dill and Caper Sauce Finely chop 30ml/2 tbsp capers and add to the sauce at step 3 with 30ml/2 tbsp finely chopped dill.

Egg and Chive Sauce Shell and finely chop 2 hard-boiled (hard-cooked) eggs. Add to the sauce at step 3 with 45ml/3 tbsp chopped chives.

Parsley Sauce Heat the milk in a pan with 1 bay leaf, 1 whole peeled onion and 12 black peppercorns and bring almost to the boil. Remove from the heat and leave to infuse (steep) for 20 minutes. Strain and make the white sauce as before. Stir in 60ml/4 tbsp finely chopped parsley at step 3.

Rosemary and Onion Sauce Finely chop 1 onion and sauté gently in the butter before adding the flour. Add 15ml/1 tbsp finely chopped rosemary at step 3.

COOK'S TIPS

• A white sauce can be made ahead and reheated. Transfer to a bowl, add a dot of butter and let it melt over the surface to prevent a skin forming. Leave to cool. Refrigerate for up to 2 days and reheat before serving. Alternatively place a circle of greaseproof (waxed) paper over the surface.

• The recipe for White Sauce gives a consistency suitable for pastry and pie fillings or as a topping for lasagne and crêpes.

• As an accompanying sauce to meat, fish and vegetables use 15g/½ oz/2 tbsp butter and flour.

• For a thicker sauce to use as a soufflé base or to bind ingredients together, use 50g/2oz/¼ cup butter and 50g/2oz/½ cup flour.

Bread Sauce

Bread sauce flavoured with cloves and bay leaves makes a comforting, wintry accompaniment to roast game, turkey, chicken and lamb.

SERVES SIX TO EIGHT

INGREDIENTS
 1 onion, peeled
 8 whole cloves
 2 bay leaves
 600ml/1 pint/2½ cups milk
 115g/4oz/2 cups fresh breadcrumbs
 15g/½ oz/1 tbsp butter
 45ml/3 tbsp single (light) cream
 salt and ground black pepper

1 Stud the onion with cloves and put in a pan with the bay leaves and milk. Bring to the boil, then remove from the heat and leave to infuse (steep) for 15 minutes.

2 Remove the onion and bay leaves and stir in the breadcrumbs. Simmer gently for about 10 minutes, or until thickened. Stir in the butter, cream and seasoning.

Below: Richly-flavoured bread sauce.

Herby Onion Gravy

The sage, thyme and parsley make this gravy delicious with roasts, sausages, liver and bacon, and toad in the hole. Make sure you really caramelize the onions in the oil before adding the remaining ingredients to achieve a rich flavour and deep, golden gravy.

MAKES ABOUT 900ML/1½ PINTS/3¾ CUPS

INGREDIENTS

30ml/2 tbsp vegetable oil
3 onions, finely sliced
2.5ml/½ tsp caster (superfine) sugar
10ml/2 tsp plain (all-purpose) flour
2 sprigs each of sage, thyme
  and parsley
900ml/1½ pints/3¾ cups chicken or
  vegetable stock
salt and ground black pepper

1 Heat the oil in a frying pan. Add the onions and sugar and sauté gently for about 10 minutes, or until the onions are just beginning to turn golden. Sprinkle on the flour and cook, stirring for 1 minute.

2 Add the herbs and stock and bring to the boil. Reduce the heat and simmer gently, uncovered, for 5 minutes, or until slightly thickened. Season to taste.

Rich Tomato Sauce

Generously flavoured with Mediterranean herbs, this intensely flavoured sauce keeps well in the refrigerator for several days and makes a lovely sauce for pasta, grilled (broiled) meats and barbecues, or as a pizza topping.

SERVES FOUR TO SIX

INGREDIENTS

45ml/3 tbsp olive oil
2 celery sticks, finely chopped
1 onion, finely chopped
3 garlic cloves, crushed
small handful of chopped mixed
  herbs, such as parsley, thyme,
  marjoram, oregano, basil
1 bay leaf
675g/1½lb ripe tomatoes, peeled
  and chopped
30ml/2 tbsp sun-dried tomato paste
150ml/¼ pint/⅔ cup vegetable stock
salt and ground black pepper

1 Heat the oil in a pan. Add the celery and onion and fry gently for 5 minutes. Add the garlic and herbs, and fry for 2 minutes.

Above: Herby onion gravy is irresistible.

2 Add the tomatoes, tomato paste and stock, and bring to the boil. Reduce the heat and simmer gently for about 20 minutes, or until thickened and pulpy. Season to taste and serve hot.

Sauce Vierge

This quick sauce adds interest to fried or grilled meat and fish. Heat 60ml/ 4 tbsp extra virgin olive oil in a small pan. Add 1.5ml/¼ tsp crushed coriander seeds and fry for 1 minute. Add 5 ripe, skinned and seeded tomatoes, a small handful of chopped parsley, tarragon and chervil and a little seasoning. Cook for 30 seconds before serving.

HERBS IN SALSAS, MAYONNAISE AND DIPS

Due largely to healthy and delicious Mediterranean ingredients, such as herbs, richly flavoured olive oils and other flavourings, we have a fabulous selection of chilled, olive-oil-based sauces to choose from. Those fresh, summery tastes, from the classic mayonnaise and all its variations to thick, aromatic olive oil dressings, will quickly enliven even the simplest meat, fish and vegetable dishes. Serve them freshly made if convenient, or store in the refrigerator, covered tightly for up to 2 days.

Salsa Verde

Nothing quite epitomizes the wonderfully aromatic, intense flavour of herbs better than a freshly blended Salsa Verde. Excellent with roast or grilled (broiled) meats as well as pan-fried fish and vegetable dishes.

SERVES FOUR

INGREDIENTS
  2 garlic cloves, chopped
  25g/1oz/1 cup flat leaf parsley
  15g/½ oz/½ cup fresh basil, mint or
    coriander (cilantro), or a mixture
    of herbs
  15ml/1 tbsp chopped chives
  15ml/1 tbsp capers, rinsed
  120ml/4fl oz/½ cup extra virgin
    olive oil
  5 anchovy fillets, rinsed
  10ml/2 tsp French mustard
  a little finely grated (shredded)
    lemon rind and juice
  salt and ground black pepper

Above: Salsa verde, one of the best known and flavoursome salsas.

2 Gradually add the remaining oil in a thin stream with the motor running to make a thick sauce.

VARIATIONS
• For a creamier, slightly milder flavour whisk in 45ml/3 tbsp crème fraîche.
• Substitute herbs such as chervil, tarragon, dill or fennel for a sauce that goes particularly well with fish, shellfish or chicken.

1 Put the first five ingredients and 15ml/1 tbsp of the oil in a blender or food processor and process lightly.

3 Transfer the herb mixture to a bowl and add the lemon rind and juice, and seasoning to taste. (You might not need additional salt as the anchovies and capers are very salty.) Serve immediately or chill until required.

Fresh Mayonnaise

Mayonnaise is definitely worth making, provided you have a little time and patience. Store in the refrigerator, covered tightly for up to 1 week. Use the freshest possible eggs. Infants, the elderly and those with compromised immune systems shold avoid eating foods containing uncooked eggs.

MAKES ABOUT 350ML/12FL OZ/1½ CUPS

INGREDIENTS
    2 egg yolks
    350ml/12fl oz/1½ cups olive oil
    15–30ml/1–2 tbsp lemon juice or
      white wine vinegar
    5–10ml/1–2 tsp Dijon mustard
    salt and ground black pepper

COOK'S TIP
• Mayonnaise can be made successfully in a food processor. Make exactly as above, pouring in the oil while the motor is running. If it separates beat another egg yolk. Gradually whisk in the curdled mixture as before.

1 Put the egg yolks in a bowl with a pinch of salt, and beat well.

2 Add the oil, a little at a time, beating constantly with an electric mixer or balloon whisk.

3 When a quarter of the oil has been added, beat in 5–10ml/1–2 tsp of the lemon juice or vinegar.

4 Continue beating in the oil in a thin, steady stream. As the mayonnaise thickens, add a little more lemon juice or vinegar.

5 When all the oil has been added, stir in the mustard, seasoning and a little more lemon juice or vinegar, if necessary. (If the mayonnaise is too thick, stir in a spoonful of water.) Store covered with plastic film or in an airtight container in the refrigerator.

VARIATIONS
Basil and Garlic Mayonnaise Tear a small handful each of green and opal basil leaves into small pieces and stir into the mayonnaise with 2 crushed garlic cloves.
Cucumber and Dill Mayonnaise Halve and scoop out the seeds from a 7.5cm/3in length of cucumber. Finely chop the flesh and add to the mayonnaise with 30ml/2 tbsp chopped dill.
Green Mayonnaise Add 25g/1oz/ ½ cup each of finely chopped parsley and watercress, 1 crushed garlic clove and 3 finely chopped spring onions (scallions).
Tartare Sauce Add 30ml/2 tbsp each of chopped tarragon and parsley, 15ml/1 tbsp each of chopped capers and gherkins and a dash of lemon juice or vinegar.

Left: Complete a fresh prawn salad with a creamy home-made mayonnaise.

DIPS

The simplest dips can be made by folding chopped herbs into mayonnaise, fromage frais or thick yogurt. You can also pep them up with garlic, lemon, ginger, spices and other aromatic ingredients. Serve with colourful crudités, interesting breads, or crisps.

Mellow Garlic Dip

Baking garlic until it is soft and succulent mellows its fiery, raw flavour, leaving it sweet and delicious.

SERVES FOUR

INGREDIENTS
  2 whole garlic heads
  15ml/1 tbsp olive oil
  60ml/4 tbsp mayonnaise
  75ml/5 tbsp natural (plain) yogurt
  5ml/1 tsp grainy mustard
  salt and ground black pepper

1 Brush the garlic heads with olive oil and wrap them tightly in kitchen foil. Bake at 200°C/400°F/Gas 6 for about 40 minutes, until soft to the touch. When cool enough to handle, separate the garlic cloves and remove their skins. Sprinkle the cloves with salt and mash on the chopping board with a knife, until puréed.

COOK'S TIPS
• The foil-wrapped garlic heads can also be cooked around the edges of a barbecue. Allow about 25 minutes, turning occasionally.
• Leftover dip will keep, well covered, in the refrigerator for 3–4 days. Use as a topping for baked potatoes, in sandwiches or serve with pan-fried meat or fish.

2 Put the garlic in a bowl and stir in the mayonnaise, yogurt and mustard. Beat well.

3 Check the seasoning, adding more salt and pepper to taste. Transfer to a serving bowl, cover and chill until ready to serve.

VARIATIONS
Garlic, Lovage and Apple Dip Make as above using 1 garlic head. Add 15ml/1 tbsp chopped lovage and 1 peeled and grated dessert apple.
Tarragon, Walnut and Roquefort Dip Make as above increasing the yogurt to 150g/5oz. Add 30ml/2 tbsp chopped tarragon, 25g/1oz/¼ cup finely chopped walnuts and 40g/1½oz crumbled Roquefort cheese.
Sage Flower and Garlic Dip Pull the sage flowers from the stems until you have a small handful. Add to the garlic dip with 30ml/2 tbsp chopped flat leaf parsley.
Anchovy, Olive and Basil Dip Make as above using 1 garlic head. Add 4 drained and chopped canned anchovy fillets, 10 pitted and sliced black olives and shredded basil leaves. Omit the salt.
Aubergine and Mint Dip Chop half a small aubergine (eggplant) and fry gently in olive oil until tender. Leave to cool. Fold into the dip omitting the mustard and add 45ml/3 tbsp chopped mint.

Saffron Dip

This herb and saffron dip is made with fromage frais for a light, refreshing texture. Substitute half the fromage frais for mayonnaise for a fuller flavour. Add more or less herbs depending on your taste.

SERVES FOUR

INGREDIENTS
  small pinch saffron threads
  200g/7oz/scant 1 cup fromage frais
  10 chives
  10 large basil leaves
  salt and ground black pepper

COOK'S TIP
Saffron has a unique flavour that cannot be substituted. Although expensive, a small pinch of the threads goes a long way, particularly if you chill the dip for a couple of hours before serving to let the flavours mingle.

Below: Herbs add subtle flavour and texture to dips.

1 Put 15ml/1 tbsp boiling water into a bowl and add the saffron threads. Leave to infuse (steep) for 5 minutes.

2 Beat the fromage frais in a large bowl until smooth. Stir in the infused saffron and liquid.

3 Chop the chives into the dip. Tear the basil leaves into small pieces and stir them in. Mix well. Season with salt and black pepper to taste. Transfer the saffron dip to a serving bowl, cover and refrigerate until ready to serve.

VARIATIONS
Ginger and Saffron Dip Finely grate (shred) a 2.5cm/1in length fresh root ginger. Stir into a little of the fromage frais, then add the rest. Add 30ml/2 tbsp chopped coriander (cilantro) instead of basil.
Apricot, Saffron and Almond Dip Finely chop 50g/2oz/¼ cup no-soak dried apricots and 40g/1½oz/⅓ cup lightly toasted flaked (sliced) almonds. Stir into the fromage frais with the saffron and add 15ml/1 tbsp chopped flat leaf parsley and 15ml/1 tbsp chopped coriander to the mixture instead of chives and basil.
Mascarpone and Rocket Dip Omit the saffron and make as above beating 115g/4oz/½ cup mascarpone into the fromage frais. Add a small handful of torn rocket (arugula) leaves (preferably wild rocket) with the herbs.
Saffron and Rosemary Dip Add 15ml/1 tbsp chopped rosemary to the saffron when infusing. Finish as above, substituting 15ml/1 tbsp grainy mustard and a handful of rosemary flowers, if available, for the chives and basil.
Parmesan and Sun-dried Tomato Dip Omit the saffron and add 25g/1oz/⅓ cup finely grated Parmesan cheese and 30ml/2 tbsp chopped sun-dried tomatoes from a jar.

BUTTERS, CREAMS AND CHEESES

Dairy produce is subtle in flavour, and cream and butter in particular are often bland, making them ideal ingredients that will carry the flavour of aromatic herbs and spices.

FLAVOURED BUTTERS

A pat of herb butter, melting over steak, fish or vegetables, turns a fairly ordinary dish into something far more interesting. Almost any herbs can be used, the butters freeze well and have infinite uses: try them spread on to warm, crusty bread, scones (US biscuits) and sandwiches or swirled into soups and sauces.

Simple Herb Butters

To add interest to plain cooked meat, fish and vegetables, make a herb butter using a herb with a natural affinity to the main ingredient.

SERVES FOUR

INGREDIENTS
    115g/4oz/½ cup softened butter
    45ml/3 tbsp chopped herbs e.g.
        parsley, thyme, rosemary, tarragon,
        chives, basil, marjoram or coriander
        (cilantro), or a mixture of several herbs
    finely grated (shredded) rind of
        ½ lemon
    good pinch cayenne pepper
    salt and ground black pepper

1 Beat the butter until creamy, then beat in the herbs, lemon rind, cayenne and a little seasoning. Transfer to a small bowl and chill until required.

COOK'S TIP
Use herbs singly such as garlic, or make up a combination of herbs.

2 Alternatively, shape while still soft as follows:

Butter Slices Transfer the butter to a piece of greaseproof (waxed) paper and shape into a neat roll. Wrap and chill. Cut into slices.

Butter Shapes Put the butter on to a sheet of greaseproof paper and flatten to about 5mm/¼in thick with a palette knife (metal spatula). Chill and stamp out shapes using a cutter.

Below: Herb butter balls make a visually attractive accompaniment to food.

VARIATIONS
As well as being the traditional accompaniment to steaks, flavoured butters can be rubbed on to meat before roasting or spread over cutlets before barbecuing. They can be spread on fish that is foil-wrapped and baked in the oven, or used as you would garlic butter to make deliciously flavoured breads.

Anchovy and Tarragon Butter Omit the herbs. Add 4 drained and finely chopped canned anchovy fillets and 45ml/3 tbsp chopped tarragon.

Lavender and Thyme Butter Omit the herbs, cayenne pepper and seasoning and add 5 chopped lavender flowers and a small handful of thyme flowers.

Roasted Pepper Butter Halve 1 large red (bell) pepper and grill (broil), skin-side uppermost until blackened. Wrap in foil or plastic for 10 minutes then peel off the skins. Discard the stalk and seeds and finely chop the pepper. Allow to cool. Add to the butter with plenty of chopped basil, parsley or coriander (cilantro).

Mixed Flower Butter *(below)* For a special lunch or tea in the garden, a block of flower-adorned butter looks stunning. Gather plenty of sage, chive and rosemary flowers and sandwich some between two thick pats of chilled butter. Press more flowers around the sides of the butter. Cover and chill in the refrigerator.

HERB CREAMS AND CHEESES

Because of their intense, aromatic flavour, herbs are great for infusing in cream or milk to create some of the simplest dessert ideas. Infuse sweet herbs such as rosemary, bay, thyme, rose geranium and lavender in the milk or cream before making ice creams, custard and rice pudding, to add a fragrant depth to the finished dish. Sprigs of herbs make lovely garnishes.

Rosemary and Ratafia Cream

Make and chill this almond-flavoured cream in advance and serve with a platter of fresh summer fruits.

SERVES SIX

INGREDIENTS
  300ml/½ pint/1¼ cups double
    (heavy) cream
  several sprigs of rosemary
  25g/1oz/½ cup ratafia biscuits
    (almond macaroons), crushed

Bring the cream slowly to the boil. Remove from the heat and add the rosemary. Leave to cool, then chill. Strain the cream into a bowl and whisk until it holds its shape. Fold in the biscuits and serve in a bowl. Chill.

VARIATIONS
Bay and Lemon Ratafia Cream Use 3 bay leaves instead of rosemary and add the finely grated (shredded) rind of 1 lemon when whisking.
Rose Geranium and Cointreau Cream Use 10 rose-geranium leaves instead of rosemary. Omit the biscuits. Add 15ml/1 tbsp Cointreau.

Above: Rosemary and ratafia-flavoured cream is ideal with summer berries.

HERB CREAMS

A platter of herb-flavoured cheeses makes a delicious finale to a light lunch. They also make delicious gifts. Use soft cheeses with a creamy consistency for best results. Store in a wrapping of waxed or baking parchment for up to 3 days.

Dill and Pink Peppercorn Cheese Finely chop several sprigs of dill and mix with 2.5ml/½ tsp crushed pink peppercorns. Using a teaspoon, spoon the mixture over the top and sides of a 150g/5oz medium-fat goat's cheese.
Thyme and Garlic Cheese Strip the leaves from several thyme stems adding any of the small flowers. Mix with a

finely chopped garlic clove. Press the mixture over a 90g/3½oz round of full-fat goat's cheese.
Minted Feta Cheese Finely chop a small bunch of mint. Drain 200g/7oz feta cheese, cut into dice and roll in the mint until coated.
Tarragon and Lemon Cheese Cut a 200g/7oz pack of low-fat cream cheese into two. Tear the leaves off some tarragon and finely chop. Grate (shred) the rind of half a lemon. Mix with the tarragon and coat the cheese.

Below: Herb cheeses are delicious served with savoury biscuits or crackers.

HERB CONDIMENTS AND SUGARS

Flavouring salt, pepper, mustard and sugar with fresh herbs adds yet another dimension to their vast range of culinary uses. Many specialist shops and supermarkets stock a supply of ready-mixed herb and spice blends, but nothing can beat the fresh, vibrant flavour of home-made versions, a selection of which can add variety and interest to all aspects of cooking. The wealth of different herbs and spices around us provides plenty of scope for experimentation. This will inevitably lead to discovering some firm favourites which can be remade each season to take you through the winter.

Herby Salt

Allow time to dry the herbs before making herb salts.

MAKES ABOUT 300G/11OZ

INGREDIENTS
  6 dried bay leaves
  90ml/6 tbsp mixed dried herbs, such as thyme, rosemary, oregano, tarragon, dill, fennel
  300g/11oz coarse salt

1 Crumble all the herbs together in a large mortar. Add the salt and crush with a pestle until the herbs are finely distributed in the salt.

2 Transfer to an airtight container and store in a cool, dry place.

COOK'S TIP
Uses for Herby Salt
• Stir into tomato juice as an alternative to Tabasco or Worcester sauce.
• Rub into meat, poultry or fish as a dry marinade before roasting or grilling (broiling). Chill for an hour in the salt if you have time.
• Stir into soups, stews, casseroles and sauces.
• Sprinkle over chips and home-made crisps.
• Use as a seasoning for boiled eggs or quail's eggs.
• Use in salad dressings.

Right: Salt infused with herb layers.

Lemon Verbena Seasoning

This delicious blend of lemony flavours makes a wonderful dry marinade for chicken, lamb or pork.

MAKES ABOUT 50G/2OZ

INGREDIENTS
  2 lemons
  30ml/2 tbsp lemon thyme, chopped
  15ml/1 tbsp lemon verbena, chopped
  15ml/1 tbsp lemon grass, chopped

1 Pare fine strips of rind from the lemons, taking care not to remove too much of the white pith. Dry the rind and herbs on a rack in a warm place, such as an airing cupboard for 24–48 hours.

2 When thoroughly dry, pound the lemon rind using a mortar and pestle. Add the remaining ingredients and crush finely. Alternatively, use the small section of a food processor to blend the ingredients together.

3 Pack into small jars or fabric bags and store in a cool, dry place.

VARIATIONS
Herb Seasoning for Fish Use one or more of the following herbs: dill, parsley, chervil, tarragon and fennel, adding crushed dill or fennel seeds and lemon or ordinary pepper.
Herb Seasoning for Meat Use a mixture of rosemary, thyme, oregano, sage, parsley and chives, adding crushed black or white mustard seeds.
Lime and Herb Pepper Home-dried lime rind gives pepper extra bite and flavour. Finely grate (shred) the rind of 3 limes and leave to dry out on a tray for 24 hours. Grind with 115g/4oz black pepper and 60ml/4 tbsp dried rosemary, parsley or tarragon.
Spicy Salt Combine 15ml/1 tbsp each of cumin seeds, coriander seeds, black peppercorns and cardamom pods with a teaspoon each of ground cloves, chilli powder and ginger. Blend with the salt.

HERB MUSTARDS

Making mustard is surprisingly easy and produces really aromatic results. Use white mustard seeds for a mild flavour and the black seeds for extra heat.

Tarragon and Champagne Mustard

Enjoy this mustard, delicately flavoured with tarragon and champagne, with cold seafood or chicken.

MAKES ABOUT 250G/9OZ

INGREDIENTS
30ml/2 tbsp mustard seeds
75ml/5 tbsp champagne or white wine vinegar
115g/4oz dry mustard powder
115g/4oz/½ cup brown sugar
2.5ml/½ tsp salt
50ml/3½ tbsp olive oil
60ml/4 tbsp chopped tarragon

1 Soak the mustard seeds overnight in the vinegar.

2 Pour the mixture into the bowl of a blender or small section of a food processor. Add the mustard powder, sugar and salt, and blend until smooth. Slowly add the oil while blending. Stir in the tarragon and pour into small, thoroughly clean jars. Store in a cool place for up to 6 weeks.

Horseradish Mustard

Traditionally associated with roast beef, fresh horseradish has a characteristically strong flavour with none of the taste of a store-bought brand. In this delicious recipe it blends with mustard to make a tangy relish for cold meats, smoked fish or cheese.

MAKES ABOUT 400G/14OZ

INGREDIENTS
25g/1oz mustard seeds
115g/4oz dry mustard powder
115g/4oz/½ cup light muscovado (molasses) sugar
120ml/4fl oz/½ cup white wine vinegar or cider vinegar
50ml/2fl oz/¼ cup olive oil
5ml/1 tsp lemon juice
45ml/3 tbsp freshly grated (shredded) horseradish

1 Put the mustard seeds in a bowl and pour over 250ml/8fl oz/1 cup boiling water. Leave for 1 hour.

2 Drain the seeds, discarding the liquid, and place in a food processor or blender with the remaining ingredients. Blend until smooth.

3 Spoon into clean jars, and store in the refrigerator. Use fresh.

HERB, FLOWER AND SPICE SUGARS

The same technique that is used to flavour sugar with a vanilla pod (bean) works equally well with herbs, flowers and spices. Rose petals, rose-geranium leaves, lavender sprigs, cloves, cinnamon, ginger, cardamom and dried orange and lemon peel all make delicious flavourings, used either individually or in simple combinations. Once infused (steeped) for two weeks they can be used as a ready-made flavouring for creamy desserts, fruit salads, ice creams and custards, or sprinkled on to sponge cakes and pastries.

Making Infused Sugars

Ensure that flower petals are clean and dry, and break larger spices, such as cinnamon sticks, into smaller pieces. Layer up in small jars with caster (superfine) or granulated sugar and store in a cool, dry place. The greater the ratio of flavourings to sugar the more intense the final result.

Do not combine more than two or three different flavourings in each sugar or they might detract from each other. Combinations like rose petal, cardamom and ginger, or lavender and orange blend really well.

Below: Many aromatic ingredients can be used to infuse flavour.

HERBAL AND FLORAL DECORATIONS

Herbs and their romantic petite flowers can be used to make some of the prettiest culinary decorations. Crystallizing edible flowers – coating them in a fine dusting of caster (superfine) sugar – both enhances their delicate flavours and makes a simple and effective way of preserving them for later use. Once dry they can be stored in an airtight container for up to a week, ready to decorate special occasion cakes and summer desserts.

Freezing fresh herb flowers in ice cubes also prolongs the enjoyment of these stunning flowers, but most impressive of all is a classic "ice-bowl".

COOK'S TIPS
• Use any herb flowers or edible flowers such as mint, sweet cicely, sage, pansy, nasturtium, marigold, viola, rosemary, lavender, borage and rosebuds or small roses. Large roses can be used if separated into petals. You can use a mixture of colours but sometimes the bowls look more delicate if just one colour is used.
• Do not pack in too many herbs and flowers or the bowl will lose its clear icy look.
• Do not worry if you hear ice-cracking sounds when releasing the ice bowl. It will not fall apart!
• Do not be tempted to leave the bowls in hot water for too long as the ice will quickly melt and become fragile. Be cautious, even if it means redipping the bowl once or twice.
• For convenience, fill the bowl with ice cream or sorbet and return to the freezer so that it is ready and waiting for you. Serve on a plate, preferably glass, with a shallow rim to catch the melting ice.
• For a special occasion, ice bowls also look stunning filled with chilled water and floating candles.

Right: Ice bowls will retain their shape for many hours before melting, although keep out of the sun where possible. For a colour co-ordinated centrepiece, why not choose herbs and flowers that complement the taste or colours of the intended contents?

Herb-flower Ice Bowl

Easy to make, this stunning flower ice bowl provides a perfect container for ice creams and sorbets.

MAKES ONE BOWL

INGREDIENTS
  ice cubes
  freshly picked herb sprigs and their
    flowers (see Cook's Tips)
  freshly picked flowers
  water

1 Find two bowls, either glass or plastic, which will fit inside one another leaving a gap of about 2cm/¾in between them. Put some ice cubes in the base of the larger bowl and tuck some herb sprigs and flowers around them.

2 Position the smaller bowl inside it and tape the bowls together across the tops so that the smaller bowl is centred. Pour cold water into the large bowl until the level starts to come up the sides. Freeze for 2–3 hours until firm.

3 Tuck more herb sprigs and flowers between the two bowls using a skewer to arrange them so that they look attractive through the sides of the bowl. Fill the large bowl with water until it comes to the rim. Carefully transfer to the freezer and freeze overnight.

4 Peel off the tape. Half-fill a washing-up bowl with hot water, sit the frozen bowls in it and pour a little hot water into the smaller bowl. Count to 30 then remove the bowls and pour the water out of the small bowl. Use a thin knife to loosen the ice from the edges of the bowls.

Making Floral Ice Cubes

Use small herb flowers that will tuck easily into ice-cube compartments, or separate larger flowers into petals. Small summer fruits such as red and white currants or raspberries can be tucked in with the flowers. Use the ice cubes in punches, cordials, sparkling table water or to decorate a platter of summer fruits.

INGREDIENTS
  a selection of freshly picked edible
    flowers
  cold water

1 Pour water into ice-cube trays until they are half full.

2 Position the flowers using tweezers, if easier to handle. Freeze for about 1 hour, or until firm. Add more water to fill the trays and refreeze until firm.

Below: Floral ice cubes make an attractive addition to a glass of summer punch or herb-flavoured cordial.

Crystallized Flowers

Pick flowers for crystallization when they are perfectly dry, and check that they are free of insects. Most herb flowers can be crystallized (candied), although some, like rosemary and thyme flowers are too fiddly to bother with. Borage, sage, nasturtium, sweet cicely fronds and rose petals work really well, as do other edible flowers like violas, violets, pansies, primroses, cowslips and pinks.

INGREDIENTS
  1 egg white
  caster (superfine) sugar
  plenty of fresh flowers or petals

1 Put the egg white into a small bowl and lightly whisk until it is broken up.

2 Coat a flower with egg white, using a paintbrush. Sprinkle the flower with sugar and shake off the excess. Transfer to a sheet of baking parchment and leave in a warm place until dry. Store in a sealed container for up to a week until ready to use.

COOK'S TIP

If you want the crystallized flowers to keep for more than a week it is best to use gum arabic (available from a chemist) instead of egg white. Dissolve 5ml/1 tsp in 25ml/ 1½ tbsp water or a colourless spirit such as gin or vodka and follow the recipe for the remaining steps. Gum arabic will make the petals very hard and brittle, so keep in a cool place away from any source of moisture.

Crystallized Roses

Coat all the petals in egg white and sugar as before, then push one end of a 15cm/6in length of fine floristry wire through the flower base. Bend and hook the other end of the wire over the rim of a tall glass or bowl so the rose is suspended. Leave until dry.

Below: Fresh roses dusted with sugar are stylish and sophisticated and deceptively simple to make.

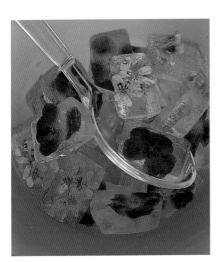

HERB DIRECTORY

These herbs appear in the following recipes and many can be grown in a kitchen garden.

ALLIUM CEPA – ONION
Description Single bulbs on each stem.
Cultivation Propagate from sets in early summer or seed sown in spring or autumn. Plant in well-drained soil, rich in nutrients.
Culinary uses Onions are among the most useful herbs. They can be eaten raw, baked, or fried, or cooked in stews, soups, sauces, casseroles or chutneys.

ALLIUM SATIVUM – GARLIC
Description A hardy perennial, often cultivated as an annual. Bulbs are made up of cloves, in a papery, white casing. The clump of flat leaves grows to 60cm/2ft. Flowers are greenish-white, but appear only in warm climates.
Cultivation Plant bulbs in autumn or winter in rich soil and a sunny position. Lift in late summer and dry in the sun before storing. Increase by dividing bulbs and replanting.
Culinary uses Bulbs, separated into cloves are a popular flavouring agent.

ALLIUM SCHOENOPRASUM – CHIVES
Description A hardy perennial with clumps of cylindrical leaves growing from small bulblets to 30cm/12in. Purple flower globes appear in early summer.
Cultivation Need a sunny or semi-shaded position. The leaves do not withstand very cold winters.
Culinary uses A prime culinary herb, it has a milder flavour than its onion cousin. Chop leaves into salads, sauces and soups. Flowers can be used as a garnish.

ANETHUM GRAVEOLENS – DILL
Description An aromatic annual, with a single stem and feathery leaves. It has tiny yellow flowers in midsummer and elliptic fruits. Resembles fennel, but is shorter and has a subtler, less strongly aniseed (anise seed) flavour.
Cultivation Plant dill seeds in well-drained but nutrient-rich soil, in full sun.
Culinary uses Leaves and seeds add a caraway-like flavour to seafood, egg dishes and bland-tasting vegetables. It can be added to curries, rice dishes, soups, pickles and chutneys.

ANTHRISCUS CEREFOLIUM – CHERVIL
Description A hardy annual, with bright-green, finely divided feathery leaves and small, flat, white flowers in early summer.
Cultivation Needs light, moist soil and a sunny situation. Propagate from seed.
Culinary uses The delicate taste of the leaves, which is more distinctive than parsley, complements most dishes. It brings out the flavour of other herbs and is an essential ingredient, along with parsley, tarragon and chives, of the classic French combination, *fines herbes*. It is best used raw.

ARMORACIA RUSTICANA – HORSERADISH
Description A perennial, with large bright-green, oblong leaves, with serrated margins.
Cultivation It flourishes in most soils.
Culinary uses The young, fresh leaves can be added to salads or chopped into smoked-fish pâtés. The fresh root is shredded to make a strong-flavoured, creamy-textured sauce, traditionally served with beef. An excellent accompaniment to cold, smoked meat and fish, hard-boiled (hard-cooked) eggs and stuffed aubergines (eggplant).

ARTEMISIA DRACUNCULUS – FRENCH TARRAGON

Description A perennial with branched stems 1m (1yd) high, and slim leaves.
Cultivation It prefers a fairly moist, but well-drained soil and full sun, and in cold climates needs protection in winter.
Culinary uses It is used in salads, pâté, cooked meat, fish and egg dishes. Well known for its affinity with chicken, it also enhances the flavour of root vegetables. Vinegar flavoured with tarragon is a classic condiment and it is a main ingredient of sauces and stuffings.

BORAGO OFFICINALIS – BORAGE

Description A short-lived hardy annual, with a sprawling habit of growth, hollow, hairy stems, downy leaves and blue (or pink) star-shaped flowers with black centres. It is attractive to bees.
Cultivation Grows in any soil. Prefers a sunny position. Propagate from seed.
Culinary uses The leaves have a faint flavour of cucumbers and are added to soft drinks and wine cups. The flowers make a pretty garnish for salads, and are candied or dried as decorations for sweet dishes and cakes.

BRASSICA NIGRA – MUSTARD

Description An erect annual, with narrow, lobed leaves and bright yellow flowers, followed by pods containing reddish-brown seeds.
Cultivation Requires rich, well-dressed soil and full sun and is propagated by seed sown in spring.
Culinary uses The ground seeds, mixed into a paste, make the familiar "hot-flavoured" condiment. The whole seeds are added to curries, soups, stews, pickles and sauces. Young leaves are eaten with cress, or added to salads.

CAPSICUM ANNUUM var. ANNUUM – BELL OR SWEET PEPPER

Description Annual, which grows into a small bushy plant 60–90cm/2–3ft high, with glossy leaves. Small white flowers are followed by large, sweet, green, ripening to red or yellow, fruits.
Cultivation Frost-tender plant, which must be grown under glass in cool temperate climates. Water freely, feed weekly and mist flowers with water daily to ensure fruit sets.
Culinary uses Fruits are used as vegetables and to flavour savoury dishes.

CAPSICUM FRUTESCENS – CHILLI

Description Most grow into small bushy plants. They have glossy lance-shaped leaves, small white flowers followed by green, ripening to red, fruits.
Cultivation Frost-tender plants, grown under glass in cool temperate climates.
Culinary uses Hot chilli peppers are added to pickles and chutneys; dried to make cayenne pepper, chilli powder or paprika.

CARUM CARVI – CARAWAY

Description A biennial 45–60cm/18–24in tall, with feathery leaves. In its second year, umbels of white flowers are followed by ridged fruits, which are popularly known as seeds.
Cultivation Prefers well-drained soil and a sunny position. Propagated from seed sown in spring, preferably in situ.
Culinary uses Seeds are used to flavour cakes, breads, cheese, baked apples, cabbage and meat dishes. Also used as a pickling spice.

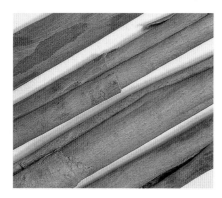

CINNAMOMUM ZEYLANICUM – CINNAMON

Description A medium-sized evergreen tree growing to about 9m/30ft, with brown, papery bark. The inner bark of young stems is wrapped round thin rods to form quills.

Cultivation Grows in sandy soils, and needs plenty of rain, sun and a minimum temperature of 15°C/59°F.

Culinary uses A popular spice for savoury and sweet dishes, it is also a traditional ingredient for Christmas puddings, mince pies and spiced drinks.

CITRUS LIMON – LEMON

Description A small evergreen tree, with light-green, oval leaves and thorny stems. Clusters of white flowers are followed by bitter-tasting yellow fruits.

Cultivation Requires well-drained, not too acid compost – 6–6.5pH – and protection from frost.

Culinary uses The juice and rind of the fruit are widely used as a flavouring in cooking, and in soft drinks, sauces, pickles, preserves and marinades. The zest of lemon, containing its oil, gives the strongest flavour.

CORIANDRUM SATIVUM – CORIANDER (CILANTRO)

Description An annual with pungent leaves. Small white flowers are followed by pale-brown fruits (seeds).

Cultivation Propagated from seed.

Culinary uses The leaves have a stronger, spicier taste than the seeds. Both are used in curries, pickles and chutneys, also in Middle Eastern, Indian, South-east Asian and South American cuisines. Leaves are added to salads, seeds are used in sweet dishes, breads and cakes, and to flavour liqueurs.

CROCUS SATIVUS – SAFFRON

Description A perennial with linear leaves growing from a rounded corm. Fragrant lilac flowers appear in autumn, the red anthers of which produce the saffron threads.

Cultivation Needs well-drained soil, sun and warm summers to flower.

Culinary uses Saffron is widely used as a flavouring and colourant in Middle Eastern and northern Indian cookery, in rice dishes and fish soups. It is sometimes used in sweets and cakes.

CURCUMA LONGA – TURMERIC

Description A perennial with shiny, lanceolate leaves and spikes of pale-yellow flowers.

Cultivation A tender, tropical plant, it requires well-drained but moist soil, a humid atmosphere and minimum temperatures of 15–18°C/59–64°F.

Culinary uses The rhizomes are boiled, skinned, dried and ground into powder. This is used in Worcestershire sauce and curry powder, and adds colour and a musky flavour to savoury dishes.

CYMBOPOGON CITRATUS – LEMON GRASS

Description A tall, clump-forming perennial, it has linear, grass-like leaves, strongly scented with lemon.

Cultivation In cool, temperate climates it must be grown as a conservatory (porch) or warm greenhouse plant, and moved outside in the summer.

Culinary uses The young white stem and leaf base are chopped and used in stir-fry dishes, also in Thai, Malaysian and South-east Asian cuisine. Leaves may also be infused (steeped) to make tea.

ELETTARIA CARDAMOMUM – CARDAMOM
Description A large perennial, with a clump of leaves growing from a fleshy rhizome. Flowers are followed by pale green capsules, which contain many small pungent black seeds.
Cultivation Needs a minimum temperature of 18°C/64°F, well-drained, rich soil, partial shade, plenty of rain and high humidity.
Culinary uses A major curry spice, the seeds are also used to flavour hot wine punches, sweet, milky rice puddings and egg custard.

ERUCA VESICARIA subsp SATIVA –
ROCKET (ARUGULA)
Description A frost-hardy annual, with dentate, deeply divided leaves. Small, four-petalled, white flowers, streaked at the centre of each petal with violet, appear in late winter to early summer.
Cultivation Propagate from seed, from late winter to early summer. Grow on poor, dry soil, with plenty of sun, for a more pungent taste.
Culinary uses The pungent leaves lend interest to lettuce, and other bland-tasting leaves, as a salad ingredient.

FICUS CARICA – FIG
Description A deciduous tree. The flowers are completely concealed within fleshy receptacles and are followed by small, pear-shaped fruits.
Cultivation Warm, sunny summers are necessary to produce fruit. Grow in well-drained, rich soil.
Culinary uses The fruits are delicious raw, or as a cooked ingredient of sweet pies, pastries, desserts and conserves. Dried figs can be stewed, or eaten as they are. They are also used in cakes.

FOENICULUM – FENNEL
Description An aromatic perennial, with erect, hollow stems and mid-green, feathery foliage. Umbels of yellow flowers are borne in summer, followed by ovoid, ridged, yellow-green seeds. The plant is scented with aniseed.
Cultivation Propagation is from seed sown in spring.
Culinary uses Leaves and seeds go well with fish, especially oily fish. Seeds add flavour to stir-fry and rice dishes. The bulbous stems of fennel are eaten raw in salads or cooked as a vegetable.

FRAGARIA VESCA – WILD STRAWBERRY
Description A low-growing perennial. It has shiny, trifoliate leaves, and small white, yellow-centred flowers, followed by red ovoid fruits with tiny yellow seeds embedded in the surface.
Cultivation Grow in fertile, well-drained soil (alkaline), in sun or partial shade.
Culinary uses Rich in vitamin C, fruits are eaten fresh or made into desserts, conserves and juices. Dried leaves are included in blended herbal teas to improve taste and aroma.

HELIANTHUS – SUNFLOWER
Description A tall annual, up to 3m/10ft in height, with erect stems and oval, hairy leaves. The daisy-shaped flower heads, and brown disc florets at the centre, are followed by the striped black-and-white seeds, about 1,000 per head.
Cultivation Propagate by seed in spring.
Culinary uses Seeds are eaten fresh or roasted in salads and breads. Oil, made from the seeds, is used for cooking and in salad dressings. It is also a constituent of margarine.

JUGLANS REGIA – WALNUT
Description A deciduous tree bearing catkins, which are followed by dark green fruits, each containing a wrinkled brown walnut.
Cultivation Requires deep, rich soil and a sunny position.
Culinary uses Walnuts are included in many dishes, sweet and savoury, for their distinctive flavour.

LAURUS NOBILIS – BAY
Description An evergreen shrub, or small tree, it has aromatic dark-green, glossy ovate leaves.
Cultivation Grow in fertile, reasonably moist but well-drained soil in a sheltered, sunny position.
Culinary uses A first-rate culinary herb, a bay leaf is always included in a bouquet garni, and adds flavour to marinades, casseroles, stews, soups and dishes requiring a long cooking time. Also used to flavour sweet sauces and as a garnish for citrus sorbets.

LAVANDULA ANGUSTIFOLIA – LAVENDER
Description An evergreen shrub with slender leaves from silvery white to green in colour and mauve to purple flower clusters held on long stems.
Cultivation Requires a well-drained soil and plenty of sun.
Culinary uses Flowers are used to flavour sugar for making cakes, biscuits, meringues, ice creams and desserts. They can be added to vinegar, marmalade or jam, or cooked (tied in a muslin bag) with blackcurrants or fruit mixtures.

LEVISTICUM OFFICINALE – LOVAGE
Description A hardy herbaceous perennial, growing on deep fleshy roots, it has glossy leaves with a spicy, celery-like scent, and umbels of dull-yellow flowers in summer, followed by seeds.
Cultivation A vigorous, spreading plant.
Culinary uses Leaves are used to flavour soups, stews, meat, fish or vegetable dishes; young shoots and stems are eaten as a vegetable (like braised celery) and may be candied; seeds are added to biscuits and bread.

MELISSA OFFICINALIS – LEMON BALM
Description A vigorous, bushy perennial, it has strongly lemon-scented, rough-textured, leaves. Clusters of pale-yellow flowers appear in late summer.
Cultivation Grows in any soil in sun or partial shade.
Culinary uses Leaves are best used fresh, as scent and therapeutic properties are lost when dried and stored. They add a lemon flavour to desserts, cordials, liqueurs and wine cups, salads, soups, sauces, stuffings, poultry, game and fish.

MYRISTICA FRAGRANS – NUTMEG
Description Evergreen tree bearing yellow globular fruits, which contain the nutmeg.
Cultivation These tropical trees require sandy, humus-rich soil and shade or partial shade. May be grown in a conservatory (greenhouse) with a minimum temperature of 18°C/64°F and humid atmosphere.
Culinary uses Ground or grated (shredded) nutmeg is used in a wide range of sweet and savoury dishes, including soups, sauces, milk and cheese dishes, fruit cakes, puddings and drinks.

MYRRHIS ODORATA – SWEET CICELY
Description A vigorous, hardy, herbaceous perennial, with a strong taproot, with hollow stems and soft, downy, fern-like leaves. Compound umbels of white flowers appear in late spring, followed by large, distinctively beaked and ridged brown fruit. The whole plant is pleasantly scented.
Cultivation Sow seeds in autumn.
Culinary uses Traditionally used as a sweetening agent and flavouring for stewed soft fruits and rhubarb. Leaves also make a pretty garnish for sweet and savoury dishes.

OCIMUM BASILICUM – BASIL
Description Basil is a half-hardy annual with oval, pale-green leaves. A purple-leaved variety is also available.
Cultivation It requires well-drained, moist, medium-rich soil and full sun. Basil is propagated from seed, and flourishes as a container plant.
Culinary uses Fresh leaves should be added towards the end of the cooking process so that its fragrance is not lost. They have an affinity with tomatoes and aubergines (eggplant), and add fragrance to ratatouille, pasta sauces, pesto sauce and pizza toppings.

OLEA EUROPAEA – OLIVE
Description An evergreen tree, with smooth, leathery, grey-green leaves. Creamy-white flowers are borne in summer, followed by fruits.
Cultivation Requires dry soil and full sun.
Culinary uses The fruits are eaten as appetizers, added to salads, sauces, bread, pizzas and pasta. The oil, pressed from the fruit, is used in salad dressings, sauces, mayonnaise and as a cooking oil. Extra-virgin, cold-pressed oil, has the best flavour and properties.

ORIGANUM MAJORANA – SWEET MARJORAM
Description Half-hardy perennial. Has greyish-green leaves and small, white, sometimes pinkish flowers in knot-like clusters surrounding the stem.
Cultivation Requires well-drained, fertile soil and full sun. Sow seed in spring, after danger of frost has passed.
Culinary uses Leaves and flowering stems are used to flavour savoury dishes, especially pasta sauces, pizza toppings, bread, oil and vinegar.

ORIGANUM VULGARE – OREGANO
Description A bushy, hardy perennial, with aromatic, ovate, dark-green leaves and panicles of pink to purple tubular flowers in summer.
Cultivation Requires well-drained soil and a sunny position.
Culinary uses Leaves are widely used in Italian, Greek and Mediterranean cuisine, especially in pasta sauces, pizza toppings, tomato sauces, vegetable dishes and to flavour bread, oil and vinegars.

PAPAVER SOMNIFERUM – OPIUM POPPY
Description A hardy annual, it has oblong, deeply lobed, blue-green leaves. Large, lilac, pink or white flowers, with papery petals, in early summer, followed by blue-green seed pods.
Cultivation Propagated by seed sown in spring, often self-seeds.
Culinary uses The seeds are dried for use whole or ground in breads, biscuits, bakery products and as a garnish. Commercially produced seed is from a subspecies of *Papaver somniferum*.

PETROSELINUM – PARSLEY
Description A frost-hardy biennial, growing to 30–60cm/1–2ft.
Cultivation Parsley requires rich, moist but well-drained soil and a sunny position, or partial shade.
Culinary uses The leaves are added to salads, sauces, salad dressings, savoury butter, stuffings, chopped into meat, fish and vegetable dishes and used as a garnish. The stalks are essential to a bouquet garni for flavouring casseroles.

PIPER NIGRUM – BLACK PEPPER
Description A perennial climber, with ovate, prominently-veined, dark-green leaves. Black pepper is produced from whole fruits, picked and dried just as they start to go red; white pepper is from ripe fruits, and green pepper is from unripe pickled fruits.
Cultivation Pepper requires deep, rich, manured soil, plenty of water, a humid atmosphere and a shady position.
Culinary uses The fruits are chiefly used as a condiment and flavouring in a wide range of dishes.

ROSA – ROSE
Description Flowering shrub.
Cultivation Fertile, moist soil and a sunny position are best for producing thriving rose plants with large flowers.
Culinary uses Hips, from R. *canina*, are used for making vinegar, syrups, preserves and wines. Flower petals, from R. *gallica*, are added to salads and desserts, crystallized, made into jellies, jams and conserves. Distilled rose water is used to flavour confectionery and desserts, especially in Middle Eastern dishes.

ROSMARINUS OFFICINALIS – ROSEMARY
Description An evergreen shrub, it has woody branches and strongly aromatic, needle-like foliage. A dense covering of small, tubular, flowers, appear in spring.
Cultivation Needs well-drained soil and a sunny position.
Culinary uses The leaves are a classic flavouring for roasted lamb, stews and casseroles, and added to marinades, vinegar, oil and dressings. Used sparingly, the leaves and flowers add spice and interest to cakes, biscuits, sorbets and stewed apples.

RUMEX ACETOSA – SORREL
Description A hardy perennial with large, pale-green, oblong to lanceolate leaves, and large terminal spikes of small, disc-shaped, reddish-brown flowers on long stalks.
Cultivation Grows best and runs to seed less quickly in rich, moist soil, in a sunny or partially shady position.
Culinary uses Young sorrel leaves add a pleasant, lemony flavour to soups, sauces, salads, egg and cheese dishes. They have the best flavour and texture in spring.

SALVIA OFFICINALIS – SAGE
Description An evergreen, highly aromatic, shrubby perennial.
Cultivation Grow in light, well-drained soil in full sun.
Culinary uses Leaves, fresh or dried, are used to give flavour to Mediterranean dishes, cheese, sausages, goose, pork and other fatty meat. In Italy sage is added to liver dishes. It is also made into stuffings – a classic combination is sage and onion. Leaves of pineapple sage may be floated in drinks.

SAMBUCUS NIGRA – ELDERFLOWER
Description Small deciduous tree, which bears flat umbels of creamy, musk-scented flowers in early summer followed by clusters of black fruit in early autumn.
Cultivation Prefers moist but well-drained, humus-rich soil in sun or partial shade.
Culinary uses Fresh or dried flowers give a muscatel flavour to gooseberries and stewed fruits and are added to desserts and sorbets. Flowers and berries are used in vinegars, cordials and wines.

SANGUISORBA MINOR – SALAD BURNET
Description A clump-forming perennial, it has pinnate leaves with numerous pairs of oval, serrated-edged leaflets and long stalks topped by rounded crimson flower-heads.
Cultivation Thrives on chalk (alkaline). Propagated by seed sown in spring.
Culinary uses The leaves have a mild, cucumber flavour, make a pleasant addition to salads and can be floated in drinks or wine punch.

SATUREJA HORTENSIS – SUMMER SAVORY
Description A small, bushy, hardy annual, it has woody stems and small, leathery, dark-green leaves. Tiny white or pale-lilac flowers appear in summer.
Cultivation Grow in well-drained soil in full sun. Propagated from seed sown in early spring.
Culinary uses Summer savory has an affinity with beans. The leaves add a spicy flavour to dried herb mixtures, stuffings, pulses, pâtés and meat dishes.

THYMUS VULGARIS – THYME
Description Common thyme is a fine-stemmed, low-growing sub-shrub with tiny leaves. Pale mauve flowers are borne in summer. There are many other species of thyme with differing flavours.
Cultivation All thymes require free-draining, gritty soil and a sunny position.
Culinary uses The leaves, fresh or dried, are widely used as a culinary flavouring in marinades, meat dishes, soups, stews and casseroles.

TROPAEOLUM MAJUS – NASTURTIUM
Description In cool temperate regions it is a half-hardy annual. Yellow or orange flowers grow on stalks.
Cultivation Grow in relatively poor soil for the best production of flowers. Easily propagated from seed sown in containers, or in situ, in spring.
Culinary uses The leaves are added to salads for their peppery taste. Flowers are also used as a flavouring for vinegar. Seeds, when still green, are pickled as a substitute for capers.

ZINGIBER OFFICINALE – GINGER
Description A perennial reed-like plant with branching rhizomes, growing to 1–1.2m/3–4ft high.
Cultivation Tender, tropical plant requiring fertile, humus-rich, well-drained soil with plenty of moisture and humidity.
Culinary uses Fresh ginger is grated (shredded) and added to stir-fry dishes, and widely used, fresh or dried, in Chinese and Thai cooking. Dried ground ginger is an ingredient of curry powder, pickles and chutneys. It is also used in biscuits, cakes and desserts.

COOKING
WITH HERBS

The fresh flavours of herbs are emphasized in chilled soups or salads — ideal for hot summer days. Piquant fusions such as sorrel, horseradish and dill, or fragrant combinations of lavender, thyme and marjoram transform summery dishes. When the weather is cooler, hot soups make ideal lunches or first courses. Golden saffron, warming garlic, pungent fennel seeds and bright bell peppers are the ingredients used here to create satisfying dishes.

Soups and
Salads

SHERRIED ONION <u>AND</u> SAFFRON SOUP <u>WITH</u> ALMONDS

THE SPANISH COMBINATION OF ONIONS, GARLIC, SAFFRON AND SHERRY GIVES THIS PALE YELLOW SOUP A BEGUILING FLAVOUR THAT MAKES IT THE PERFECT OPENING COURSE FOR A SPECIAL MEAL.

SERVES FOUR

INGREDIENTS
40g/1½oz/3 tbsp butter
2 large yellow onions, thinly sliced
1 small garlic clove, finely chopped
good pinch of saffron threads (about
   12 threads)
50g/2oz/⅓ cup blanched almonds,
   toasted and finely ground
750ml/1¼ pints/3 cups good chicken
   or vegetable stock
45ml/3 tbsp dry sherry
salt and ground black pepper
30ml/2 tbsp toasted flaked (sliced)
   almonds and chopped fresh parsley,
   to garnish

1 Melt the butter in a heavy pan over a low heat. Add the onions and garlic, stirring to coat them thoroughly in the butter. Cover the pan and cook very gently, stirring frequently, for 15–20 minutes, or until the onions are soft and golden yellow.

COOK'S TIP
This soup is also delicious served chilled. Add a little more chicken or vegetable stock to make a slightly thinner soup, then leave to cool and chill for at least 4 hours (or overnight). Just before serving, taste for seasoning. Float one or two ice cubes in each bowl.

2 Add the saffron threads and cook, uncovered, for 3–4 minutes, then add the ground almonds and continue to cook, stirring constantly, for another 2–3 minutes.

3 Pour in the chicken or vegetable stock and sherry and stir in 5ml/1 tsp salt. Season with plenty of black pepper. Bring the mixture to the boil, then lower the heat and simmer gently for about 10 minutes.

4 Process the soup in a food processor or blender until smooth, then return it to the rinsed pan. Reheat slowly, without allowing the soup to boil, stirring occasionally. Taste for seasoning, adding more salt and ground black pepper if required.

5 Ladle the soup into four heated bowls, garnish with the toasted flaked almonds and chopped fresh parsley, and serve immediately.

CHILLED GARLIC <u>AND</u> ALMOND SOUP <u>WITH</u> GRAPES

USE PLUMP GARLIC CLOVES FOR THIS RICHLY FLAVOURED AND CREAMY CHILLED SOUP, WHICH IS BASED ON AN ANCIENT MOORISH RECIPE FROM ANDALUCIA IN SOUTHERN SPAIN. ALMONDS AND PINE NUTS COMPLETE THE FULL FLAVOUR.

3 Soak the bread in 300ml/½ pint/ 1¼ cups of the water for 10 minutes, then squeeze dry. Process the garlic, bread, nuts and 5ml/1 tsp salt to a paste in a food processor or blender.

4 Gradually blend in the olive oil and sherry vinegar, followed by sufficient water to make a smooth soup with a creamy consistency.

5 Stir in 30ml/2 tbsp of the sherry. Adjust the seasoning and add more dry sherry to taste. Chill for at least 3 hours, then adjust the seasoning again and stir in a little more iced water if the soup has thickened. Reserve a few of the grapes for the garnish and stir the remainder into the soup.

6 Ladle the soup into bowls (glass bowls look good) and garnish with ice cubes, the reserved grapes and chopped chives. Serve with additional extra virgin olive oil for drizzling to taste over the soup just before it is eaten.

SERVES SIX

INGREDIENTS
- 75g/3oz/½ cup blanched almonds
- 50g/2oz/½ cup pine nuts
- 6 large garlic cloves, peeled but left whole
- 200g/7oz good-quality day-old bread, crusts removed
- 900ml–1 litre/1½–1¾ pints/3¾– 4 cups still mineral water, chilled
- 120ml/4fl oz/½ cup extra virgin olive oil, plus extra to serve
- 15ml/1 tbsp sherry vinegar
- 30–45ml/2–3 tbsp dry sherry
- 250g/9oz grapes, peeled, halved and seeded
- salt and ground white pepper
- ice cubes and chopped fresh chives, to garnish

1 Roast the almonds and pine nuts together in a dry pan over a moderate heat until they are very lightly browned. Allow to cool, then grind to a powder.

2 Blanch the peeled garlic cloves in boiling water for 3 minutes, then drain and rinse.

COOK'S TIPS
- Blanching the garlic softens its flavour.
- Toasting the nuts slightly accentuates their flavour, but you can omit this step if you prefer a paler soup.

GARLIC AND CORIANDER SOUP

THIS RECIPE IS BASED ON THE WONDERFUL BREAD SOUPS OR ACORDAS OF PORTUGAL. USING THE BEST-QUALITY INGREDIENTS WILL ENSURE THIS SIMPLE SOUP IS A SUCCESS.

SERVES SIX

INGREDIENTS
    25g/1oz/1 cup fresh coriander
      (cilantro), leaves and stalks
      chopped separately
    1.5 litres/2½ pints/6¼ cups
      vegetable or chicken stock, or water
    5–6 plump garlic cloves, peeled
    6 eggs
    275g/10oz day-old bread, with most
      of the crust removed, torn into
      bitesize pieces
    90ml/6 tbsp extra virgin olive oil,
      plus extra to serve
    salt and ground black pepper

1 Place the coriander stalks in a pan. Add the stock or water and bring to the boil. Lower the heat and simmer for 10 minutes, then process in a food processor or blender. Sieve the soup and return it to the pan.

2 Crush the garlic with 5ml/1 tsp salt, then stir in 120ml/4fl oz/½ cup of the hot soup. Return the mixture to the rest of the soup in the pan.

3 Meanwhile, poach the eggs in a frying pan of simmering water for 3–4 minutes, or until just set. Use a draining spoon to remove them from the pan and transfer to a warmed plate. Trim off any untidy bits of white.

4 Meanwhile, bring the soup back to the boil and add seasoning to taste. Stir in the chopped coriander leaves and remove from the heat.

5 Place the bread in six soup plates or bowls and drizzle the oil over it. Ladle in the soup and stir. Add a poached egg to each bowl and serve immediately, offering olive oil at the table so that it can be drizzled over the soup as desired.

ITALIAN PEA AND BASIL SOUP

THE PUNGENT FLAVOUR OF BASIL LIFTS THIS APPETIZING ITALIAN SOUP OF PETITS POIS, WHILE THE ONION AND GARLIC GIVE DEPTH. SERVE IT WITH GOOD CRUSTY BREAD TO ENJOY IT AT ITS BEST.

2 Add the peas and stock to the pan and bring to the boil. Reduce the heat, add the basil and seasoning, then simmer for 10 minutes.

3 Spoon the soup into a food processor or blender (you may have to do this in batches) and process until the soup is smooth.

4 Return the soup to the rinsed pan and reheat gently until piping hot. Ladle into warm bowls, sprinkle with shaved Parmesan and garnish with basil.

SERVES FOUR

INGREDIENTS
  75ml/5 tbsp olive oil
  2 large onions, chopped
  1 celery stick, chopped
  1 carrot, chopped
  1 garlic clove, finely chopped
  400g/14oz/3½ cups frozen
    petits pois (baby peas)
  900ml/1½ pints/3¾ cups
    vegetable stock
  25g/1oz/1 cup fresh basil leaves,
    roughly torn, plus extra to garnish
  salt and ground black pepper
  shaved Parmesan cheese,
    to serve

1 Heat the oil in a large pan and add the onions, celery, carrot and garlic. Cover the pan and cook over a low heat for 45 minutes, or until the vegetables are soft, stirring occasionally to prevent the vegetables sticking.

VARIATION
You can also use mint or a mixture of parsley, mint and chives in place of the basil, if you like.

TOMATO AND FRESH BASIL SOUP

FRESH BASIL AND FULL-FLAVOURED TOMATOES ARE A FAVOURITE COMBINATION. MAKE THIS DELICIOUS ITALIAN SOUP IN LATE SUMMER WHEN TOMATOES ARE AT THEIR BEST AND THERE IS STILL PLENTY OF FRESH BASIL TO BE PICKED.

SERVES FOUR

INGREDIENTS

15ml/1 tbsp olive oil
1 onion, finely chopped
900g/2lb ripe Italian plum tomatoes,
   roughly chopped
1 garlic clove, roughly chopped
about 750ml/1¼ pints/3 cups
   chicken or vegetable stock
120ml/4fl oz/½ cup dry white wine
30ml/2 tbsp sun-dried tomato purée
   (paste)
30ml/2 tbsp chopped fresh basil,
   plus a few whole leaves to garnish
30ml/2 tbsp single (light) cream
salt and ground black pepper

1 Heat the olive oil in a large pan over a medium heat. Add the chopped onion and cook it gently for about 5 minutes, stirring frequently, until it is softened but not brown.

2 Stir in the chopped tomatoes and garlic, then add the stock, white wine and tomato purée, with seasoning to taste. Bring to the boil, then reduce the heat, half-cover the pan and simmer for 20 minutes, stirring occasionally.

3 Purée the soup with the chopped basil in a food processor or blender, then press through a sieve into a clean pan. Discard the residue in the sieve.

4 Add the cream to the pan and heat through, stirring. Do not allow the soup to boil. Check the consistency and add more hot stock if necessary, then add the seasoning. Pour into bowls and garnish with basil leaves. Serve at once.

CUCUMBER AND GARLIC SOUP WITH WALNUTS

YOGURT AND CUCUMBER MAKE REFRESHING PARTNERS FOR CHILLED SOUP. HERE, THE FAMILIAR COMBINATION IS GIVEN A RICHER DIMENSION USING PUNGENT GARLIC AND DILL.

SERVES FIVE TO SIX

INGREDIENTS
½ cucumber
4 garlic cloves, peeled but left whole
2.5ml/½ tsp salt
75g/3oz/¾ cup walnut pieces
40g/1½oz day-old bread, torn
  into pieces
30ml/2 tbsp walnut or sunflower oil
400ml/14fl oz/1⅔ cups natural
  (plain) yogurt
120ml/4fl oz/½ cup cold water or
  chilled still mineral water
5–10ml/1–2 tsp lemon juice
For the garnish
40g/1½oz/scant ⅓ cup coarsely
  chopped walnuts
25ml/1½ tbsp olive oil
sprigs of fresh dill

1 Dice the cucumber flesh and set aside.

2 Using a large mortar and pestle, crush the garlic cloves and salt together well. Add the walnut and bread pieces and crush everything together until the consistency is smooth.

3 Add the walnut or sunflower oil slowly, and use the pestle to combine the mixture well.

4 Transfer the mixture into a large bowl and beat in the yogurt and the diced cucumber flesh.

5 Add the cold water or mineral water and lemon juice to taste, then pour the soup into chilled bowls to serve. Garnish with the coarsely chopped walnuts, a little olive oil drizzled over the nuts and sprigs of fresh dill.

COOK'S TIP
If you prefer your soup to be smooth, purée it in a food processor or blender before serving.

SORREL, SPINACH <u>AND</u> DILL SOUP

THE WARM FLAVOUR OF HORSERADISH AND THE ANISEED FLAVOUR OF DILL MELD WITH SORREL AND SPINACH TO MAKE THIS UNUSUAL RUSSIAN SOUP. AN EXCELLENT SUMMER SOUP, SERVED CHILLED.

SERVES SIX

INGREDIENTS
  25g/1oz/2 tbsp butter
  225g/8oz sorrel, stalks removed
  225g/8oz young spinach,
    stalks removed
  25g/1oz fresh horseradish, grated
    (shredded)
  750ml/1¼ pints/3 cups cider
  1 pickled cucumber, finely chopped
  30ml/2 tbsp chopped fresh dill
  225g/8oz cooked fish, such as pike,
    perch or salmon, skinned and boned
  salt and ground black pepper
  sprig of dill, to garnish

1 Melt the butter in a large pan. Add the prepared sorrel and spinach leaves together with the grated fresh horseradish. Cover the pan and allow to cook gently for 3–4 minutes, or until the sorrel and spinach leaves have wilted.

2 Tip into a food processor or blender and process to a fine purée (paste). Ladle into a tureen or bowl and stir in the cider, cucumber and dill.

3 Chop the fish into bitesize pieces. Add to the soup, then season well. Chill for at least 3 hours before serving, garnished with a sprig of dill.

MUSHROOM <u>AND</u> PARSLEY SOUP

A HANDFUL OF PARSLEY HARMONIZES WITH WHOLESOME FIELD MUSHROOMS, ENHANCING WITHOUT DOMINEERING THEIR FLAVOUR. THIS SOUP MAKES A HEARTY LUNCH, SERVED WITH CRUSTY BREAD, ON COLD AUTUMN DAYS.

SERVES EIGHT

INGREDIENTS
75g/3oz/6 tbsp unsalted (sweet)
  butter
2 onions, roughly chopped
600ml/1 pint/2½ cups milk
900g/2lb field (portabello)
  mushrooms, sliced
8 slices white bread
60ml/4 tbsp chopped fresh parsley,
  plus extra to garnish
300ml/½ pint/1¼ cups double
  (heavy) cream
salt and ground black pepper

COOK'S TIP
Use fresh flat leaf parsley in this soup. It
has a superior flavour to the curly variety.

1 Melt the butter and sauté the
chopped onion for about 5 minutes,
or until it is soft but not coloured. Add
the milk.

2 Add the sliced mushrooms to the
pan and continue cooking for a further
5 minutes.

3 Tear the bread into pieces, drop them
into the soup and leave to soak for
15 minutes. Purée the soup and return
it to the pan. Add the chopped parsley,
cream and salt and pepper to taste.
Reheat gently, but do not allow the soup
to boil. Serve at once, garnished with
extra chopped parsley.

MELON AND BASIL SOUP

BASIL AND LIME GIVE ZEST TO SWEET MELON IN THIS CHILLED SUMMER SOUP. SIMPLE TO PREPARE, BUT STRIKINGLY UNUSUAL, IT MAKES A PERFECT START TO A SUMMER MEAL.

3 Place the sugar, water and lime rind in a small pan over a low heat. Stir until dissolved, then bring to the boil and simmer for 2–3 minutes.

4 Remove the pan from the heat and leave to cool slightly. Pour half the mixture into the food processor or blender with the melon flesh. Blend until smooth, adding the remaining syrup and lime juice to taste.

5 Pour the mixture into a bowl, then stir in the basil.

6 Cover the bowl with clear film and transfer to the refrigerator to chill for 2–3 hours. When ready to serve, pour into individual bowls and serve garnished with basil leaves and melon balls.

SERVES FOUR TO SIX

INGREDIENTS
   2 Charentais or cantaloupe melons
   75g/3oz/6 tbsp caster
    (superfine) sugar
   175ml/6fl oz/¾ cup water
   finely grated (shredded) rind and
    juice of 1 lime
   45ml/3 tbsp finely chopped
    fresh basil
   fresh basil leaves, to garnish

1 Cut the melons in half across the middle. Scrape out the seeds with a spoon and discard.

2 Using a melon baller, scoop out 20–24 balls and set aside for the garnish. Scoop out the remaining flesh and place in the bowl of a food processor or blender.

COOK'S TIP
Add the syrup in two stages, as the amount of sugar needed will depend on the sweetness of the melon.

CAULIFLOWER AND BEAN SOUP WITH FENNEL SEED AND PARSLEY

FENNEL SEEDS SAUTÉED WITH GARLIC AND ONION GIVE A DELICIOUS EDGE TO THE MILD FLAVOURS OF CAULIFLOWER AND FLAGEOLET BEANS IN THIS SUBSTANTIAL AND WARMING SOUP.

SERVES FOUR TO SIX

INGREDIENTS
15ml/1 tbsp olive oil
1 garlic clove, crushed
1 onion, chopped
10ml/2 tsp fennel seeds
1 cauliflower, cut into small florets
2 × 400g/14oz cans flageolet or
  cannellini beans, drained and rinsed
1.2 litres/2 pints/5 cups vegetable
  stock or water
60–90ml/4–6 tbsp chopped fresh
  parsley
salt and ground black pepper
toasted slices of French bread,
  to serve

1 Heat the olive oil in a large, flameproof casserole or heavy pan. Add the garlic, onion and fennel seeds and cook them gently for 5 minutes, or until they are softened.

2 Add the cauliflower florets and half of the flageolet beans and pour in the stock or water.

3 Bring to the boil. Reduce the heat and simmer for 10 minutes, or until the cauliflower is tender.

4 Pour the soup into a food processor or blender and blend until smooth. Return to the pan, and stir in the remaining flageolet beans. Season to taste.

5 Reheat the soup and pour into bowls. Sprinkle with chopped parsley and serve with toasted slices of French bread.

LEEK, POTATO AND ROCKET SOUP

ROCKET ADDS ITS DISTINCTIVE, PEPPERY TASTE TO THIS WONDERFULLY SATISFYING SOUP. SERVE IT HOT, GARNISHED WITH A GENEROUS SPRINKLING OF TASTY CIABATTA CROÛTONS.

SERVES FOUR TO SIX

INGREDIENTS
50g/2oz/¼ cup butter
1 onion, chopped
3 leeks, chopped
2 medium floury potatoes, diced
900ml/1½ pints/3¾ cups light
   chicken stock or water
2 large handfuls of rocket (arugula),
   roughly chopped
150ml/¼ pint/⅔ cup double (heavy)
   cream
salt and ground black pepper
garlic-flavoured ciabatta croûtons,
   to serve (see Cook's Tip)

1 Melt the butter in a large, heavy pan then add the chopped onion and leeks and the diced potatoes. Stir until the vegetables are coated in melted butter. Heat the ingredients until they are sizzling then reduce the heat to low.

2 Cover and sweat the vegetables for 15 minutes. Pour in the chicken stock or water and bring to the boil then reduce the heat, cover again and allow to simmer for 20 minutes, or until the vegetables are tender.

3 Press the soup through a sieve or pass through a food mill and return to the rinsed-out pan. (When puréeing the soup, don't use a food processor or blender, as these will give the soup a gluey texture.) Add the chopped rocket to the pan.

4 Allow the soup to cook gently, uncovered, for 5 minutes.

5 Stir in the cream, then season to taste and reheat gently. Ladle into warmed bowls and serve with a scattering of garlic-flavoured ciabatta croûtons.

COOK'S TIP
For the croûtons, cut 1cm/½in cubes of ciabatta bread. Heat a peeled garlic clove in 60ml/4 tbsp olive oil. Remove, then fry the croûtons until golden.

POTATO AND GARLIC BROTH

ALTHOUGH THERE IS PLENTY OF GARLIC IN THIS SOUP, THE END RESULT IS NOT OVERPOWERING.
SERVE PIPING HOT WITH BREAD, AS THE PERFECT WINTER WARMER.

SERVES FOUR

INGREDIENTS
2 small or 1 large whole head of
  garlic (about 20 cloves)
4 potatoes, diced
1.75 litres/3 pints/7½ cups
  vegetable stock
salt and ground black pepper
chopped flat leaf parsley, to garnish
  (optional)

VARIATION
Make the soup more substantial by
placing in each bowl a slice of French
bread which has been toasted and
topped with melted cheese. Pour the
soup over so that the bread soaks it up.

1 Preheat the oven to 190°C/375°F/
Gas 5. Place the unpeeled garlic bulbs
or bulb in a small roasting pan and
bake for 30 minutes, or until they are
soft in the centre.

2 Meanwhile, par-boil the potatoes in a
large pan of boiling, lightly salted water
for 10 minutes.

3 Simmer the stock for 5 minutes. Drain
the par-boiled potatoes and then add to
the stock.

4 Squeeze the garlic pulp into the soup,
reserving a few cloves to garnish, stir
and season to taste. Simmer the soup
for 15 minutes and serve garnished with
garlic cloves and parsley, if you like.

ROASTED PEPPER AND ONION SOUP

GRILLING INTENSIFIES THE FLAVOUR OF SWEET RED AND YELLOW BELL PEPPERS AND HELPS THIS SOUP KEEP ITS STUNNING COLOUR. THE GARLIC AND ONION ADD CHARACTER. PEPPERS ARE NOW AVAILABLE ALL YEAR ROUND AND MAKE A BRIGHT AND WELCOME SOUP WHATEVER THE TIME OF YEAR.

SERVES FOUR

INGREDIENTS

   3 red (bell) peppers
   1 yellow (bell) pepper
   1 onion, chopped
   1 garlic clove, crushed
   750ml/1¼ pints/3 cups good
     vegetable stock
   15ml/1 tbsp plain (all-purpose) flour
   salt and ground black pepper
   red and yellow (bell) peppers diced,
     to garnish

1 Preheat the grill (broiler). Halve the peppers and cut out their stalks and white pith. Scrape out the seeds.

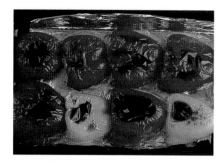

2 Line a grill (broiling) pan with foil and arrange the halved peppers, skin-side up, in a single layer. Grill (broil) until the skins have blackened and blistered.

VARIATION

If preferred, garnish the soup with a swirl of natural (plain) yogurt instead of sprinkling it with the diced bell peppers.

3 Transfer the peppers to a plastic bag. Seal and leave until cool, then peel away their skins and discard. Roughly chop the pepper flesh.

4 Put the onion and garlic clove into a large pan with 150ml/¼ pint/⅔ cup stock. Boil for about 5 minutes, or until most of the stock has reduced. Lower the heat and stir until softened and just beginning to colour.

5 Sprinkle the flour over the onions, then gradually stir in the remaining stock. Add the chopped, roasted peppers and bring to the boil. Cover and simmer for a further 5 minutes.

6 Leave to cool slightly, then purée in a food processor or blender. Season to taste. Return to the pan and reheat until piping hot. Ladle into four soup bowls and garnish with diced peppers.

CUCUMBER AND DILL SALAD

AROMATIC DILL IS A PARTICULARLY USEFUL HERB TO USE WITH SALADS. HERE, ITS ANISEED FLAVOUR IS PARTNERED WITH FRESH-TASTING CUCUMBER IN A SOUR CREAM DRESSING.

3 Rinse well under cold running water, then pat dry with kitchen paper.

4 Finely chop about 45ml/3 tbsp fresh dill, setting aside one sprig for the garnish. Put the slices of cucumber in a bowl, add the chopped dill and combine the ingredients together, either mixing with your hands or with a fork.

5 In another bowl, stir the vinegar into the sour cream and season the mixture with pepper.

SERVES FOUR

INGREDIENTS
    2 cucumbers
    5ml/1 tsp salt
    5 sprigs fresh dill
    15ml/1 tbsp white wine vinegar
    150ml/¼ pint/⅔ cup sour cream
    ground black pepper

1 Use a cannelle knife (zester) to peel away strips of rind from along the length of the cucumbers, creating a striped effect. Slice thinly.

2 Put the slices in a sieve or colander set over a bowl and sprinkle with the salt. Leave for 1 hour to drain.

6 Pour the sour cream over the cucumber and chill for 1 hour before turning into a serving dish. Garnish with the sprig of dill, and serve.

COOK'S TIP
Salting the cucumber draws out some of the moisture, thereby making it firmer. Make sure you rinse it thoroughly before using or the salad will be too salty.

FENNEL, ORANGE AND ROCKET SALAD

AN UNUSUAL COMBINATION OF FENNEL, ROCKET, ORANGE AND OLIVES IS BROUGHT TOGETHER IN THIS REFRESHING SALAD THAT IS IDEAL SERVED WITH SPICY OR RICH FOOD.

SERVES FOUR

INGREDIENTS
    2 oranges
    1 fennel bulb
    115g/4oz rocket (arugula) leaves
    50g/2oz/⅓ cup black olives
For the dressing
    30ml/2 tbsp extra virgin olive oil
    15ml/1 tbsp balsamic vinegar
    1 small garlic clove, crushed
    salt and ground black pepper

1 With a vegetable peeler, cut strips of rind from the oranges, leaving the pith behind, and cut into thin julienne strips. Cook in boiling water for a few minutes. Drain. Peel the oranges, removing all the white pith. Slice them into thin rounds and discard any seeds.

2 Cut the fennel bulb in half lengthways with a sharp knife and slice across the bulb as thinly as possible, preferably in a food processor fitted with a slicing disc or using a mandolin.

3 Combine the oranges and fennel slices in a serving bowl and toss with the rocket leaves.

4 To make the dressing, mix together the olive oil, balsamic vinegar, crushed garlic and seasoning and pour over the salad in the bowl.

5 Toss the salad ingredients together well and leave to stand for a few minutes. Sprinkle with the black olives and julienne strips of orange rind.

CHICKEN SALAD <u>WITH</u> HERBS <u>AND</u> LAVENDER

THE DELIGHTFUL SCENT OF LAVENDER HAS A NATURAL AFFINITY WITH SWEET GARLIC, THYME, MARJORAM AND ORANGE. THE ADDITION OF FRIED POLENTA OR CORN MEAL MAKES THIS SALAD BOTH FILLING AND DELICIOUS.

SERVES FOUR

INGREDIENTS
  4 boneless chicken breasts
  900ml/1½ pints/3¾ cups light
    chicken stock
  175g/6oz/1½ cups fine polenta
    or corn meal
  50g/2oz/¼ cup butter, plus extra
    for greasing
  450g/1lb young spinach
  175g/6oz lamb's lettuce
  8 small tomatoes, halved
  salt and ground black pepper
  8 sprigs fresh lavender, to garnish
For the marinade
  6 fresh lavender flowers
  10ml/2 tsp finely grated (shredded)
    orange rind
  2 garlic cloves, crushed
  10ml/2 tsp clear honey
  30ml/2 tbsp olive oil
  10ml/2 tsp chopped fresh thyme
  10ml/2 tsp chopped fresh marjoram
  salt

1 To make the marinade, strip the lavender flowers from the stems and combine with the orange rind, garlic, honey and salt. Add the oil and herbs.

2 Slash the chicken deeply, spread the mixture over and leave to marinate in the refrigerator for 20 minutes.

3 To make the polenta, bring the chicken stock to the boil in a heavy pan. Add the polenta or corn meal in a steady stream, stirring all the time until thick. Turn the cooked polenta or corn meal out on to a shallow, buttered tray and leave to cool.

COOK'S TIP
When preparing the spinach, tear the leaves into smaller pieces just before you are ready to serve. Do not cut them with a knife, as this tends to make the edges turn brown.

4 Cook the chicken on a medium barbecue or under the grill (broiler) for 15 minutes, basting with the marinade and turning once, until cooked through.

5 Cut the polenta into 2.5cm/1in cubes using a wet knife.

6 Heat the butter in a large frying pan and fry the polenta until it is golden.

7 Divide the spinach and lamb's lettuce among four dinner plates. Slice each chicken breast and arrange among the salad. Add the polenta and tomato halves to each plate.

8 Season each salad with salt and ground black pepper and garnish with sprigs of lavender. Serve immediately.

ROASTED TOMATO AND MOZZARELLA SALAD WITH BASIL DRESSING

FRESH BASIL MAKES AN APPETIZING AND VIVIDLY COLOURED OIL FOR SERVING WITH MOZZARELLA AND TOMATOES. ROASTING THE TOMATOES BRINGS OUT THEIR FLAVOUR AND ADDS A NEW DIMENSION TO THIS SALAD.

SERVES FOUR

INGREDIENTS
    olive oil, for brushing
    6 large plum tomatoes
    2 balls fresh mozzarella cheese,
        cut into 8–12 slices
    salt and ground black pepper
    basil leaves, to garnish
For the basil oil
    25 basil leaves
    60ml/4 tbsp extra virgin olive oil
    1 garlic clove, crushed

COOK'S TIP
Make the basil oil just before serving to retain its fresh flavour and bright colour.

1 Preheat the oven to 200°C/400°F/ Gas 6 and oil a baking tray. Cut the tomatoes in half lengthways and remove the seeds. Place skin-side down on the baking tray and roast for 20 minutes, or until the tomatoes are tender but still retain their shape.

2 Meanwhile, make the basil oil. Place the basil leaves, olive oil and garlic in a food processor or blender and process until smooth. Transfer to a bowl and chill until required.

3 For each serving, place the tomato halves on top of two or three slices of mozzarella and drizzle over the oil. Season well. Garnish with basil leaves and serve at once.

COOK'S TIP
The best mozzarella to use for this salad is the traditional kind made from buffalo's milk, which has the best flavour.

MIXED HERB SALAD WITH TOASTED SUNFLOWER AND PUMPKIN SEEDS

THE FUSION OF CORIANDER, PARSLEY, BASIL AND ROCKET WITH SUNFLOWER AND PUMPKIN SEEDS GIVES THIS SALAD ITS CRUNCHY AND CRISPY TEXTURES.

SERVES FOUR

INGREDIENTS
    25g/1oz/3 tbsp pumpkin seeds
    25g/1oz/3 tbsp sunflower seeds
    90g/3½oz mixed salad leaves
    50g/2oz/2 cups mixed salad herbs,
        such as coriander (cilantro), parsley,
        basil and rocket (arugula)
For the dressing
    60ml/4 tbsp extra virgin olive oil
    15ml/1 tbsp balsamic vinegar
    2.5ml/½ tsp Dijon mustard
    salt and ground black pepper

COOK'S TIP
Use your hands to toss the salad to avoid bruising the leaves.

1 To make the dressing, combine the ingredients in a bowl or screw-top jar, and shake or mix with a small whisk or fork until combined.

2 Toast the pumpkin and sunflower seeds in a dry frying pan over a medium heat for 2 minutes, or until golden, tossing frequently to prevent them burning. Allow to cool slightly.

3 Put the salad and herb leaves in a large bowl and then sprinkle with the cooled seeds.

4 Pour the dressing over the salad and toss carefully until the leaves are well coated, then serve.

FENNEL <u>AND</u> EGG TABBOULEH <u>WITH</u> HERBS

TABBOULEH IS A MIDDLE EASTERN SALAD OF STEAMED BULGUR WHEAT, FLAVOURED WITH LOTS OF PARSLEY, MINT, LEMON JUICE AND GARLIC. HERE, THE SALAD ALSO INCLUDES THE SWEET, ANISEED FLAVOUR OF FENNEL AND THE TANG OF BLACK OLIVES.

SERVES FOUR

INGREDIENTS

  250g/9oz/1⅓ cups bulgur wheat
  4 small eggs
  1 fennel bulb
  1 bunch of spring onions (scallions),
    chopped
  25g/1oz/½ cup drained sun-dried
    tomatoes in oil, sliced
  45ml/3 tbsp chopped fresh parsley
  30ml/2 tbsp chopped fresh mint
  75g/3oz/½ cup black olives
  60ml/4 tbsp olive oil
  30ml/2 tbsp garlic oil
  30ml/2 tbsp lemon juice
  50g/2oz/½ cup chopped hazelnuts,
    toasted
  1 open-textured loaf or 4 pitta
    breads, warmed
  salt and ground black pepper

1 In a bowl, pour boiling water over the bulgur wheat, and leave to soak for about 15 minutes.

2 Drain the bulgur wheat in a metal sieve, and place the sieve over a pan of boiling water. Cover and steam for about 10 minutes. Fluff up the grains with a fork and spread out on a metal tray. Set aside to cool.

3 Hard-boil (hard-cook) the eggs for 8 minutes. Cool under running water, peel and quarter.

4 Halve and finely slice the fennel. Boil in salted water for 6 minutes, then drain and cool under running water.

5 Combine the eggs, fennel, spring onions, sun-dried tomatoes, parsley, mint and olives with the bulgur wheat. Dress with olive oil, garlic oil and lemon juice, then add the nuts. Season well, then tear the bread into pieces and add to the salad. Serve immediately.

COOK'S TIP

If you are short of time, simply soak the bulgur wheat in boiling water for about 20 minutes. Drain and rinse under cold water to cool, then drain thoroughly.

LENTIL AND SPINACH SALAD WITH ONION, CUMIN AND GARLIC

THIS EARTHY SALAD IS A BLEND OF HERBY FLAVOURS. PUY LENTILS ARE TOSSED WITH ONIONS, BAY, THYME, PARSLEY AND CUMIN AND THEN DRESSED IN A MEDLEY OF MUSTARD, GARLIC AND LEMON.

SERVES SIX

INGREDIENTS
- 225g/8oz/1 cup Puy lentils
- 1 fresh bay leaf
- 1 celery stick
- fresh thyme sprig
- 30ml/2 tbsp olive oil
- 1 onion or 3–4 shallots, finely chopped
- 10ml/2 tsp crushed toasted cumin seeds
- 400g/14oz young spinach
- 30–45ml/2–3 tbsp chopped fresh parsley
- toasted French bread, to serve
- salt and ground black pepper

For the dressing
- 75ml/5 tbsp extra virgin olive oil
- 5ml/1 tsp Dijon mustard
- 15–25ml/1–1½ tbsp red wine vinegar
- 1 small garlic clove, finely chopped
- 2.5ml/½ tsp finely grated (shredded) lemon rind

1 Rinse the lentils and place them in a large pan. Add plenty of water to cover. Tie the bay leaf, celery and thyme into a bundle and add to the pan, then bring to the boil. Reduce the heat so that the water just boils steadily. Cook the lentils for 30–45 minutes, or until just tender. Do not add salt at this stage, as it toughens the lentils.

2 Meanwhile, to make the dressing, mix the oil, mustard and 15ml/1 tbsp vinegar with the garlic and lemon rind, and season well with salt and pepper.

3 Thoroughly drain the lentils and turn them into a bowl. Add most of the dressing and toss well, then set the lentils aside, stirring occasionally.

COOK'S TIP
Named after Puy in France, these small, greyish-green lentils are considered to have the best and most distinctive flavour. They keep both their shape and colour well when cooked.

4 Heat the olive oil in a pan or deep frying pan and sauté the chopped onion or shallots over a low heat for 4–5 minutes, or until they are beginning to soften. Add the cumin and cook for a further 1 minute.

5 Add the spinach and season to taste, then cover and cook for 2 minutes. Stir and cook again briefly until wilted.

6 Stir the spinach into the lentils and leave the salad to cool. Bring back to room temperature, if necessary. Stir in the remaining dressing and chopped parsley. Adjust the seasoning, and add extra red wine vinegar, if necessary.

7 Turn the salad on to a serving platter and serve with slices of toasted French bread.

GRIDDLED FENNEL <u>AND</u> HERB SALAD <u>WITH</u> SPICY TOMATO DRESSING

THIS IS AN EXCELLENT SALAD TO MAKE IN THE EARLY AUTUMN WHEN DELICATELY SWEET FENNEL AND YOUNG LEEKS ARE AT THEIR BEST. THYME, BAY LEAVES, SHALLOTS, OLIVES AND A DASH OF CHILLI COMPLETE THE FUSION OF FLAVOURS. SERVE WITH GRILLED FISH OR SIMPLY WITH BREAD.

SERVES SIX AS A FIRST COURSE

INGREDIENTS
  675g/1½lb leeks
  2 large fennel bulbs
  120ml/4fl oz/½ cup extra virgin
    olive oil
  2 shallots, chopped
  150ml/¼ pint/⅔ cup dry white wine
    or white vermouth
  5ml/1 tsp fennel seeds, crushed
  6 fresh thyme sprigs
  2–3 bay leaves
  good pinch of dried red chilli flakes
  350g/12oz tomatoes, peeled, seeded
    and diced
  5ml/1 tsp sun-dried tomato
    paste (optional)
  good pinch of sugar (optional)
  75g/3oz/½ cup small black olives
  salt and ground black pepper

2 Trim the fennel bulbs with a sharp knife, reserving any feathery tops for the garnish and cut the bulbs either into thin slices or into thicker wedges, according to taste.

3 Cook the fennel in the reserved cooking water for about 5 minutes, then drain thoroughly and toss with 30ml/ 2 tbsp of the olive oil. Season to taste with black pepper.

6 Add the diced tomatoes and cook briskly for 5–8 minutes, or until reduced and thickened.

7 Add the tomato paste, if using, and adjust the seasoning, adding a good pinch of sugar, if you think the dressing needs it.

1 Cook the leeks in boiling salted water for 4–5 minutes. Use a draining spoon to remove the leeks, place them in a colander to drain thoroughly and cool. Reserve the cooking water in the pan. Then squeeze out excess water and cut the leeks into 7.5cm/3in lengths.

COOK'S TIP
When buying fennel, look for rounded bulbs; flatter ones are immature. The flesh should be crisp and white, with no signs of bruising. Avoid specimens with broken leaves or that appear to be either soggy or dried out.

4 Heat a ridged cast-iron griddle. Arrange the leeks and fennel slices or wedges on the griddle and cook until they are tinged deep brown. Remove the vegetables from the griddle, place in a large, shallow dish and set aside.

5 Place the remaining olive oil in a large pan with the shallots, white wine or vermouth, crushed fennel seeds, thyme, bay leaves and chilli flakes, and bring to the boil over a medium heat. Lower the heat and simmer for 10 minutes.

8 Pour the dressing over the leeks and fennel, toss to mix and leave to cool. The salad may be made several hours in advance and kept in the refrigerator, but bring it back to room temperature before serving.

9 When ready to serve, stir the salad and scatter the black olives and chopped fennel tops over the top.

VARIATION
If you prefer, the black olives can be served in a separate bowl, so that guests can help themselves if they wish.

POTATO AND MUSSEL SALAD WITH SHALLOT AND CHIVE DRESSING

SHALLOT AND CHIVES IN A CREAMY DRESSING ADD BITE TO THIS SALAD OF POTATO AND SWEET MUSSELS AND PARSLEY. SERVE WITH FULL-FLAVOURED WATERCRESS AND PLENTY OF WHOLEMEAL BREAD.

SERVES FOUR

INGREDIENTS
675g/1½lb salad potatoes
1kg/2¼lb mussels, scrubbed and
    beards removed
200ml/7fl oz/scant 1 cup dry
    white wine
15g/½oz/¼ cup chopped flat
    leaf parsley
salt and ground black pepper
chopped fresh chives or chive
    flowers, to garnish
For the dressing
105ml/7 tbsp mild olive oil
15–30ml/1–2 tbsp white
    wine vinegar
5ml/1 tsp Dijon mustard
1 large shallot, very finely chopped
15ml/1 tbsp chopped fresh chives
45ml/3 tbsp double (heavy) cream
pinch of caster (superfine) sugar

1 Cook the potatoes in boiling, salted water for 15–20 minutes, or until tender. Drain, cool, then peel. Slice the potatoes into a bowl and toss with 30ml/2 tbsp of the oil for the dressing.

2 Discard any open mussels that do not close when sharply tapped. Bring the white wine to the boil in a large, heavy pan. Add the mussels, cover and boil vigorously, shaking the pan occasionally, for 3–4 minutes, or until the mussels have opened. Discard any mussels which have not opened after 5 minutes' cooking. Drain and shell the mussels, reserving the cooking liquid.

3 Boil the reserved cooking liquid until reduced to about 45ml/3 tbsp. Strain this through a fine sieve over the potatoes and toss to mix.

4 For the dressing, whisk together the remaining oil, 15ml/1 tbsp vinegar, the mustard, shallot and chives.

5 Add the cream and whisk again to form a thick dressing. Adjust the seasoning, adding more vinegar and a pinch of sugar to taste.

6 Toss the mussels with the potatoes, then mix in the dressing and chopped parsley. Serve sprinkled with chopped chives or chive flowers separated into florets.

COOK'S TIP
Potato salads, such as this one, should not be chilled if at all possible as the cold alters the texture of the potatoes and of the creamy dressing. For the best flavour and texture, serve this salad just cool or at room temperature.

CHICKEN AND CORIANDER SALAD

SERVE THIS SUBSTANTIAL SUMMER SALAD WARM TO MAKE THE MOST OF THE WONDERFUL FLAVOURS OF CHICKEN AND CORIANDER. THE CHICKEN CAN BE GRILLED OR IS ALSO EXCELLENT BARBECUED.

2 Cook the mangetouts for 2 minutes in boiling water, then refresh in cold water. Tear the lettuces into small pieces and mix all the salad ingredients and the bacon together. Arrange the salad in individual dishes.

3 Season the chicken breasts with salt and pepper, then grill (broil) them on medium heat for 10–15 minutes, or cook on a medium barbecue. Baste with the marinade and turn once during cooking, until cooked through.

4 Slice the chicken into thin pieces. Divide among the bowls of salad and add some of the dressing to each dish. Combine quickly and scatter some fresh coriander over each bowl, to garnish.

SERVES SIX

INGREDIENTS
4 medium chicken breasts, skinned and boned
225g/8oz mangetouts (snow peas)
2 heads decorative lettuce such as lollo rosso or feuille de chêne
3 carrots, cut into matchsticks
175g/6oz/2⅓ cups sliced button (white) mushrooms
6 bacon rashers (strips), fried and chopped
salt and ground black pepper
60ml/4 tbsp fresh coriander (cilantro) leaves
For the coriander dressing
120ml/4fl oz/½ cup lemon juice
30ml/2 tbsp wholegrain mustard
250ml/8fl oz/1 cup olive oil
75ml/2½fl oz/⅓ cup sesame oil
5ml/1 tsp coriander seeds, crushed

1 Mix all the dressing ingredients in a bowl. Place the prepared chicken breasts in a shallow dish and pour over half the dressing. Leave to marinate overnight in the refrigerator. Chill the remaining dressing.

COOK'S TIP
Use any of your favourite herbs in this dish, basil, parsley and thyme all work well.

SALAD OF FRESH CEPS WITH PARSLEY AND WALNUT DRESSING

THE DISTINCTIVE FLAVOUR OF WALNUTS IS A NATURAL PARTNER TO MUSHROOMS. HERE, WILD MUSHROOMS AND WALNUTS MELD WITH FRENCH MUSTARD, LEMON, PARSLEY AND NUT OILS IN A RICHLY FLAVOURED SALAD.

SERVES FOUR

INGREDIENTS
  350g/12oz/4¾ cups fresh small
    cep mushrooms
  50g/2oz/½ cup broken walnut pieces
  175g/6oz mixed salad leaves, to
    include Batavia, young spinach
    and frisée
  50g/2oz/⅔ cup freshly shaved
    Parmesan cheese
  salt and ground black pepper
For the dressing
  2 egg yolks
  2.5ml/½ tsp French mustard
  75ml/5 tbsp groundnut (peanut) oil
  45ml/3 tbsp walnut oil
  30ml/2 tbsp lemon juice
  30ml/2 tbsp chopped fresh parsley
  1 pinch caster (superfine) sugar

1 To make the dressing, place the egg yolks in a screw-top jar with the mustard, groundnut and walnut oils, lemon juice, parsley and sugar. Shake well to combine.

COOK'S TIP
The dressing for this salad uses raw egg yolks. Be sure to use only the freshest eggs from a reputable supplier. Pregnant women, young children and the elderly are advised not to eat raw egg yolks. This dressing can be made without the egg yolks if necessary.

2 Slice the mushrooms thinly with a sharp knife, keeping the slices intact if you can.

3 Transfer the sliced mushrooms to a large bowl and combine with the dressing. Set aside for 10–15 minutes to allow the flavours to mingle.

4 Meanwhile, preheat the grill (broiler) to medium-hot, place the walnut pieces in a grill (broiling) pan and toast for about a minute, shaking the pan to ensure they toast evenly. Alternatively, dry-fry them on a griddle.

5 Wash and spin the mixed salad leaves, then add to the mushrooms in the bowl and toss to combine.

6 To serve, spoon the salad on to four large plates, season well then scatter with the toasted walnuts and shavings of Parmesan cheese.

COOK'S TIP
If fresh ceps are unavailable, this salad can also be made with a range of other fresh mushrooms. Chestnut mushrooms, fresh shiitake mushrooms and even the familiar button (white) mushrooms would all work well.

VARIATION
For special occasions, two or three drops of truffle oil will impart a deep and mysterious flavour.

Enjoy the variety of flavours herbs bring to brunches, light lunches or suppers. Serve scrambled egg with chives, or appreciate the creaminess of baked garlic. Frittatas feature here, as well as pasta dishes, making use of crisp rocket, garlic, bell peppers and stunning combinations of aromatic herbs. Or, for the delicate touch, the flowers and leaves of sweet cicely add scent to roasted peppers for a special meal.

Light Meals

CHIVE SCRAMBLED EGGS IN BRIOCHE

DELICIOUSLY CREAMY SCRAMBLED EGG WITH A HINT OF CHIVES CONCEALS A LAYER OF MUSHROOMS IN THESE BRIOCHE BASKETS. SERVE FOR A LIGHT LUNCH OR A DELIGHTFULLY INDULGENT BREAKFAST.

SERVES FOUR

INGREDIENTS
   115g/4oz/½ cup unsalted (sweet)
     butter
   75g/3oz/1¼ cups finely sliced brown
     cap (cremini) mushrooms
   4 individual brioches
   8 eggs
   15ml/1 tbsp chopped fresh chives,
     plus extra to garnish
   salt and ground black pepper

1 Preheat the oven to 180°C/350°F/ Gas 4. Place a quarter of the butter in a frying pan and heat until melted. Fry the mushrooms for about 3 minutes, or until soft. Set aside and keep warm.

COOK'S TIP
Timing and temperature are crucial for perfect scrambled eggs. When cooked for too long over too high a heat, eggs become dry and crumbly; cooked briefly over a low heat and they are sloppy and unappealing.

2 Slice the tops off the brioches, then scoop out the centres and discard. Put the brioches and lids on a baking sheet and bake for 5 minutes, or until hot and slightly crisp.

3 Meanwhile, beat the eggs lightly and season to taste with salt and ground black pepper. Heat the remaining butter in a heavy pan over a gentle heat. When the butter has melted and is foaming slightly, add the eggs. Using a wooden spoon, stir constantly, to ensure the egg does not stick to the pan.

4 Continue to stir gently until about three-quarters of the egg is semi-solid and creamy – this process should take 2–3 minutes. Remove the pan from the heat – the egg will continue to cook in the heat from the pan – then stir in the chopped chives.

5 To serve, spoon a little of the mushrooms into the bottom of each brioche and top with the scrambled eggs. Sprinkle with extra chives, balance the brioche lids on top and serve immediately.

QUAIL'S EGGS AND FOCACCIA WITH HERBS

*ITALIAN FOCACCIA BREAD IS TRANSFORMED WITH A SIMPLE TOPPING OF FRESH MIXED HERBS AND
GARLIC AND IS THE PERFECT PARTNER FOR QUAIL'S EGGS. A DIP FLAVOURED WITH CAPERS, SHALLOT,
SPRING ONIONS AND BEETROOT PROVIDES CONTRASTING TEXTURE.*

SERVES SIX

INGREDIENTS

    1 large Italian focaccia or 2–3 Indian
      parathas or other flatbreads
    olive oil, for brushing and dipping
    1 large garlic clove, finely chopped
    small handful of fresh mixed herbs,
      such as coriander (cilantro), mint,
      parsley and oregano, chopped
    18–24 quail's eggs
    30ml/2 tbsp home-made mayonnaise
    30ml/2 tbsp sour cream
    5ml/1 tsp chopped capers
    5ml/1 tsp finely chopped shallot
    225g/8oz fresh beetroot (beet),
      cooked in water, peeled and sliced
    ½ bunch spring onions (scallions),
      halved lengthways
    60ml/4 tbsp red onion chutney
    salt and ground black pepper
    coarse salt and mixed peppercorns,
      roughly ground, to serve

1 Preheat the oven to 190°C/375°F/
Gas 5. Brush the bread with olive oil,
sprinkle with garlic, mixed herbs and
seasoning, and bake for 10–15 minutes,
or until golden. Keep warm.

2 Put the quail's eggs into a pan of cold
water. Bring the water to the boil and
cook for 5 minutes. Carefully lift the
eggs out of the pan, using a slotted
spoon, and place in a bowl of cold
water. Leave to cool.

3 To make the mayonnaise dip, mix
together the mayonnaise, sour cream,
capers, shallot and seasoning. Peel the
eggs and arrange in a serving dish.

4 Cut the bread into wedges and serve
with the eggs and mayonnaise dip,
along with dishes of beetroot, spring
onions and chutney. Serve with bowls
of coarse salt, ground peppercorns and
olive oil for dipping.

LITTLE ONIONS WITH CORIANDER, WINE AND OLIVE OIL

CHILLIES AND TOASTED CORIANDER SEEDS ADD PIQUANCY TO THE SMALL ONIONS USED HERE. BAY, GARLIC, THYME, OREGANO, LEMON AND PARSLEY PROVIDE AN UNMISTAKABLY MEDITERRANEAN KICK.

SERVES SIX

INGREDIENTS

    105ml/7 tbsp olive oil
    675g/1½lb small onions, peeled
    150ml/¼ pint/⅔ cup dry white wine
    2 bay leaves
    2 garlic cloves, bruised
    1–2 small dried red chillies
    15ml/1 tbsp coriander seeds, toasted
      and lightly crushed
    2.5ml/½ tsp sugar
    a few fresh thyme sprigs
    30ml/2 tbsp currants
    10ml/2 tsp chopped fresh oregano
      or marjoram
    5ml/1 tsp grated (shredded) lemon rind
    15ml/1 tbsp chopped fresh flat
      leaf parsley
    30–45ml/2–3 tbsp pine nuts, toasted
    salt and ground black pepper

1 Place 30ml/2 tbsp of the olive oil in a wide pan. Add the onions, place over a medium heat and cook gently for about 5 minutes, or until the onions begin to colour. Use a draining spoon to remove from the pan and set aside.

2 Add the remaining oil, the wine, bay leaves, garlic, chillies, coriander seeds, sugar and thyme to the pan.

3 Bring to the boil and cook briskly for 5 minutes. Return the onions to the pan. Add the currants, reduce the heat and cook gently for 15–20 minutes, or until the onions are tender but not falling apart.

4 Use a draining spoon to transfer the onions to a serving dish, then boil the liquid vigorously until it reduces considerably. Taste and adjust the seasoning, if necessary, then pour the liquid over the onions.

5 Scatter the chopped oregano or marjoram over the onions in the dish, then cool and chill them.

6 Just before you are ready to serve the onions, stir in the grated lemon rind, chopped flat leaf parsley and toasted pine nuts.

COOK'S TIP
You might like to serve this dish as part of a mixed hors d'oeuvre – an antipasto – perhaps accompanied by mild mayonnaise-dressed celeriac salad and some thinly sliced prosciutto or other air-dried ham.

SPICED ONION KOFTAS

CORIANDER, CUMIN, TURMERIC AND CHILLIES CREATE THE TRADITIONAL FLAVOURING FOR THESE INDIAN ONION FRITTERS. CHICKPEA FLOUR IS AVAILABLE FROM SUPERMARKETS AND INDIAN STORES.

SERVES FOUR TO FIVE

INGREDIENTS
675g/1½lb onions, halved and
  thinly sliced
5ml/1 tsp salt
5ml/1 tsp ground coriander seeds
5ml/1 tsp ground cumin
2.5ml/½ tsp ground turmeric
1–2 fresh green chillies, seeded and
  finely chopped
45ml/3 tbsp chopped fresh
  coriander (cilantro)
90g/3½oz/scant ¾ cup chickpea flour
2.5ml/½ tsp baking powder
vegetable oil, for deep-frying
To serve
  lemon wedges
  fresh coriander (cilantro) sprigs
  yogurt and herb dip or yogurt and
    cucumber dip (see Cook's Tips)

1 Place the onions in a colander, add the salt and toss well. Stand the colander on a plate for 45 minutes, tossing once or twice. Rinse, then squeeze out excess moisture. Place in a bowl. Add the ground coriander, cumin, turmeric, chillies and fresh coriander. Mix well.

COOK'S TIPS
• To make a yogurt and herb dip, stir 30ml/2 tbsp each of chopped fresh coriander and mint into about 250ml/ 8fl oz/1 cup set yogurt. Season with salt, ground toasted cumin seeds and a pinch of muscovado (molasses) sugar.
• For a cucumber dip, stir half a diced cucumber and one seeded and chopped green chilli into 250ml/8fl oz/1 cup set yogurt. Season with salt and cumin.

2 Add the chickpea flour and baking powder to the onion mixture, then use your hand to mix all the ingredients together thoroughly.

3 Shape the mixture by hand into 12–15 kofta, which should be about the size of golf balls.

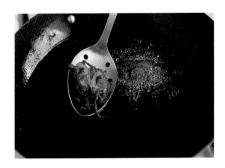

4 Heat the oil for deep-frying to 180–190°C/350–375°F or until a cube of day-old bread browns in 30–45 seconds. Fry the kofta, four to five at a time, until deep golden brown all over.

5 Drain each batch on kitchen paper and keep warm until all the kofta are cooked. Serve with lemon wedges, coriander sprigs and a yogurt dip.

ROASTED GARLIC TOASTS

GARLIC ROASTED OR BARBECUED IN ITS SKIN BECOMES A SOFT, AROMATIC PURÉE WITH A SWEET, NUTTY FLAVOUR, WHICH IS PERFECTLY COMPLEMENTED BY AROMATIC ROSEMARY. SPREAD ON CRISP TOAST TO MAKE A DELICIOUS STARTER OR ACCOMPANIMENT TO MEAT OR VEGETABLE DISHES.

SERVES FOUR

INGREDIENTS
    2 whole garlic heads
    extra virgin olive oil, for brushing
        and drizzling
    fresh rosemary sprigs
    ciabatta loaf or thick baguette
    chopped fresh rosemary
    salt and ground black pepper

4 Slice the ciabatta or baguette and brush each slice generously with olive oil. Toast the slices until they are crisp and golden, turning once.

5 Squeeze the garlic cloves from their skins on to the toasts. Sprinkle with the chopped fresh rosemary and olive oil, and add salt and black pepper to taste.

1 Preheat the oven to 200°C/400°F/ Gas 6 or light the barbecue, if using. Remove the tops from both of the whole heads of garlic, by slicing them with a sharp kitchen knife.

2 Brush the garlic heads with extra virgin olive oil and add a few sprigs of fresh rosemary, before wrapping in kitchen foil.

3 Bake the foil parcels in the oven for 25–30 minutes, or until the garlic is soft. Alternatively, cook the parcels on a medium-hot barbecue, turning them over occasionally.

VEGETABLES <u>WITH</u> TAPENADE <u>AND</u> HERB AIOLI

THE DELICATE BUT DISTINCTIVE FLAVOURS OF CHERVIL, TARRAGON AND PARSLEY ARE COMBINED WITH GARLIC FOR THIS HERB AIOLI. HERE, IT ACCOMPANIES A FULL-FLAVOURED TAPENADE AND IS SERVED WITH A PLATTER OF SUMMER VEGETABLES AND QUAIL'S EGGS.

SERVES SIX

INGREDIENTS

  2 red (bell) peppers, cut into
    wide strips
  30ml/2 tbsp olive oil
  225g/8oz new potatoes
  115g/4oz green beans
  225g/8oz baby carrots
  225g/8oz young asparagus
  12 quail's eggs
  fresh herbs, to garnish
  coarse salt, for sprinkling
For the tapenade
  175g/6oz/1½ cups pitted black olives
  50g/2oz can anchovy fillets, drained
  30ml/2 tbsp capers
  about 120ml/4fl oz/½ cup olive oil
  finely grated (shredded) rind of
    1 lemon
  15ml/1 tbsp brandy (optional)
For the herb aioli
  5 garlic cloves, crushed
  2 egg yolks
  5ml/1 tsp Dijon mustard
  about 10ml/2 tsp white wine vinegar
  250ml/8fl oz/1 cup light olive oil
  45ml/3 tbsp chopped mixed fresh
    herbs, such as chervil, parsley
    and tarragon
  30ml/2 tbsp chopped watercress
  salt and ground black pepper

1 To make the tapenade, finely chop the olives, anchovies and capers and beat together with the oil, lemon rind and brandy, if using. (Alternatively, lightly process the ingredients in a blender or food processor.)

2 Season the tapenade with pepper and blend in a little more oil if the mixture seems very dry. Transfer to a serving dish.

3 To make the aioli, beat together the garlic, egg yolks, mustard and vinegar. Gradually blend in the olive oil, a drop at a time, whisking the mixture well until thick and smooth.

4 Stir in the mixed herbs and chopped watercress. Season with salt and pepper to taste, adding a little more vinegar if necessary. Cover with clear film and chill until ready to serve.

5 Brush the peppers with oil, and place on a hot barbecue or under a hot grill (broiler) until they begin to char.

6 Cook the potatoes in a large pan of boiling, salted water until tender. Add the beans and carrots and blanch for 1 minute. Add the asparagus and cook for a further 30 seconds. Drain the vegetables. Cook the quail's eggs in boiling water for 2 minutes.

7 Arrange all the vegetables, eggs and sauces on a serving platter. Garnish with fresh herbs and serve with coarse salt, for sprinkling.

COOK'S TIPS
• Stir any leftover tapenade into pasta or spread on to warm toast.
• If you are making this dish as part of a picnic, allow the vegetables to cool before packing in an airtight container. Pack the quail's eggs in the original box.

ROASTED PEPPERS WITH SWEET CICELY

THE SWEET ANISEED FLAVOURS OF SWEET CICELY AND FENNEL COMBINE BEAUTIFULLY WITH THE SUCCULENT TASTES OF THE PEPPERS AND TOMATOES AND THE PIQUANCY OF CAPERS. SWEET CICELY LEAVES MAKE AN EXCELLENT GARNISH AND THEY TASTE JUST LIKE THE FLOWERS. THIS DISH CAN BE SERVED AS A LIGHT LUNCH OR AS AN UNUSUAL STARTER FOR A DINNER PARTY.

3 Place a whole small or half a medium tomato in each half of a pepper cavity.

4 Cover with a scattering of semi-ripe sweet cicely seeds, fennel seeds and capers and about half the sweet cicely flowers. Drizzle the olive oil all over.

5 Bake in the top of the oven for 1 hour. Remove from the oven and add the rest of the flowers. Garnish with fresh sweet cicely leaves and flowers, and serve with lots of crusty bread to soak up the juices.

SERVES FOUR

INGREDIENTS
    4 red (bell) peppers, halved
       and deseeded
    8 small or 4 medium tomatoes
    15ml/1 tbsp semi-ripe sweet
       cicely seeds
    15ml/1 tbsp fennel seeds
    15ml/1 tbsp capers
    8 sweet cicely flowers, newly
       opened, stems removed
    60ml/4 tbsp olive oil
For the garnish
    a few small sweet cicely leaves
    8 more flowers

1 Preheat the oven to 180°C/350°F/ Gas 4. Place the red pepper halves in a large ovenproof dish and set aside.

2 To skin the tomatoes, cut a cross at the base, then pour over boiling water and leave them to stand for 30 seconds to 1 minute. Cut them in half if they are of medium size.

COOK'S TIP
Try adding the stems from the sweet cicely to the water in which fruit is stewed. They will add a delightful flavour and reduce the need for sugar.

VARIATION
If sweet cicely is not available, this dish can also be made with a range of different herbs, although they will all impart a distinctive flavour. Celery leaves, chervil and lovage are some you might like to try.

FRIED PEPPERS WITH CHEESE AND PARSLEY

FETA CHEESE GOES PARTICULARLY WELL WITH PARSLEY AND A HINT OF CHILLI, AND IS USED HERE AS A FILLING FOR RIPE PEPPERS IN A TRADITIONAL BULGARIAN DISH. RED, GREEN OR YELLOW PEPPERS ARE EQUALLY DELICIOUS SERVED THIS WAY.

SERVES TWO TO FOUR

INGREDIENTS

4 long (bell) peppers
50g/2oz/½ cup plain (all-purpose)
  flour, seasoned
1 egg, beaten
olive oil, for shallow frying
cucumber and tomato salad, to serve

For the filling

1 egg
90g/3½oz feta cheese, finely
  crumbled
30ml/2 tbsp chopped fresh parsley
1 small fresh chilli, seeded and
  finely chopped

1 Slit open the peppers lengthways, scoop out the seeds. Remove the cores, leaving the peppers in one piece.

2 Carefully open out the peppers and place under a preheated grill (broiler), skin-side uppermost. Cook until the skin is charred and blackened. Place the peppers on a plate, cover with clear film and leave for 10 minutes.

3 Using a sharp knife, carefully peel away the skin from the peppers.

4 In a bowl, thoroughly mix all the filling ingredients together. Divide evenly among the four peppers.

5 Reshape the peppers to look whole. Dip them into the seasoned flour, then the egg, then the flour again.

6 Fry the peppers gently in a little olive oil for 6–8 minutes, turning once, or until golden brown and the filling is set. Drain the peppers on kitchen paper before serving with a cucumber and tomato salad.

COOK'S TIP
Feta cheese is traditionally made from ewe's or goat's milk, although it is now sometimes made from cow's milk. It keeps well if stored in a screw-top jar or polythene wrapper in the fridge.

PROVENÇAL THYME MUSHROOMS

THYME FLOWERS HAVE A ZINGY, OFTEN LEMONY, FLAVOUR AND ADD PUNCH TO YOUR COOKING. HERE, THEY COMBINE WITH THYME LEAVES AND GARLIC TO MAKE A DELICIOUS MUSHROOM STUFFING.

SERVES EIGHT

INGREDIENTS
   8 flat or field (portabello) mushrooms
   25g/1oz/½ cup white breadcrumbs
   30ml/2 tbsp thyme leaves
   2 garlic cloves
   45ml/3 tbsp olive oil
   30ml/2 tbsp thyme flowers
   coarse salt and ground black pepper

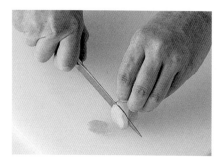

1 Preheat the oven to 200°C/400°F/ Gas 6. Clean and skin the mushrooms. Remove the stalks.

2 Finely slice the stalks and set aside. Place the mushrooms cup-side up in a large ovenproof dish.

3 Blend the breadcrumbs, mushroom stalks, thyme leaves and garlic in a food processor. Add plenty of salt and pepper, and 15ml/1 tbsp olive oil. Then mix in 15ml/1 tbsp thyme flowers.

4 Divide the bread mixture among the mushrooms and drizzle over the remaining olive oil.

5 Cook in the oven until the mushrooms are soft and the breadcrumbs lightly browned. Scatter over the remaining flowers just before serving.

STUFFED GARLIC MUSHROOMS WITH PROSCIUTTO AND HERBS

LARGE FIELD MUSHROOMS, WITH THEIR RICH, EARTHY FLAVOUR, ARE EXCELLENT STUFFED AND BAKED. THE STUFFING USED HERE COMBINES ONION, GARLIC, PARSLEY AND THYME WITH STRONGLY FLAVOURED WILD MUSHROOMS, AND IS SIMPLY MOUTHWATERING.

SERVES FOUR

INGREDIENTS

1 onion, chopped
75g/3oz/6 tbsp unsalted (sweet)
  butter
8 flat or field (portabello) mushrooms
15g/½oz/¼ cup dried porcini
  mushrooms, soaked in warm water
  for 20 minutes
1 garlic clove, crushed
75g/3oz/2½ cups fresh breadcrumbs
1 egg
75ml/5 tbsp chopped fresh parsley
15ml/1 tbsp chopped fresh thyme
115g/4oz prosciutto, thinly sliced
salt and ground black pepper
fresh parsley, to garnish

1 Preheat the oven to 190°C/375°F/
Gas 5. Fry the onion gently in half the
butter for 6–8 minutes, or until soft but
not coloured.

2 Meanwhile, break off the stems of
the field mushrooms, setting the
caps aside.

3 Drain the porcini mushrooms and
chop these and the stems of the field
mushrooms finely. Add to the onion
together with the garlic and cook for
a further 2–3 minutes.

VARIATION
For a vegetarian version of this dish, omit
the prosciutto and top the mushrooms
with sun-dried tomatoes instead.

4 Transfer the mixture to a bowl, add
the breadcrumbs, egg, herbs and
seasoning. Melt the remaining butter in
a small pan and generously brush over
the mushroom caps. Arrange the
mushrooms on a baking sheet and
spoon in the filling.

5 Bake the mushrooms in the
preheated oven for 20–25 minutes,
or until the filling is well browned.

6 Top each filled mushroom cap with a
strip of prosciutto, garnish with fresh
parsley and serve.

COOK'S TIPS
• These stuffed garlic mushrooms can be
easily prepared in advance ready to go
into the oven.
• Do not discard the porcini soaking water.
Strain it, then use for thinning sauces.

BAKED FENNEL <u>WITH A</u> CRUMB CRUST

GARLIC AND PARSLEY BLEND PERFECTLY WITH THE DELICATE, ANISEED FLAVOUR OF FENNEL IN THIS TASTY GRATIN. IT GOES WELL WITH PASTA DISHES AND RISOTTOS.

<u>SERVES FOUR</u>

INGREDIENTS
    3 fennel bulbs, cut lengthways
        into quarters
    30ml/2 tbsp olive oil
    1 garlic clove, chopped
    50g/2oz/1 cup day-old wholemeal
        (whole-wheat) breadcrumbs
    30ml/2 tbsp chopped fresh flat
        leaf parsley
    salt and ground black pepper
    fennel leaves, to garnish (optional)

VARIATION
To make a cheese-topped version of this dish, simply add 60ml/4 tbsp finely grated strong-flavoured cheese, such as mature Cheddar, Red Leicester or Parmesan, to the breadcrumb mixture in step 4. Sprinkle the mixture over the fennel as described.

1 Cook the fennel in a pan of boiling salted water for 10 minutes, or until just tender.

2 Drain the fennel quarters and place them in a baking dish or roasting pan, then brush them all over with half of the olive oil.

3 Preheat the oven to 190°C/375°F/ Gas 5.

4 In a small bowl, mix together the garlic, breadcrumbs and parsley with the rest of the oil. Sprinkle the mixture evenly over the fennel, then season well with salt and pepper.

5 Bake for 30 minutes, or until the fennel is tender and the breadcrumbs are crisp and golden. Serve hot, garnished with a few fennel leaves, if you wish.

LEMON AND HERB RISOTTO CAKE

CHIVES AND PARSLEY COMBINE WITH THE RIND OF LEMON TO FLAVOUR THIS UNUSUAL MOZZARELLA AND RICE DISH. IT CAN BE SERVED AS A MAIN COURSE WITH SALAD, OR AS A SATISFYING SIDE DISH. IT'S ALSO GOOD SERVED COLD, AND PACKS WELL FOR PICNICS.

SERVES FOUR

INGREDIENTS

oil, for greasing
1 small leek, thinly sliced
600ml/1 pint/2½ cups chicken stock
225g/8oz/generous 1 cup risotto rice
finely grated (shredded) rind of
  1 lemon
30ml/2 tbsp chopped fresh chives
30ml/2 tbsp chopped fresh parsley
75g/3oz/¾ cup grated (shredded)
  mozzarella cheese
salt and ground black pepper
parsley and lemon wedges, to garnish

1 Preheat the oven to 200°C/400°F/ Gas 6. Use a pastry brush to lightly oil the base and sides of a 21cm/8½in round, loose-bottomed cake tin (pan).

2 Cook the leek in a large pan with 45ml/3 tbsp stock, stirring over a moderate heat, to soften. Add the rice and the remaining stock.

3 Bring to the boil. Cover the pan and simmer gently, stirring occasionally, for about 20 minutes, or until all the liquid is absorbed.

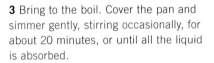

4 Stir in the lemon rind, herbs, cheese and seasoning. Spoon into the tin, cover with foil and bake for 30–35 minutes, or until lightly browned. Turn out and serve in slices, garnished with parsley and lemon wedges.

COOK'S TIP
The best type of rice to choose for this recipe is the Italian round-grain arborio rice, but if it is not available, use pudding rice instead.

ONION, FENNEL AND LAVENDER TARTS

FRAGRANT LAVENDER COMBINES PERFECTLY WITH THE AROMATIC FLAVOUR OF FENNEL AND MILDLY FLAVOURED SPANISH ONION. THESE UNUSUAL AND MOUTH-WATERING TARTLETS MAKE AN APPEALING LIGHT SUMMER MEAL.

SERVES FOUR

INGREDIENTS
　75g/3oz/6 tbsp butter
　1 large Spanish onion, finely sliced
　1 fennel bulb, trimmed and sliced
　30ml/2 tbsp fresh lavender florets or
　　15ml/1 tbsp roughly chopped dried
　　culinary lavender
　2 egg yolks
　150ml/¼ pint/⅔ cup crème fraîche
　salt and ground black pepper
　fresh lavender florets, to garnish
　　(optional)
For the pastry
　115g/4oz/1 cup plain (all-purpose)
　　flour
　pinch of salt
　50g/2oz/¼ cup chilled butter, cut
　　into cubes
　10ml/2 tsp cold water

1 To make the pastry, sift the flour and salt together. Rub the butter into the flour until the mixture resembles breadcrumbs. Stir in the water and bring the dough together to form a ball.

2 Roll the pastry out on a lightly floured surface to line four 7.5cm/3in round, loose-based flan tins (quiche pans). Prick the bases with a fork and chill. Preheat the oven to 200°C/400°F/Gas 6.

3 Melt the butter in a shallow pan and add the sliced onion and fennel and the chopped lavender. Reduce the heat to low. Cover the pan with wet greaseproof (waxed) paper and cook gently for 15 minutes, or until golden.

4 Line the pastry cases with greaseproof paper and bake blind for 5 minutes. Remove the paper, return to the oven and bake for a further 4 minutes.

5 Reduce the oven temperature to 180°C/350°F/Gas 4. Mix the egg yolks, crème fraîche and seasoning together.

6 Spoon the onion mixture into the pastry cases. Spoon the crème fraîche mixture on top and bake for 10–15 minutes, or until the mixture has set and the filling is puffed up and golden.

7 Sprinkle a little extra lavender on top, if you like, and serve warm or cold.

ROAST GARLIC WITH GOAT'S CHEESE, WALNUT AND HERB PÂTÉ

THE COMBINATION OF SWEET, MELLOW ROASTED GARLIC AND GOAT'S CHEESE IS A CLASSIC ONE. COOKING THE GARLIC WITH SPRIGS OF ROSEMARY AND THYME MAKES IT MORE AROMATIC. THE PÂTÉ IS PARTICULARLY GOOD MADE WITH FRESH THYME AND PARSLEY, AND THE NEW SEASON'S WALNUTS.

SERVES FOUR

INGREDIENTS
 4 large garlic bulbs
 4 fresh rosemary sprigs
 8 fresh thyme sprigs
 60ml/4 tbsp olive oil
 coarse salt and ground black pepper
For the pâté
 175g/6oz/¾ cup soft goat's cheese
 5ml/1 tsp finely chopped fresh thyme
 15ml/1 tbsp finely chopped
  fresh parsley
 50g/2oz/½ cup chopped
  shelled walnuts
 15ml/1 tbsp walnut oil (optional)
To serve
 4–8 slices sourdough bread
 shelled walnuts

1 Preheat the oven to 180°C/350°F/
Gas 4. Strip the papery outer skin from
the garlic bulbs. Place them in an
ovenproof dish large enough to hold
them snugly.

2 Tuck the rosemary and thyme sprigs
between the garlic bulbs, drizzle the oil
over and season to taste with coarse
salt and black pepper.

VARIATION
If you prefer, the pâté can also be made
with other kinds of chopped nuts, such
as hazelnuts and cashews.

3 Cover the garlic closely with foil and
bake for 50–60 minutes, basting once.
Leave to cool.

4 Preheat the grill (broiler). To make the
pâté, cream the cheese with the thyme,
parsley and chopped walnuts. Beat in
15ml/1 tbsp of the cooking oil from the
garlic and season to taste, then transfer
the pâté to a serving bowl.

5 Brush the sourdough bread with the
remaining cooking oil from the garlic,
then grill (broil) until toasted.

6 Drizzle the walnut oil, if using, over
the pâté and grind some black pepper
over it. Place a bulb of garlic on each
plate and serve with the pâté and
toasted bread. Serve with a few shelled
walnuts and a little coarse salt.

LIVER PÂTÉ PIE WITH MUSTARD AND PARSLEY

A PORK AND HAM PÂTÉ IS FLAVOURED WITH ONION, MUSTARD, PARSLEY AND KIRSCH IN THIS RICH AND SATISFYING PIE. DELICIOUS SERVED FOR LUNCH WITH A GLASS OF PILSNER BEER.

3 Process half the minced (ground) pork and the liver until fairly smooth. Stir in the remaining pork, ham, onion, parsley, mustard, Kirsch and seasoning. Spoon the filling into the tin, smoothing it down and levelling the surface.

SERVES TEN

INGREDIENTS
    675g/1½lb minced (ground) pork
    350g/12oz pork liver
    350g/12oz/2 cups diced cooked ham
    1 small onion, finely chopped
    30ml/2 tbsp chopped fresh parsley
    5ml/1 tsp German mustard
    30ml/2 tbsp Kirsch
    salt and ground black pepper
    beaten egg, for sealing and glazing
    25g/1oz sachet aspic jelly
    250ml/8fl oz/1 cup boiling water
    mustard, bread and dill pickles,
        to serve
For the pastry
    450g/1lb/4 cups plain (all-purpose)
        flour, plus extra for dusting
    pinch of salt
    275g/10oz/1¼ cups butter
    2 eggs and 1 egg yolk
    30ml/2 tbsp water

1 Preheat the oven to 200°C/400°F/ Gas 6. To make the pastry, sift the flour and salt and rub in the butter. Beat the eggs, egg yolk and water, add to the dry ingredients and mix.

2 Knead the dough briefly until smooth. Roll out two-thirds on a lightly floured surface and use to line a 10 × 25cm/ 4 × 10in loaf tin (pan). Trim any excess dough neatly from around the edges.

4 Roll out the remaining pastry on the lightly floured surface and use it to top the pie, sealing the edges with some of the beaten egg. Decorate with the pastry trimmings and glaze with the remaining beaten egg. Using a fork, make three or four holes in the top, for the steam to escape.

5 Bake for 40 minutes, then reduce the oven temperature to 180°C/350°F/Gas 4 and cook for a further 1 hour. Cover the pastry with foil if the top begins to brown too much. Allow to cool in the tin.

6 Make up the aspic jelly, using the boiling water. Stir to dissolve. When it is cool, make a small hole near the edge of the pie with a skewer, then pour in the aspic through a greaseproof- (waxed-) paper funnel. Chill for at least 2 hours before serving the pie in slices with mustard, bread and dill pickles.

MINTED POTATO AND RED PEPPER FRITTATA

FRESH MINT TASTES WONDERFUL WITH NEW POTATOES. IN THIS ITALIAN-STYLE OMELETTE IT COMBINES WITH GARLIC, ONION AND BRIGHT RED PEPPERS TO MAKE A LIGHT AND TEMPTING LUNCH DISH THAT IS SIMPLY BURSTING WITH FLAVOUR.

SERVES THREE TO FOUR

INGREDIENTS

- 450g/1lb small new or salad potatoes
- 6 eggs
- 30ml/2 tbsp chopped fresh mint
- 30ml/2 tbsp olive oil
- 1 onion, chopped
- 2 garlic cloves, crushed
- 2 red (bell) peppers, seeded and roughly chopped
- salt and ground black pepper
- mint sprigs, to garnish

1 Cook the potatoes in their skins in boiling salted water until just tender. Drain, cool slightly, then slice thickly.

2 Whisk together the eggs, chopped fresh mint and seasoning in a bowl, then set aside. Heat the olive oil in a large frying pan that can be used under the grill (broiler).

3 Add the onion, garlic, peppers and potatoes to the pan and cook, stirring occasionally, for 5 minutes.

4 Pour the egg mixture over the vegetables in the frying pan and stir gently with a wooden spoon to ensure the egg is evenly distributed.

5 Push the mixture towards the centre of the pan as it cooks to allow the liquid egg to run on to the base. Meanwhile preheat the grill.

6 When the frittata is lightly set, place the frying pan under the hot grill for 2–3 minutes until the top is a light golden brown colour.

7 Serve the frittata hot or cold, cut into wedges. Garnish with extra sprigs of mint.

TAGLIATELLE <u>WITH</u> HERBS

IN SUMMER, WHEN HERBS ARE PLENTIFUL, ENJOY THIS SIMPLE PASTA DISH THAT IS SO FULL OF FLAVOUR. ROSEMARY, PARSLEY, MINT, SAGE, BASIL, BAY AND GARLIC ARE ALL HERE, MERGING TOGETHER TO CREATE A LIGHT, AND TASTY MEAL.

<u>SERVES SIX</u>

INGREDIENTS

3 rosemary sprigs
1 small handful fresh flat leaf parsley
5–6 fresh mint leaves
5–6 fresh sage leaves
8–10 large fresh basil leaves
30ml/2 tbsp extra virgin olive oil
50g/2oz/¼ cup butter
1 shallot, finely chopped
2 garlic cloves, finely chopped
pinch of chilli powder, to taste
400g/14oz fresh egg tagliatelle
1 bay leaf
120ml/4fl oz/½ cup dry white wine
90–120ml/6–8 tbsp vegetable stock
salt and ground black pepper
basil leaves, to garnish

1 Strip the rosemary and parsley leaves from their stalks and chop them together with the other fresh herbs.

2 Heat the oil and half the butter in a large pan. Add the shallot, garlic and chilli powder. Cook on a very low heat, stirring frequently, for 2–3 minutes.

3 Cook the fresh pasta in a large pan of boiling salted water according to the packet instructions.

4 Add the chopped herbs and the bay leaf to the shallot mixture and stir for 2–3 minutes, then add the wine and increase the heat. Boil rapidly for 1–2 minutes, or until reduced. Lower the heat, add the stock and simmer gently for 1–2 minutes. Season.

5 Drain the pasta and add it to the herb mixture. Toss well to mix and remove and discard the bay leaf.

6 Put the remaining butter in a warmed large bowl, tip the dressed pasta into it and toss well to mix. Serve immediately, garnished with basil.

LINGUINE <u>WITH</u> ROCKET

THIS IS A FIRST COURSE THAT YOU WILL FIND IN MANY A FASHIONABLE RESTAURANT IN ITALY. THE DISTINCTIVE PEPPERY FLAVOUR OF ROCKET IS WELL DEFINED IN THIS QUICK AND EASY-TO-PREPARE DISH, WHICH COULD ALSO BE MADE WITH SPAGHETTI.

SERVES FOUR

INGREDIENTS

   350g/12oz fresh or dried linguine
   120ml/4fl oz/½ cup extra virgin olive oil
   150g/5oz rocket (arugula)
   75g/3oz/1 cup freshly grated
     (shredded) Parmesan cheese
   salt and ground black pepper

1 Cook the pasta in a large pan of boiling salted water, then drain.

2 Heat about 60ml/4 tbsp of the olive oil in the pasta pan, then add the drained pasta, then the rocket. Toss over a medium to high heat for 1–2 minutes or until the rocket is just wilted, then remove from the heat.

3 Tip the pasta and rocket into a warmed large bowl. Add half the freshly grated Parmesan and the remaining olive oil. Add a little salt and black pepper to taste.

4 Toss the mixture quickly to mix. Serve immediately, sprinkled with the remaining Parmesan.

COOK'S TIP

Buy rocket by the bunch from the greengrocer. The type sold in small cellophane packets in supermarkets is very expensive for this kind of dish. Always check when buying rocket that all the leaves are bright green. In hot weather, rocket quickly turns yellow.

PASTA SALAD <u>WITH</u> PRAWNS <u>AND</u> HERBS

THIS PRAWN AND PASTA SALAD IS ENLIVENED WITH A LEMON, BASIL AND CORIANDER DRESSING, SPIKED WITH A LITTLE RED CHILLI. IT MAKES AN ATTRACTIVE AND DELICIOUS LUNCH SERVED WITH WARM CIABATTA BREAD.

SERVES FOUR

INGREDIENTS

225g/8oz/2 cups dried farfalle
juice of ½ lemon
1 small fresh red chilli, seeded and
  very finely chopped
60ml/4 tbsp chopped fresh basil
30ml/2 tbsp chopped fresh
  coriander (cilantro)
60ml/4 tbsp extra virgin olive oil
15ml/1 tbsp mayonnaise
250g/9oz/1½ cups peeled cooked
  prawns (shrimp)
1 avocado
salt and ground black pepper

1 Cook the pasta in a large pan of boiling salted water until *al dente*.

2 Meanwhile, put the lemon juice and chilli in a bowl with half the basil and coriander, and salt and pepper to taste. Whisk well to mix, then whisk in the oil and mayonnaise until thick.

3 Add the prawns and gently stir to coat them with the dressing.

4 Drain the pasta into a colander, and rinse under cold running water until cold. Leave to drain and dry, shaking the colander occasionally.

5 Halve, stone and peel the avocado, then cut the flesh into neat dice. Add to the prawns and dressing with the pasta, toss well to mix and taste for seasoning. Serve immediately, sprinkled with the remaining basil and coriander.

COOK'S TIP

This pasta salad can be made several hours ahead of time, without the avocado. Cover the bowl with clear film and chill. Prepare the avocado and add it to the salad just before serving, or it will discolour.

ORECCHIETTE WITH ROCKET AND OREGANO

GARLIC AND TOMATOES ARE FREQUENT PARTNERS IN ITALIAN COOKING. IN THIS HEARTY DISH FROM PUGLIA IN SOUTH-EAST ITALY, ROCKET ADDS A PEPPERY DEFINITION TO A PASTA SAUCE.

SERVES FOUR TO SIX

INGREDIENTS
45ml/3 tbsp olive oil
1 small onion, finely chopped
300g/11oz canned chopped
  Italian plum tomatoes or passata
  (bottled strained tomatoes)
2.5ml/½ tsp dried oregano
pinch of chilli powder or
  cayenne pepper
30ml/2 tbsp red or white wine
2 potatoes, total weight about
  200g/7oz, diced
300g/11oz/2¾ cups dried orecchiette
2 garlic cloves, finely chopped
150g/5oz rocket (arugula) leaves,
  stalks removed
90g/3½oz/scant ½ cup ricotta cheese
salt and ground black pepper
freshly grated (shredded) Pecorino
  cheese, to serve

1 Heat 15ml/1 tbsp of the olive oil in a medium pan, add half the finely chopped onion and cook gently, stirring frequently, for about 5 minutes, or until softened. Add the canned tomatoes or passata, oregano and chilli powder or cayenne pepper to the onion. Pour the wine over, and add a little salt and pepper to taste. Cover the pan and simmer for about 15 minutes, stirring the mixture occasionally.

2 Bring a large pan of salted water to the boil. Add the potatoes and pasta. Stir well and let the water return to the boil. Lower the heat and simmer for 15 minutes, or according to the instructions on the packet, until the pasta is cooked.

3 Heat the remaining oil in a large pan, add the rest of the onion and the garlic and fry for 2–3 minutes, stirring occasionally. Add the rocket, toss over the heat for about 2 minutes, or until wilted, then stir in the tomato sauce and the ricotta. Mix well.

4 Drain the pasta and potatoes, add them both to the pan of sauce and toss to mix. Taste the sauce for seasoning and then serve immediately in warmed bowls, with grated Pecorino offered separately.

PANSOTTI WITH HERBS AND CHEESE

HERB-FLAVOURED PASTA ENCLOSES A FILLING OF RICOTTA CHEESE, BASIL, PARSLEY, MARJORAM AND GARLIC. THE PANSOTTI ARE THEN SERVED WITH A RICH AND SATISFYING WALNUT SAUCE — HEAVENLY.

SERVES SIX TO EIGHT

INGREDIENTS

For the herb-flavoured pasta
  300g/11oz/2¾ cups flour
  3 eggs
  5ml/1 tsp salt
  3 small handfuls of fresh herbs,
    finely chopped
  flour, for dusting
  50g/2oz/¼ cup butter
  freshly grated (shredded) Parmesan
    cheese, to serve

For the filling
  250g/9oz/generous 1 cup ricotta cheese
  150g/5oz/1⅔ cups freshly grated
    (shredded) Parmesan cheese
  1 large handful fresh basil leaves,
    finely chopped
  1 large handful fresh flat leaf parsley,
    finely chopped
  a few sprigs fresh marjoram or
    oregano, leaves removed and
    finely chopped
  1 garlic clove, crushed
  1 small egg
  salt and ground black pepper

For the sauce
  90g/3½oz/½ cup shelled walnuts
  1 garlic clove
  60ml/4 tbsp extra virgin olive oil
  120ml/4fl oz/½ cup double
    (heavy) cream

1 Mound the flour on the work surface and make a deep well in the centre.

2 Crack the eggs into the well, then add the salt and herbs. With a table knife, mix the eggs, salt and herbs together, then start incorporating the flour from the sides of the well.

3 As soon as the mixture is no longer liquid dip your fingers in the flour and use them to work the ingredients into a sticky dough. Press the dough into a ball and knead it as you would bread, for 10 minutes until smooth and elastic. Wrap in clear film and leave to rest at room temperature for 20 minutes.

4 To make the filling, put the ricotta, Parmesan, herbs, garlic and egg in a bowl with salt and pepper to taste and beat well to mix.

5 To make the sauce, put the walnuts, garlic clove and olive oil in a food processor and process to a paste, adding up to 120ml/4fl oz/½ cup warm water through the feeder tube to lighten the consistency.

6 Spoon the mixture into a large bowl and add the cream. Beat well to mix, then add salt and pepper to taste.

7 Using a pasta machine, roll out one-quarter of the pasta into a 90cm/36in strip. Cut the strip with a sharp knife into two 45cm/18in lengths (you can do this during rolling if the strip gets too long to manage).

8 Using a 5cm/2in square ravioli cutter, cut eight or nine squares from one of the pasta strips. Using a teaspoon, put a mound of filling in the centre of each square.

9 Brush a little water around the edge of each square, then fold the square diagonally in half over the filling to make a triangular shape. Press the edges gently to seal.

10 Spread out the pansotti on clean, floured dish towels, sprinkle lightly with flour and leave to dry. Repeat the process with the remaining dough to make 64–80 pansotti altogether.

11 Cook the pansotti in a large pan of salted boiling water for 4–5 minutes. Meanwhile, put the walnut sauce in a large, warmed bowl and add a ladleful of the pasta cooking water to thin it down. Melt the butter in a small pan until sizzling.

12 Drain the pansotti and tip them into the bowl of walnut sauce. Drizzle the butter over them, toss well, then sprinkle with Parmesan. Alternatively, toss the pansotti in the melted butter, spoon into warmed individual bowls and drizzle over the sauce. Serve immediately, with more Parmesan offered separately.

PENNE WITH ROCKET AND MOZZARELLA

LIKE A WARM SALAD, THIS PASTA DISH IS VERY QUICK AND EASY TO MAKE — PERFECT FOR AN AL FRESCO SUMMER LUNCH. CRISP ROCKET AND GOOD-QUALITY, FRESH AND RIPE TOMATOES PROVIDE THE ESSENTIAL FLAVOURINGS HERE.

SERVES FOUR

INGREDIENTS

400g/14oz/3½ cups fresh or
    dried penne
6 ripe plum tomatoes, peeled, seeded
    and diced
2 × 150g/5oz packets mozzarella
    cheese, drained and diced
2 large handfuls of rocket (arugula),
    total weight about 150g/5oz
75ml/5 tbsp extra virgin olive oil
salt and ground black pepper

VARIATION
For a change, a mixture of basil and
rocket leaves also works well.

1 Cook the fresh or dried pasta in a
large pan of boiling salted water
according to the packet instructions
until it is *al dente*.

2 Meanwhile, put the diced tomatoes,
mozzarella, rocket and olive oil into a
large bowl with a little salt and ground
black pepper to taste and toss
everything together well to mix.

3 Drain the cooked pasta and tip it into
the bowl with the other ingredients. Toss
well to mix and serve immediately.

COOK'S TIP
To keep the pasta shapes separate, stir
it frequently during cooking. This is
especially important at the start of the
cooking process.

FUSILLI WITH BASIL AND PEPPERS

CHARGRILLED PEPPERS HAVE A WONDERFUL, SMOKY FLAVOUR THAT MARRIES WELL WITH GARLIC, OLIVES, BASIL AND TOMATOES IN THIS DELECTABLE PASTA DISH.

SERVES FOUR

INGREDIENTS

3 large (bell) peppers (red, yellow
    and orange)
350g/12oz/3 cups fresh or
    dried fusilli
60ml/4 tbsp extra virgin olive oil
1–2 garlic cloves, to taste,
    finely chopped
4 ripe plum tomatoes, peeled, seeded
    and diced
50g/2oz/½ cup pitted black olives,
    halved or quartered lengthways
1 handful of fresh basil leaves
salt and ground black pepper

VARIATION
Add a few slivers of bottled or canned
anchovy fillets at step 5.

1 Put the whole peppers under a hot
grill (broiler) and grill (broil) for about
10 minutes, turning frequently until
charred on all sides.

2 Put the hot peppers in a plastic bag,
seal the bag and set aside until the
peppers are cold.

3 Remove the peppers from the bag
and hold them, one at a time, under
cold running water. Peel off the charred
skins with your fingers, split the
peppers open and pull out the cores.
Rub off all the seeds under the running
water, then pat the peppers dry on
kitchen paper.

4 Cook the pasta in salted boiling water
until *al dente*.

5 Meanwhile, thinly slice the peppers
and place them in a large bowl with the
olive oil, garlic, tomatoes, olives, basil,
salt and pepper to taste.

6 Drain the cooked pasta and tip it into
the bowl with the other ingredients. Toss
well to mix and serve immediately.

VERMICELLI WITH HERB FRITTATA

HERE, ROASTED RED PEPPER, BASIL, PARSLEY, GARLIC AND ONION CREATE A FULL AND FRESH FLAVOUR.
IT MAKES A SUBSTANTIAL AND TASTY LUNCHEON DISH AND IS ALSO EXCELLENT FOR PICNICS.

SERVES FOUR TO SIX

INGREDIENTS
  50g/2oz dried vermicelli
  6 eggs
  60ml/4 tbsp double (heavy) cream
  1 handful fresh basil
    leaves, chopped
  1 handful fresh flat leaf
    parsley, chopped
  75g/3oz/1 cup freshly grated
    (shredded) Parmesan cheese
  25g/1oz/2 tbsp butter
  15ml/1 tbsp olive oil
  1 onion, finely sliced
  3 large pieces bottled roasted red
    (bell) pepper, drained, rinsed,
    dried and cut into strips
  1 garlic clove, crushed
  salt and ground black pepper
  rocket (arugula) leaves, to serve

1 Preheat the oven to 190°C/375°F/
Gas 5. Cook the pasta in a pan
of boiling salted water for 8 minutes.

2 Meanwhile, break the eggs into a bowl
and add the cream and herbs. Whisk in
about two-thirds of the grated Parmesan
and add salt and pepper to taste.

3 Drain the pasta well and allow to cool;
snip it into short lengths with scissors.
Add to the egg mixture and whisk again.

4 Melt the butter in the oil in a large,
ovenproof, non-stick frying pan. Add
the onion and cook gently, stirring
frequently, until softened. Add the
pepper and garlic.

5 Pour the egg and pasta mixture into
the pan and stir well. Cook over a low
to medium heat, without stirring, for
3–5 minutes, or until the frittata is just
set underneath.

6 Sprinkle over the remaining Parmesan
and bake in the oven for 5 minutes or
until set.

7 Before serving, leave to stand for at
least 5 minutes. Cut into wedges and
serve warm or cold, accompanied by
rocket leaves.

PENNE WITH AUBERGINE AND MINT PESTO

WALNUTS, MINT AND PARSLEY MAKE A SPLENDID AND UNUSUAL VARIATION ON THE CLASSIC ITALIAN
PESTO. HERE IT IS TOSSED INTO PASTA AND AUBERGINES, WHERE THE MINTY AROMA IS EMPHASIZED.

SERVES FOUR

INGREDIENTS
  2 large aubergines (eggplant)
  450g/1lb penne
  50g/2oz/⅓ cup walnut halves
  salt
For the pesto
  25g/1oz/1 cup fresh mint leaves
  15g/½oz/½ cup flat leaf parsley
  40g/1½oz/scant ⅓ cup walnuts
  40g/1½oz/½ cup freshly grated
    (shredded) Parmesan cheese
  2 garlic cloves
  90ml/6 tbsp olive oil
  salt and ground black pepper

1 Cut the aubergines lengthways into
1cm/½in slices, then cut the slices
crossways into short strips.

2 Layer the strips in a colander with salt
and leave to stand for 30 minutes over
a plate to catch any juices. Rinse well in
cool water and drain.

3 Place all the pesto ingredients, except
the oil, in a blender or food processor.

4 Blend until smooth, then gradually
add the oil in a thin stream until the
mixture amalgamates. Season to taste
with salt and ground black pepper.

5 Cook the pasta in boiling salted water
according to the packet instructions.
Add the aubergine 3 minutes before
the end.

6 Drain well and mix in the mint pesto
and walnut halves. Serve immediately.

There are so many ways to complement or contrast the flavour of fish using fresh herbs. Try sealing in the flavours by baking "en papillote", for example. Gently enhance the flavour of grilled (broiled) fish by adding rosemary or thyme and garlic, or add fragrance with a melting herb butter. Salsas, sauces and crispy herb crusts are all here to tempt your taste buds.

Fish

GRILLED COD FILLET <u>WITH</u> FRESH MIXED-HERB CRUST

DELICATELY FLAVOURED CHERVIL AND PARSLEY GO ESPECIALLY WELL WITH FISH. HERE, THEY ARE COMBINED WITH CHIVES AND WHOLEMEAL BREADCRUMBS TO MAKE A DELICIOUS CRUST FOR GRILLED OR BARBECUED COD.

<u>SERVES FOUR</u>

INGREDIENTS
    25g/1oz/2 tbsp butter
    4 thick pieces of cod fillet, about
        225g/8oz each, skinned
    175g/6oz/3 cups wholemeal (whole-
        wheat) breadcrumbs
    15ml/1 tbsp chopped fresh chervil
    15ml/1 tbsp chopped fresh parsley,
        plus extra sprigs to garnish
    15ml/1 tbsp chopped fresh chives
    15ml/1 tbsp olive oil
    salt and ground black pepper
    lemon wedges, to garnish

1 Melt the butter and brush over the cod fillets. Mix any remaining butter with the breadcrumbs, fresh herbs and plenty of salt and ground black pepper.

2 Cook the fish under a medium grill (broiler) for about 10 minutes, turning once. Increase the heat, then press a quarter of the crust mixture on to each fillet, spreading evenly to cover. Lightly sprinkle olive oil over the top and cook for a further 2 minutes, or until the topping is golden brown.

3 Serve the fish garnished with lemon wedges and the sprigs of fresh parsley.

VARIATION
This mixed-herb crust works well with any firm white fish.

SALMON EN PAPILLOTE <u>WITH</u> CHILLIES <u>AND</u> CHIVES

COOKING FISH "EN PAPILLOTE" ENSURES THAT THE AROMATIC INGREDIENTS RETAIN THEIR FLAVOUR, AND THAT THE SALMON REMAINS MOIST AND SUCCULENT. IT IS ALSO EXCELLENT WHEN ENTERTAINING, AS THE PARCELS MAY BE PREPARED AHEAD OF COOKING.

SERVES SIX

INGREDIENTS
   25ml/1½ tbsp groundnut (peanut) oil
   2 yellow (bell) peppers, seeded and
      thinly sliced
   4cm/1½in fresh root ginger, peeled
      and finely grated (shredded)
   1 large fennel bulb, finely sliced,
      feathery tops chopped and reserved
   1 fresh green chilli, seeded and
      finely sliced
   2 large leeks, cut into 10cm/4in
      lengths and sliced lengthways
   60ml/4 tbsp chopped chives
   10ml/2 tsp light soy sauce
   6 portions salmon fillet, about
      175g/6oz each, skinned
   10ml/2 tsp toasted sesame oil
   salt and ground black pepper

1 Heat the oil in a large, non-stick frying pan and cook the peppers, ginger and fennel for 5–6 minutes, or until they are softened but not browned. Add the chilli and leeks and cook for a further 2–3 minutes. Stir in half the chives and the soy sauce with seasoning to taste. Set aside to cool.

2 Preheat the oven to 190°C/375°F/ Gas 5. Cut six 35cm/14in circles of baking parchment or foil. Divide the vegetable mixture among the circles and place a portion of salmon on top. Drizzle with sesame oil and sprinkle with the remaining chives and the chopped fennel tops. Season to taste.

3 Fold the paper or foil over to enclose the fish, rolling and twisting the edges together to seal the parcels.

4 Place the parcels on a baking tray and bake for 15–20 minutes, or until the parcels are puffed up and, if made with paper, lightly browned. Transfer the parcels to warmed individual plates and serve immediately.

COOK'S TIP
This dish is excellent served with a simple accompaniment such as buttered new potatoes or plain egg noodles.

HERB-TOPPED PISSALADIÈRE

GENTLY COOKED, SWEET SPANISH ONIONS FLAVOURED WITH GARLIC, THYME AND ROSEMARY MAKE A MELLOW BACKDROP TO THE ANCHOVIES AND OLIVES IN THIS DISH. IT CAN BE MADE USING EITHER SHORTCRUST PASTRY OR, AS HERE, YEASTED DOUGH, SIMILAR TO A PIZZA BASE.

SERVES SIX

INGREDIENTS

   250g/9oz/2¼ cups strong white
     (bread) flour, plus extra
     for dusting
   50g/2oz/½ cup fine polenta
     or semolina
   5ml/1 tsp salt
   175ml/6fl oz/¾ cup lukewarm water
   5ml/1 tsp dried yeast
   5ml/1 tsp caster (superfine) sugar
   30ml/2 tbsp extra virgin olive oil,
     plus extra for greasing
For the topping
   60–75ml/4–5 tbsp extra virgin olive oil
   6 large sweet onions, thinly sliced
   2 large garlic cloves, thinly sliced
   5ml/1 tsp chopped fresh thyme, plus
     several sprigs
   1 fresh rosemary sprig
   1–2 × 50g/2oz cans anchovies in
     olive oil
   50–75g/2–3oz/⅓–½ cup small
     black olives, preferably small
     Niçoise olives
   salt and ground black pepper

1 Mix the flour, polenta or semolina and salt in a large mixing bowl. Pour half the water into a bowl. Add the yeast and sugar, then leave in a warm place for 10 minutes, or until frothy. Pour the yeast mixture into the flour mixture with the remaining water and the olive oil.

2 Using your hands, mix all the ingredients together to form a dough, then turn out and knead for 5 minutes, or until smooth, springy and elastic.

3 Return the dough to the clean, floured bowl and place it in a plastic bag or cover with oiled clear film, then set the dough aside at room temperature for 30–60 minutes to rise and double in bulk.

4 Meanwhile, start to prepare the topping. Heat 45ml/3 tbsp of the olive oil in a large, heavy pan and add the sliced onions. Stir well to coat the onions in the oil, then cover the pan and cook over a very low heat, stirring occasionally, for 20–30 minutes. (Use a heat-diffuser mat to keep the heat low, if possible.)

5 Add a little salt to taste and the garlic, chopped thyme and rosemary sprig. Stir well and continue cooking for another 15–25 minutes, or until the onions are soft and deep golden yellow but not browned. Uncover the pan for the last 5–10 minutes if the onions seem very wet. Remove and discard the rosemary. Set the onions aside to cool.

6 Preheat the oven to 220°C/425°F/ Gas 7. Roll out the dough and use to line a large baking sheet, about 30 × 23cm/ 12 × 9in. Taste the onions for seasoning before spreading them over the dough.

7 Drain the anchovies, cut them in half lengthways and arrange them in a lattice pattern over the onions. Scatter the olives and thyme sprigs over the top of the pissaladière and drizzle with the remaining olive oil. Bake for about 20–25 minutes, or until the dough is browned and cooked. Season with pepper and serve warm, cut into slices.

VARIATIONS
• Shortcrust pastry can be used instead of yeast dough as a base: bake it blind for 10–15 minutes at 200°C/400°F/ Gas 6 before adding the filling.
• With either base, if you are fond of anchovies, try spreading about 60ml/ 4 tbsp anchovy purée (paste) (anchoïade) over the base before adding the onions. Alternatively, spread black olive paste over the base.

PAN-FRIED COD <u>WITH</u> CREAMY VERMOUTH <u>AND</u> HERB SAUCE

CHUNKY COD IS TEAMED WITH A QUICK PAN SAUCE OF VERMOUTH, CREAMY GOAT'S CHEESE, PARSLEY AND CHERVIL. GRILLED PLUM TOMATOES MAKE THE PERFECT ACCOMPANIMENT.

2 Heat a non-stick frying pan, then add 15ml/1 tbsp of the oil, swirling it around to coat the bottom. Add the pieces of cod and cook, without turning or moving them, for 4 minutes, or until nicely caramelized.

3 Turn each piece over and cook the other side for a further 3 minutes, or until just firm. Remove it to a serving plate and keep hot.

4 Heat the remaining oil and stir-fry the spring onions for 1 minute. Add the vermouth and cook until reduced by half. Add the stock and cook again until reduced by half.

SERVES FOUR

INGREDIENTS
 4 pieces of cod fillet, about
   150g/5oz each, skinned
 30ml/2 tbsp olive oil
 4 spring onions (scallions), chopped
 150ml/¼ pint/⅔ cup dry vermouth,
   preferably Noilly Prat
 300ml/½ pint/1¼ cups fish stock
 45ml/3 tbsp crème fraîche or
   double (heavy) cream
 65g/2½oz goat's cheese, rind
   removed, and chopped
 30ml/2 tbsp chopped fresh parsley
 15ml/1 tbsp chopped fresh chervil
 salt and ground black pepper
 flat leaf parsley, to garnish
 grilled plum tomatoes, to serve

1 Remove any stray bones from the cod fillets. Rinse the fish under cold running water and pat dry with kitchen paper. Place on a plate and season well.

COOK'S TIP
The cooking time may change according to the thickness of the fish fillets.

5 Stir in the crème fraîche or cream and goat's cheese and simmer for 3 minutes. Add salt and pepper, stir in the herbs and spoon over the fish. Garnish with parsley and serve with grilled tomatoes.

VARIATION
Instead of cod you could use salmon, haddock or plaice.

PAN-FRIED SALMON <u>WITH</u> TARRAGON <u>AND</u> MUSHROOM SAUCE

TARRAGON HAS A DISTINCTIVE ANISEED FLAVOUR THAT IS GOOD WITH FISH, CRÈME FRAÎCHE AND MUSHROOMS. OYSTER MUSHROOMS HAVE BEEN INCLUDED HERE TO PROVIDE TEXTURE AND FLAVOUR.

SERVES FOUR

INGREDIENTS
50g/2oz/¼ cup unsalted (sweet) butter
4 salmon steaks, about 175g/6oz each
1 shallot, finely chopped
175g/6oz/2½ cups assorted wild and cultivated mushrooms such as oyster mushrooms, saffron milk-caps, bay boletus or cauliflower fungus, trimmed and sliced
200ml/7fl oz/scant 1 cup chicken or vegetable stock
10ml/2 tsp cornflour (cornstarch)
2.5ml/½ tsp mustard
50ml/3½ tbsp crème fraîche
45ml/3 tbsp chopped fresh tarragon
5ml/1 tsp white wine vinegar
salt and cayenne pepper
new potatoes and a green salad, to serve

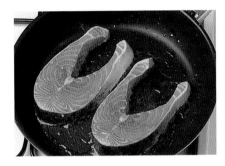

1 Melt half of the butter in a large, non-stick frying pan, season the salmon and cook in batches over a moderate heat for 8 minutes, turning once. Transfer to a plate, cover and keep warm.

COOK'S TIP
Fresh tarragon will bruise and darken quickly after chopping, so prepare the herb just before you use it.

2 Heat the remaining butter in the pan and gently fry the shallot to soften without letting it colour. Add the mushrooms and cook until the juices begin to flow. Add the stock and simmer for 2–3 minutes.

3 Put the cornflour and mustard in a cup and blend with 15ml/1 tbsp water. Stir into the mushroom mixture and bring to a simmer, stirring, to thicken. Add the crème fraîche, tarragon, vinegar, and salt and pepper.

4 Spoon the mushrooms over each salmon steak and serve with new potatoes and a green salad.

ROAST MONKFISH WITH GARLIC AND BAY LEAVES

MONKFISH QUICKLY ROASTED WITH GARLIC AND BAY IS DELICIOUS SERVED WITH NEW POTATOES FOR A SUMMERTIME MEAL.

SERVES SIX

INGREDIENTS
1.2kg/2½lb monkfish tail
8 garlic cloves
15ml/1 tbsp olive oil
2 fennel bulbs, sliced
juice and grated (shredded) rind of
  1 lemon
2 bay leaves, plus extra to garnish
salt and ground black pepper

3 Tie the separated fillets together with string to reshape as a tailpiece.

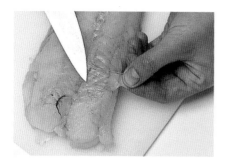

1 Preheat the oven to 220°C/425°F/ Gas 7. With a sharp filleting knife, carefully cut away the thin membrane covering the outside of the monkfish; keep the knife flat against the fish to avoid cutting too much of the flesh away. When finished, discard the membrane.

4 Peel and slice the garlic cloves and cut incisions into the fish flesh. Place the garlic slices in the incisions.

2 Cut along one side of the central bone to remove the fillet. Repeat on the other side. Discard the bone.

5 Heat the oil in a large, heavy pan and cook the fish until sealed on all sides, then place in a roasting pan together with the fennel slices, lemon juice, bay leaves and seasoning.

VARIATION
Monkfish is usually available all the year round, but if it is not available then you could substitute another firm white fish.

6 Roast the fish in the oven for about 20 minutes, until tender and cooked through. Serve immediately, garnished with bay leaves and lemon rind.

GRILLED RED MULLET WITH ROSEMARY

THIS RECIPE IS VERY SIMPLE — THE TASTE OF GRILLED RED MULLET IS SO GOOD IN ITSELF THAT IT NEEDS VERY LITTLE TO BRING OUT THE FLAVOUR: GARLIC AND JUST A HINT OF ROSEMARY ARE ALL THAT ARE NEEDED.

SERVES FOUR

INGREDIENTS

    4 red mullet or snapper, about
       275g/10oz each, cleaned
    4 garlic cloves, cut lengthways into
       thin slivers
    75ml/5 tbsp olive oil
    30ml/2 tbsp balsamic vinegar
    10ml/2 tsp very finely chopped fresh
       rosemary or 5ml/1 tsp dried
    ground black pepper
    fresh rosemary sprigs and lemon
       wedges, to garnish
    coarse salt, to serve

COOK'S TIP
Red mullet are extra delicious cooked on the barbecue. If possible, enclose them in a basket grill so that they are easy to turn over.

1 Cut three diagonal slits in both sides of each fish with a sharp kitchen knife. Push the garlic slivers into the slits in the fish.

2 Place the fish in a single layer in a shallow dish. Make a marinade by whisking the olive oil, balsamic vinegar and rosemary with ground black pepper to taste.

3 Pour the liquid over the fish, cover with clear film and leave to marinate in the refrigerator for at least 1 hour. Grill (broil) for 5–6 minutes on each side, turning once and brushing with the marinade.

4 Serve hot, sprinkled with coarse salt and garnished with fresh rosemary sprigs and lemon wedges.

GRILLED SOLE <u>WITH</u> CHIVE, LIME <u>AND</u> LEMON GRASS BUTTER

CHIVES MIXED WITH PIQUANT LIME AND LEMON GRASS MAKE A DELICIOUS BUTTER TO SERVE WITH SIMPLE GRILLED FISH. SOLE IS THE IDEAL CHOICE, BUT HALIBUT AND TURBOT ARE ALSO GOOD. SERVE WITH STEAMED NEW POTATOES AND A SIMPLE VEGETABLE ACCOMPANIMENT.

SERVES FOUR

INGREDIENTS

115g/4oz/½ cup unsalted (sweet) butter, softened, plus a little extra melted butter
5ml/1 tsp minced (ground) or very finely chopped lemon grass
pinch of finely grated (shredded) lime rind
1 kaffir lime leaf, very finely sliced (optional)
45ml/3 tbsp finely chopped chives or chive flowers
2.5–5ml/½–1 tsp Thai fish sauce (*nam pla*)
4 sole, skinned
salt and ground black pepper
a few whole chives and/or chive flowers, to garnish
lemon or lime wedges, to serve

1 Cream the butter with the lemon grass, lime rind, kaffir lime leaf, if using, and chives or chive flowers. Season to taste with Thai fish sauce (*nam pla*), salt and pepper.

2 Chill the butter to firm it for a short while, then form it into a roll and wrap in foil or clear film. Chill until firm.

3 Heat the grill (broiler). Brush the sole with a little melted butter and season to taste. Grill (broil) for about 5 minutes on each side, or until firm and just cooked.

4 Slice the butter. Place the fish on warmed plates and top with butter. Decorate with chives and hand round lemon or lime wedges.

COD, BASIL, TOMATO AND POTATO PIE

NATURAL AND SMOKED FISH MAKE A GREAT COMBINATION, ESPECIALLY WITH A HINT OF TOMATO AND BASIL. SERVED WITH A GREEN SALAD, IT MAKES AN IDEAL DISH FOR LUNCH OR A FAMILY SUPPER.

SERVES EIGHT

INGREDIENTS

1kg/2¼lb smoked cod
1kg/2¼lb white cod
900ml/1½ pints/3¾ cups milk
1.2 litres/2 pints/5 cups water
2 basil sprigs
1 lemon thyme sprig
150g/5oz/10 tbsp butter
1 onion, chopped
75g/3oz/⅔ cup plain (all-purpose)
  flour
30ml/2 tbsp chopped fresh basil
4 firm plum tomatoes, peeled
  and chopped
12 medium maincrop floury potatoes
salt and ground black pepper
crushed black peppercorns, to garnish
salad leaves, to serve

1 Place both kinds of fish in a roasting pan with 600ml/1 pint/2½ cups of the milk, the water and the herb sprigs. Bring to a simmer and cook gently for 3–4 minutes. Leave the fish to cool in the liquid for about 20 minutes. Drain the fish, reserving the cooking liquid for use in the sauce. Flake the fish, removing any skin and bone.

2 Melt 75g/3oz/6 tbsp of the butter in a large pan, add the onion and cook for about 5 minutes, or until softened and tender but not browned. Sprinkle over the flour and half the chopped basil. Gradually add the reserved fish cooking liquid, adding a little more milk if necessary to make a fairly thin sauce, and stirring constantly to make a smooth consistency. Bring to the boil, season with salt and pepper, and add the remaining basil.

3 Remove the pan from the heat, then add the fish and tomatoes and stir gently to combine. Pour into an ovenproof dish.

4 Preheat the oven to 180°C/350°F/ Gas 4. Cook the potatoes in boiling water until tender. Drain, then add the remaining butter and milk, and mash.

5 Season to taste and spoon over the fish mixture, using a fork to create a pattern. (You can freeze the pie at this stage.) Bake in the oven for 30 minutes, or until the top is golden. Sprinkle with the crushed peppercorns and serve hot with salad leaves.

SALMON RISOTTO WITH CUCUMBER AND TARRAGON

THE SUBTLE FLAVOUR OF CUCUMBER IS A FAMILIAR COMPANION FOR SALMON. IN THIS SIMPLE RISOTTO FRESH TARRAGON ADDS ITS UNMISTAKABLE, DELICATE AROMA AND FLAVOUR.

SERVES FOUR

INGREDIENTS
  25g/1oz/2 tbsp butter
  small bunch of spring onions
    (scallions), white parts only,
    chopped
  ½ cucumber, peeled, seeded
    and chopped
  350g/12oz/1¾ cups risotto rice
  1.2 litres/2 pints/5 cups hot chicken
    or fish stock
  150ml/¼ pint/⅔ cup dry white wine
  450g/1lb salmon fillet, skinned
    and diced
  45ml/3 tbsp chopped fresh tarragon
  salt and ground black pepper

1 Heat the butter in a large pan and add the spring onions and cucumber. Cook for 2–3 minutes, stirring occasionally. Do not let the spring onions colour.

2 Stir in the risotto rice, then pour in the stock and white wine. Bring to the boil, then lower the heat and allow to simmer, uncovered, for 10 minutes, stirring occasionally.

3 Stir in the diced salmon and then season to taste with salt and ground black pepper. Continue cooking for a further 5 minutes, stirring occasionally to avoid sticking, then remove from the heat. Cover the pan and leave the risotto to stand for 5 minutes.

4 Remove the lid, add the chopped fresh tarragon and mix lightly. Spoon the risotto into a warmed bowl and serve immediately.

COOK'S TIP
Carnaroli risotto rice would be an excellent choice for this risotto, although, if it is not available, arborio rice can be used instead.

TUNA STEAKS WITH CORIANDER AND LIME BUTTER

CORIANDER AND LIME COMPLEMENT EACH OTHER PERFECTLY IN THIS HERB BUTTER MELTED OVER TUNA STEAKS. A HERB BUTTER CAN TRANSFORM A SIMPLE MEAL AND CAN BE PREPARED IN ADVANCE, SO IT IS IDEAL FOR ENTERTAINING.

SERVES FOUR

INGREDIENTS

675g/1½lb tuna or swordfish, cut
   into 4 steaks, 2.5cm/1in thick
60ml/4 tbsp vegetable oil
30ml/2 tbsp tablespoons lemon juice
15ml/1 tbsp lime juice
salt and ground black pepper
slices of lime and parsley sprigs,
   to garnish
steamed asparagus, to serve (optional)
For the coriander and lime butter
25g/1oz/1 cup fresh coriander
   (cilantro)
225g/8oz/1 cup unsalted (sweet)
   butter, softened
grated (shredded) rind and juice of
   1 lime

1 To make the coriander and lime butter, finely chop the coriander leaves. Mix into the butter with the grated lime rind and juice. Transfer to greaseproof (waxed) paper and shape into a log. Chill.

2 Arrange the fish steaks in a dish. Combine the oil, citrus juices, salt and pepper, and pour over the fish. Cover and chill for 1–2 hours, turning the fish once or twice. Preheat the grill (broiler).

VARIATIONS
• For Salmon Steaks with Citrus Butter, lightly brush four salmon steaks, 2.5cm/ 1in thick, with oil, and season. Grill for 4–5 minutes on each side. Serve topped with pats of citrus butter.

3 Drain the fish and arrange on the rack in the grill pan (broiler). Grill (broil) for 3–4 minutes, or until just firm to the touch but still moist in the centre, turning the steaks over once. Slice the butter.

4 Transfer the fish to warmed plates and top each fish steak with a pat of coriander-lime butter. Garnish with slices of lime and parsley sprigs and serve the fish immediately, accompanied by steamed asparagus, if you like.

HERBY FISHCAKES <u>WITH</u> LEMON <u>AND</u> CHIVE SAUCE

THESE PIQUANT FISHCAKES ARE A CUT ABOVE THE REST. FLAVOURED WITH HORSERADISH AND PARSLEY, THEY ARE SERVED WITH A FRAGRANT GINGER, LEMON AND CHIVE SAUCE.

SERVES FOUR

INGREDIENTS
   350g/12oz potatoes, peeled
   75ml/5 tbsp milk
   350g/12oz haddock or hoki
     fillets, skinned
   15ml/1 tbsp lemon juice
   15ml/1 tbsp creamed horseradish
   30ml/2 tbsp chopped fresh parsley
   flour, for dusting
   115g/4oz/2 cups fresh wholemeal
     (whole-wheat) breadcrumbs
   salt and ground black pepper
   flat leaf parsley sprig, to garnish
   mangetouts (snow peas) and a sliced
     tomato and onion salad, to serve
For the lemon and chive sauce
   thinly pared rind and juice of
     ½ small lemon
   120ml/4fl oz/½ cup dry white wine
   2 thin slices fresh root ginger
   10ml/2 tsp cornflour (cornstarch)
   30ml/2 tbsp chopped fresh chives

1 Cook the potatoes in a large pan of boiling water for 15–20 minutes. Drain and mash with the milk, and season with salt and ground black pepper to taste.

2 Purée the fish together with the lemon juice and horseradish sauce in a food processor or blender. Mix together with the potatoes and parsley.

3 With floured hands, shape the mixture into eight fishcakes and coat with the breadcrumbs. Chill in the refrigerator for 30 minutes.

4 Cook the fishcakes under a preheated moderate grill (broiler) for 8 minutes on each side, or until browned.

5 To make the sauce, cut the lemon rind into strips and put into a pan with the lemon juice, wine and ginger and seasoning. Simmer for 6 minutes.

6 Blend the cornflour with 15ml/1 tbsp of cold water. Add to the pan and simmer until clear. Stir in the chives immediately before serving. Serve the sauce hot with the fishcakes, garnished with flat leaf parsley and accompanied by mangetouts and a tomato and onion salad.

BAKED COD <u>WITH</u> HORSERADISH SAUCE

FISH KEEPS MOIST WHEN BAKED IN A SAUCE. IN THIS UKRAINIAN RECIPE, A CREAMY HORSERADISH SAUCE IS SERVED ALONGSIDE, FOR ADDED FLAVOUR.

2 Melt the butter in a small, heavy pan. Stir in the flour and cook for 3–4 minutes, or until lightly golden. Stir to stop the flour sticking to the pan. Remove from the heat.

3 Gradually whisk the milk, and then the fish stock, into the flour mixture. Season with salt and ground black pepper. Bring to the boil, stirring, and simmer for 3 minutes, still stirring.

4 Pour the sauce over the fish and bake for 20–25 minutes, depending on the thickness. Check by gently inserting a knife into the thickest part: the flesh should be opaque.

5 For the horseradish sauce, blend the tomato purée and horseradish with the sour cream in a small pan. Slowly bring to the boil, stirring, and then simmer for 1 minute.

6 Pour the horseradish sauce into a serving bowl and serve alongside the baked fish. Serve the fish immediately. Garnish with the parsley sprigs and serve with potato wedges and fried sliced leeks.

SERVES FOUR

INGREDIENTS
    4 thick cod fillets or steaks
    15ml/1 tbsp lemon juice
    25g/1oz/2 tbsp butter
    25g/1oz/¼ cup plain (all-purpose)
      flour, sifted
    150ml/¼ pint/⅔ cup milk
    150ml/¼ pint/⅔ cup fish stock
    salt and ground black pepper
    sprigs of flat leaf parsley, to garnish
    potato wedges and fried sliced leeks,
      to serve
For the horseradish sauce
    30ml/2 tbsp tomato purée (paste)
    30ml/2 tbsp grated (shredded)
      fresh horseradish
    150ml/¼ pint/⅔ cup sour cream

1 Preheat the oven to 180°C/350°F/ Gas 4. Place the fish in a buttered ovenproof dish in a single layer. Sprinkle with lemon juice.

SALMON <u>WITH</u> SUMMER HERB MARINADE

MAKE THE BEST USE OF SUMMER HERBS IN THIS MARINADE. TRY ANY COMBINATION OF HERBS, DEPENDING ON WHAT YOU HAVE TO HAND. SALMON IS PERFECT, BUT THE MARINADE CAN ALSO BE USED WITH OTHER FISH, MEAT AND POULTRY.

<u>SERVES FOUR</u>

INGREDIENTS
large handful of fresh herb sprigs,
  such as chervil, thyme, parsley,
  sage, chives, rosemary, oregano
90ml/6 tbsp olive oil
45ml/3 tbsp tarragon vinegar
1 garlic clove, crushed
2 spring onions (scallions), chopped
4 salmon steaks or thick fillets
salt and ground black pepper
salad leaves and lemon wedges,
  to serve

1 Discard any coarse stalks or damaged leaves from the herbs, then chop them very finely.

2 Put the chopped herbs into a large bowl and add the oil, tarragon vinegar, garlic and chopped spring onions. Stir to mix thoroughly.

3 Place the salmon in a bowl and pour over the marinade. Cover and leave to marinate in a cool place for 4–6 hours.

4 Drain the salmon. Cook under a medium grill (broiler) for 10–15 minutes, turning once. Use the marinade to baste the fish occasionally.

5 The fish is cooked when the flesh separates into flakes when it is gently lifted with a knife. Serve with salad leaves and lemon wedges.

SEARED SCALLOPS WITH CHIVE SAUCE ON LEEK AND CARROT RICE

THE SWEET FLESH OF SCALLOPS PAIRS SUPERBLY WITH THE DELICATE FLAVOUR OF CHIVES. SERVED ON A BED OF WILD AND WHITE RICE WITH LEEKS, CARROTS AND CHERVIL, THIS IS AN IMPRESSIVE DISH.

SERVES FOUR

INGREDIENTS

12–16 shelled scallops
45ml/3 tbsp olive oil
50g/2oz/⅓ cup wild rice
65g/2½oz/5 tbsp butter
4 carrots, cut into long, thin strips
2 leeks, cut into thick diagonal slices
1 small onion, finely chopped
90g/3½oz/½ cup long grain rice
1 fresh bay leaf
200ml/7fl oz/scant 1 cup white wine
450ml/¾ pint/scant 2 cups well-
  flavoured fish stock
60ml/4 tbsp double (heavy) cream
a little lemon juice
25ml/1½ tbsp chopped fresh chives
30ml/2 tbsp chopped fresh chervil
salt and ground black pepper

1 Lightly season the scallops, brush with 15ml/1 tbsp of the olive oil and set aside.

2 Cook the wild rice in plenty of boiling water for about 30 minutes, until tender, then drain.

3 Melt half the butter in a small frying pan and sauté the carrots fairly gently for 4–5 minutes. Add the leeks and fry for another 2 minutes.

4 Season to taste and add 30–45ml/ 2–3 tbsp water, then cover and cook for a few minutes. Uncover and cook until the liquid evaporates. Set aside off the heat.

5 Melt half the rest of the butter with 15ml/1 tbsp of the remaining oil in a heavy pan. Add the onion and fry for 3–4 minutes, or until softened but not browned.

6 Add the long grain rice and bay leaf and cook, stirring constantly, until the rice looks translucent and the grains are coated with oil.

7 Pour in half the wine and half the stock. Season with 2.5ml/½ tsp salt and bring to the boil. Stir, then cover and cook very gently for 15 minutes, or until the liquid is absorbed and the rice is cooked and tender.

8 Reheat the carrots and leeks gently, then stir them into the long grain rice with the wild rice. Add seasoning to taste, if necessary.

9 Meanwhile, pour the remaining wine and stock into a small pan and boil rapidly until the liquid has reduced by about half.

COOK'S TIP
To shell a fresh scallop, hold it firmly with the flat-side up, and insert a strong knife blade between the shells to cut the top muscle. Separate the two shells. Slide the knife blade under the skirt to cut the second muscle. Remove the scallop. The edible part is the round white part and the coral, or roe, if present. Discard the beard-like fringe and intestinal thread.

10 Heat a heavy frying pan over a high heat. Add the remaining butter and olive oil. Sear the scallops for 1–2 minutes each side, or until browned, then remove and keep warm.

11 Pour the reduced stock into the frying pan and heat until bubbling, then add the double cream and boil until the mixture is thickened. Season with lemon juice, salt and black pepper. Stir in the chopped chives.

12 Stir the chervil into the rice and vegetable mixture and pile it on to plates. Arrange the scallops on top and spoon the sauce over the rice.

SARDINES WITH WARM HERB SALSA

PLAIN GRILLING OR BARBECUING IS THE VERY BEST WAY TO COOK FRESH SARDINES. SERVED WITH THIS LUSCIOUS SALSA OF PARSLEY, CHIVES AND BASIL, THE ONLY OTHER ESSENTIAL INGREDIENT IS FRESH, CRUSTY BREAD, TO MOP UP THE TASTY JUICES.

SERVES FOUR

INGREDIENTS

   12–16 fresh sardines
   oil for brushing
   juice of 1 lemon
   crusty bread, to serve
For the salsa
   15ml/1 tbsp butter
   4 spring onions (scallions), chopped
   1 garlic clove, finely chopped
   rind of 1 lemon
   30ml/2 tbsp finely chopped
     fresh parsley
   30ml/2 tbsp finely chopped
     fresh chives
   30ml/2 tbsp finely chopped
     fresh basil
   30ml/2 tbsp green olive paste
   10ml/2 tsp balsamic vinegar
   salt and ground black pepper

3 Add the lemon rind and remaining salsa ingredients to the onions and garlic in the pan and keep warm, stirring occasionally. Do not allow the mixture to boil.

4 Brush the sardines lightly with oil and sprinkle with lemon juice and seasoning. Cook for about 2 minutes on each side, on a barbecue or under a moderate grill (broiler). Serve with the salsa and bread.

1 To clean the sardines, use a pair of small kitchen scissors to slit the fish along the belly and pull out the innards. Wipe the fish with kitchen paper, and then arrange on a grill rack (broiler).

2 To make the salsa, melt the butter in a small pan and gently sauté the spring onions and garlic for about 2 minutes, shaking the pan occasionally, until softened but not browned.

COOK'S TIP

It is important to remove the innards as soon as possible, or they will start to taint the surrounding flesh.

HALIBUT FILLETS WITH FRESH TOMATO AND BASIL SALSA

A FRESH-TASTING TOMATO SALSA ENLIVENED WITH JALAPEÑO PEPPER AND BASIL IS IDEAL WITH SIMPLY GRILLED OR BARBECUED HALIBUT.

SERVES FOUR

INGREDIENTS
    4 halibut fillets, about 175g/
      6oz each
    45ml/3 tbsp olive oil
    basil leaves, to garnish
For the salsa
    1 tomato, roughly chopped
    ¼ red onion, finely sliced
    1 small jalapeño pepper, chopped
    30ml/2 tbsp balsamic vinegar
    10 large fresh basil leaves
    15ml/1 tbsp olive oil
    salt and ground black pepper

1 To make the salsa, mix together the chopped tomato, red onion, jalapeño pepper and balsamic vinegar in a bowl. Slice the fresh basil leaves finely, using a sharp kitchen knife.

2 Stir the basil and the olive oil into the tomato mixture. Season to taste. Cover the bowl with clear film and leave to marinate for at least 3 hours.

3 Rub the halibut fillets with oil, and season. Cook under a medium grill (broiler), or on a barbecue, for 8 minutes, basting with oil and turning once. Garnish with basil and serve with the salsa.

COOK'S TIP
It is easy to overcook halibut, which will make it turn dry and spoil its excellent flavour.

HERBY PLAICE CROQUETTES

FENNEL HAS A SUBTLE FLAVOUR, WITH A HINT OF ANISEED, WHICH LENDS ITSELF TO THE FINE FLAVOUR OF PLAICE. THESE HERBY CROQUETTES WOULD MAKE A DELICIOUS LUNCH OR SUPPER DISH AND A MIXED SALAD MAKES THE IDEAL ACCOMPANIMENT.

SERVES FOUR

INGREDIENTS
    450g/1lb plaice (flounder) fillets
    300ml/½ pint/1¼ cups milk
    450g/1lb cooked potatoes
    1 bulb fennel, finely chopped
    1 garlic clove, finely chopped
    45ml/3 tbsp chopped fresh parsley
    2 eggs
    15ml/1 tbsp unsalted (sweet) butter
    225g/8oz/4 cups white breadcrumbs
    25g/1oz/2 tbsp sesame seeds
    oil for deep-frying
    salt and ground black pepper

1 Poach the fish fillets in the milk for about 15 minutes, or until the fish flakes. Drain and reserve the milk.

2 Remove the fish skin and bones. In a food processor fitted with a metal blade, process the fish, potatoes, fennel, garlic, parsley, eggs and butter.

VARIATION
If plaice is unavailable, other white fish, such as sole, haddock or cod, could be used for these croquettes.

3 Add 30ml/2 tbsp of the reserved cooking milk, and season to taste.

4 Chill for 30 minutes, then shape the mixture into 20 croquettes with your floured hands.

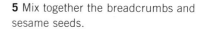

5 Mix together the breadcrumbs and sesame seeds.

6 Roll the croquettes in the mixture to form a good coating. Heat the oil in a large, heavy pan to 190°C/375°F, or until a cube of day-old bread fries to golden brown in under 1 minute. Deep-fry in batches for about 4 minutes, or until golden brown. Drain well on kitchen paper and serve hot.

COOK'S TIP
Always deep-fry with clean oil as the fish will flavour the oil and taint any other foods fried in it.

FILLETS <u>OF</u> HAKE BAKED <u>WITH</u> THYME <u>AND</u> GARLIC

QUICK COOKING IS THE ESSENCE OF THIS SIMPLE DISH. GARLIC, LEMON AND A HINT OF THYME ARE ALL THAT ARE NEEDED TO ENHANCE THE FLAVOUR OF THE HAKE.

<u>SERVES FOUR</u>

INGREDIENTS

    4 hake fillets, about 175g/6oz each
    1 shallot, finely chopped
    2 garlic cloves, thinly sliced
    4 sprigs fresh thyme, plus extra
      to garnish
    grated (shredded) rind and juice
      of 1 lemon
    30ml/2 tbsp extra virgin olive oil
    salt and ground black pepper

1 Preheat the oven to 180°C/350°F/ Gas 4. Lay the hake fillets in the base of a large roasting tin (pan). Scatter the shallot, garlic and thyme on top.

2 Season the fish well with salt and ground black pepper.

VARIATION
If hake is not available, you can use cod or haddock fillets for this recipe.

3 Drizzle the lemon juice and olive oil over the fish. Bake in the preheated oven for about 15 minutes. Serve immediately, scattered with finely grated lemon rind and garnished with the extra thyme sprigs.

SMOKED HADDOCK FILLETS <u>WITH</u> QUICK PARSLEY SAUCE

A GOOD, STRONG, FRESH PARSLEY SAUCE IS GREAT WITH FULL-FLAVOURED SMOKED HADDOCK. THIS RECIPE IS QUICK TO PREPARE AND MAKES A TASTY MIDWEEK MEAL.

SERVES FOUR

INGREDIENTS
 4 smoked haddock fillets, about
  225g/8oz each
 75g/3oz/6 tbsp butter, softened
 25g/1oz/¼ cup plain (all-purpose) flour
 300ml/½ pint/1¼ cups milk
 60ml/4 tbsp chopped fresh parsley
 salt and ground black pepper
 parsley sprigs, to garnish

1 Smear the fish on both sides with 50g/2oz/¼ cup butter. Preheat the grill (broiler).

2 Beat the remaining 25g/1oz butter and flour together with a wooden spoon to make a thick and smooth paste.

3 Grill (broil) the fish over a medium high heat for 10–15 minutes, turning when necessary.

4 Meanwhile, heat the milk until just below boiling point. Add the flour mixture in small knobs, whisking constantly over the heat. Continue until the sauce is smooth and thick.

5 Stir in the seasoning and parsley, and serve poured over the fillets, or in a serving jug. Serve immediately, garnished with parsley and your choice of vegetables.

BAKED TUNA <u>WITH A</u> CORIANDER CRUST

FRESH TUNA IS VERY MEATY AND FILLING AND IS EXCELLENT ACCOMPANIED BY A LIGHT SALSA OF MANGO AND LIME WITH JUST A DASH OF CHILLI. TOPPING THE FISH WITH A FRESH CORIANDER AND LEMON CRUST ADDS A TASTY CRISPNESS.

2 Mix together the lemon rind, black peppercorns, chopped onion and fresh coriander in a mortar and pestle to make a coarse paste.

3 Spread the paste on to one side of each tuna steak, pressing on well to ensure it sticks.

4 Heat the olive oil in a heavy frying pan until it begins to smoke. Add the tuna, paste-side down, and fry until a crust forms. Lower the heat and turn the steaks to cook for 1 minute more.

5 Pat off any excess oil on to absorbent kitchen paper, and serve with the mango salsa.

SERVES FOUR

INGREDIENTS
  finely grated rind of 1 lemon
  5ml/1 tsp black peppercorns
  ½ small onion, finely chopped
  30ml/2 tbsp chopped fresh
    coriander (cilantro)
  4 fresh tuna steaks, about 175g/
    6oz each
  120ml/4fl oz/½ cup olive oil
For the salsa
  1 mango, peeled, stone removed and
    cut into dice
  finely grated (shredded) rind and
    juice of 1 lime
  ½ red chilli, deseeded and chopped

1 To make the mango salsa, mix the mango, lime rind and juice, and chilli in a bowl and leave to marinate for at least 1 hour.

Enrich the flavour of meat using herbs. Add the subtle fragrance of lavender or lemon grass to lamb or rabbit, or permeate tender chicken with garlic for a pronounced flavour. Use herbs for sauces or for dressings, or to flavour accompaniments for meat, such as horseradish dumplings or coriander (cilantro) yogurt. Whether grilling (broiling), braising, barbecuing or frying, herbs will give your meat a whole new dimension.

Meat and Poultry

BEEF STROGANOFF <u>WITH</u> CHANTERELLE MUSHROOMS <u>AND</u> PARSLEY CREAM

DIJON MUSTARD AND PARSLEY ARE THE ESSENTIAL HERBS THAT FLAVOUR THE CREAMY SAUCE IN THIS FAMOUS DISH. CHANTERELLE MUSHROOMS AND FILLET BEEF MAKE IT AN EXQUISITE CHOICE FOR A DINNER-PARTY, ALTHOUGH BUTTON OR CUP MUSHROOMS COULD BE SUBSTITUTED IF NECESSARY.

SERVES FOUR

INGREDIENTS

    450g/1lb fillet or rump steak,
       trimmed and cut into thin strips
    30ml/2 tbsp olive oil
    45ml/3 tbsp brandy
    2 shallots, finely chopped
    225g/8oz/3¼ cups chanterelle
       mushrooms, trimmed and halved
    150ml/¼ pint/⅔ cup beef stock
    75ml/5 tbsp sour cream
    5ml/1 tsp Dijon mustard
    ½ sweet gherkin, chopped
    45ml/3 tbsp chopped fresh parsley
    salt and ground black pepper
    buttered noodles dressed with poppy
       seeds, to serve

1 Season the steak with pepper, heat half of the oil in a pan and cook for 2 minutes. Transfer to a plate.

COOK'S TIP
Fillet steak will give the best flavour and texture, but rump or sirloin would also work well.

2 Place the pan over a high heat to brown the sediment. Add the brandy, and carefully ignite with a match to burn off the alcohol. Pour these juices over the meat, cover and keep warm.

3 Wipe the pan, heat the remaining oil and lightly brown the shallots. Add the mushrooms and sauté for 3–4 minutes.

4 Add the stock, simmer for a few minutes, then add the cream, mustard and gherkin together with the steak and its juices. Simmer briefly, season, and stir in the parsley. Serve with buttered noodles dressed with poppy seeds.

LEMON GRASS PORK CHOPS WITH MUSHROOMS

THAI FLAVOURINGS WITH LEMON GRASS, CHILLI AND SPRING ONIONS ARE USED TO MAKE AN AROMATIC MARINADE AND A SPICY SAUCE FOR GRILLED OR BARBECUED PORK. THE SAUCE CAN BE PUT TOGETHER IN A PAN ON THE BARBECUE WHILE THE CHOPS AND MUSHROOMS ARE COOKING.

SERVES FOUR

INGREDIENTS

    4 pork chops, about 225g/8oz each
    4 large field (portabello) mushrooms
    45ml/3 tbsp vegetable oil
    4 fresh red chillies, seeded and
        finely sliced
    45ml/3 tbsp Thai fish sauce (*nam pla*)
    90ml/6 tbsp lime juice
    4 shallots, chopped
    5ml/1 tsp roasted ground rice
    30ml/2 tbsp spring onions
        (scallions), chopped
    fresh coriander (cilantro) leaves and
        4 spring onions (scallions) sliced
        lengthways, to garnish
For the marinade
    2 garlic cloves, chopped
    15ml/1 tbsp sugar
    15ml/1 tbsp Thai fish sauce (*nam pla*)
    30ml/2 tbsp soy sauce
    15ml/1 tbsp sesame oil
    15ml/1 tbsp whisky or dry sherry
    2 lemon grass stalks, finely chopped
    2 spring onions (scallions), chopped

2 Place the mushrooms and marinated pork chops on a grill rack (broiler), and brush with 15ml/1 tbsp vegetable oil.

3 Cook the pork chops under a medium-hot grill, or on a barbecue, for 10–15 minutes and the mushrooms for 2 minutes, turning once. Brush both with the marinade while cooking.

4 Meanwhile, heat the remaining oil in a small frying pan, then remove from the heat and mix in the remaining ingredients except the garnishes.

5 Put the pork chops and mushrooms on a serving plate and spoon over the sauce. Garnish with the fresh coriander and spring onions.

1 To make the marinade, mix all the ingredients together. Arrange the pork chops in a shallow dish. Pour over the marinade and leave for 1–2 hours.

COOK'S TIP

Thai fish sauce, or *nam pla*, is actually anchovy essence (paste). It has a clean, salty taste and enhances other flavours rather than swamping them.

CHICKEN WITH FRESH HERBS AND GARLIC

THYME, SAGE, GARLIC AND LEMON COMBINE TO GIVE ROAST CHICKEN A SUMMERY FLAVOUR.
IF YOU PREFER, COOK THE CHICKEN ON A SPIT ON THE BARBECUE.

SERVES FOUR

INGREDIENTS

2kg/4½lb free-range chicken
finely grated (shredded) rind and
　juice of 1 lemon
1 garlic clove, crushed
30ml/2 tbsp olive oil
2 fresh thyme sprigs
2 fresh sage sprigs
90ml/6 tbsp unsalted (sweet) butter,
　softened
salt and ground black pepper

COOK'S TIP

If you are roasting a chicken to serve
cold, cooking it in foil helps to keep it
succulent – open the foil for the last
20 minutes to brown the skin, then close
it as the chicken cools.

1 Season the chicken well and place in
a shallow non-metallic dish.

2 Mix the lemon rind and juice, crushed
garlic and olive oil together and pour
them over the chicken. Leave to
marinate in the refrigerator for at least
2 hours. Preheat the oven to 230°C/
450°F/Gas 8.

3 Place the herbs in the cavity of the
bird and smear the butter over the skin.
Roast in the oven for 1½–1¾ hours,
reducing the heat to 190°C/375°F/Gas 5
after the first 10 minutes. Baste with
marinade during cooking. The chicken
is cooked when the juices run clear
when the thigh is pierced with a skewer.
Leave for 15 minutes before carving.

TURKEY ESCALOPES WITH LEMON AND SAGE

SAGE IS A USEFUL HERB THAT CAN BE HARVESTED ALL THE YEAR ROUND. ITS WELL-DEFINED FLAVOUR BLENDS PERFECTLY WITH LEMON IN A MARINADE FOR TURKEY ESCALOPES USED HERE.

2 In a small bowl, combine the lemon rind, sage, lemon juice, and 30ml/ 2 tbsp of the oil. Stir well to mix.

3 Arrange the turkey cutlets, in one layer, in one or two shallow baking dishes. Divide the lemon mixture evenly between the dishes and rub well into the turkey. Leave to marinate for 20 minutes.

4 Heat the remaining oil in a frying pan. Dredge the turkey cutlets in the breadcrumbs, shaking off the excess.

SERVES FOUR

INGREDIENTS
4 turkey cutlets (boneless slices of breast, about 175g/6oz each)
15ml/1 tbsp freshly grated (shredded) lemon rind
15ml/1 tbsp chopped fresh sage or 5ml/1 tsp dried sage
50ml/2fl oz/¼ cup fresh lemon juice
90ml/6 tbsp vegetable oil
50g/2oz/scant 1 cup fine dry breadcrumbs
salt and ground black pepper
fresh sage leaves and lemon slices, to garnish
steamed courgettes (zucchini) and new potatoes, to serve

1 Place each turkey cutlet between two sheets of greaseproof (waxed) paper or clear film. With the flat side of a meat mallet, pound until about 5mm/¼in thick, being careful not to split the meat. Remove the paper or clear film. Sprinkle the cutlets with salt and pepper.

VARIATION
For an equally delicious alternative, substitute fresh tarragon leaves for the sage used here.

5 Fry in the hot oil for about 2 minutes on each side. Garnish with sage leaves and lemon slices, and serve with courgettes and new potatoes.

Baked Chicken <u>with</u> Shallots, Garlic <u>and</u> Fennel

This is a very simple and delicious way to cook chicken. Leave the chicken to marinate for a few hours before baking so that the complementary flavours of garlic, shallots and fennel seeds can really permeate the flesh.

SERVES FOUR

INGREDIENTS

   1.6–1.8kg/3½–4lb chicken, cut into
     8 pieces or 8 chicken joints
   250g/9oz shallots, chopped
   1 head garlic, separated into cloves
     and peeled
   60ml/4 tbsp extra virgin olive oil
   45ml/3 tbsp tarragon vinegar
   45ml/3 tbsp white wine or
     vermouth (optional)
   5ml/1 tsp fennel seeds,
     lightly crushed
   2 bulbs fennel, cut into wedges,
     feathery tops reserved
   150ml/¼ pint/⅔ cup double
     (heavy) cream
   5ml/1 tsp redcurrant jelly
   15ml/1 tbsp tarragon mustard
   caster (superfine) sugar (optional)
   30ml/2 tbsp chopped fresh flat
     leaf parsley
   salt and ground black pepper

1 Place the chicken, shallots and all but one of the garlic cloves in a flameproof dish or roasting pan. Add the oil, vinegar, wine or vermouth, if using, and fennel seeds. Season with pepper and mix well, then marinate for 2–3 hours.

2 Preheat the oven to 190ºC/375ºF/ Gas 5. Add the fennel to the chicken, season with salt, and stir to mix. Cook for 50–60 minutes, stirring once or twice. The juices should run clear when the thigh is pierced with a skewer.

3 Transfer the chicken and vegetables to a serving dish and keep warm. Skim off some of the fat and bring the juices to the boil, then pour in the cream. Stir, then whisk in the redcurrant jelly and mustard. Check the seasoning, adding a little sugar, if you like.

4 Chop the remaining garlic with the reserved fennel tops and mix with the chopped parsley. Pour the sauce over the chicken and scatter the chopped garlic and herb mixture over the top. Serve immediately.

COOK'S TIPS
• If possible, use the fresh new season's garlic for this dish, as it is plump, moist and full of flavour. Purple-skinned garlic is considered to have the best flavour.
• The cut surfaces of fennel tend to discolour quickly, so try not to prepare it much in advance of using it. If you must, then put the wedges into a bowl of cold water that has been acidulated with a little lemon juice.

CHICKEN WITH FORTY CLOVES OF GARLIC

THIS DISH DOES NOT HAVE TO BE MATHEMATICALLY EXACT — THE IMPORTANT THING IS THAT THERE SHOULD BE LOTS OF GARLIC. THE SMELL THAT EMANATES FROM THE OVEN AS THE CHICKEN AND GARLIC COOK IS INDESCRIBABLY DELICIOUS.

3 Sprinkle in 5ml/1 tsp flour and cook for 1 minute. Add the port or wine. Tuck in the whole heads of garlic and the peeled cloves with the herb sprigs. Pour over the remaining oil and season to taste with salt and pepper.

4 Mix the main batch of flour with sufficient water to make a firm dough. Roll it out into a long sausage and press it around the rim of the casserole, then press on the lid, folding the dough up and over the lid to create a tight seal. Cook in the oven for 1½ hours.

5 To serve, break the seal and remove the chicken and whole garlic to a serving platter and keep warm.

6 Remove and discard the herb sprigs, then place the casserole on the hob and whisk the contents to combine the garlic with the juices. Add the crème fraîche, if using, and a little lemon juice to taste, if liked. Process the sauce in a food processor or blender or press it through a sieve if a smoother result is required. Serve the garlic purée with the chicken.

SERVES FOUR TO FIVE

INGREDIENTS
  5–6 whole heads of garlic
  15g/½oz/1 tbsp butter
  45ml/3 tbsp olive oil
  1.8–2kg/4–4½lb chicken
  150g/5oz/1¼ cups plain (all-purpose)
    flour, plus 5ml/1 tsp
  75ml/5 tbsp white port, Pineau
    de Charentes or other white,
    fortified wine
  2–3 fresh tarragon or rosemary sprigs
  30ml/2 tbsp crème fraîche (optional)
  few drops of lemon juice (optional)
  salt and ground black pepper

1 Separate three of the heads of garlic into cloves and peel them. Remove the first layer of papery skin from the remaining heads of garlic and cut off the tops to expose the cloves, but leave them whole. Preheat the oven to 180°C/350°F/Gas 4.

2 Heat the butter and 15ml/1 tbsp of the olive oil in a flameproof casserole which is just large enough to take the chicken and garlic. Add the chicken and cook over a medium heat, turning frequently, for 10–15 minutes, or until it is browned all over.

PAN-FRIED PORK WITH THYME AND GARLIC RISOTTO

LEAN PORK CHUMP CHOPS ARE DELICIOUS MARINATED IN GARLIC AND LEMON. SERVED WITH A SMOOTH, CREAMY, BUT ROBUST, RISOTTO, VIBRANTLY FLAVOURED WITH GARLIC AND THYME, THEY MAKE A TASTY MEAL.

3 To make the risotto, heat the butter with the oil in a large, heavy pan until foaming. Sauté the chopped shallots and garlic gently until the shallots are softened, but not coloured. Add the rice and thyme and stir until the grains are well coated.

4 Add a ladleful of boiling stock and cook gently, stirring occasionally. When all the stock is absorbed, add another ladleful. Continue cooking in this way until all the stock is absorbed. Keep the stock simmering and do not add too much at a time. This should take 25–30 minutes. Season to taste.

SERVES FOUR

INGREDIENTS
    4 large pork chump or loin chops,
      each weighing about 175g/6oz,
      rind removed
    1 garlic clove, finely chopped
    juice of ½ lemon
    5ml/1 tsp soft light brown sugar
    25g/1oz/2 tbsp butter
    fresh thyme sprigs, to garnish
For the risotto
    25g/1oz/2 tbsp butter
    15ml/1 tbsp olive oil
    2 shallots, chopped
    2 garlic cloves, finely chopped
    250g/9oz/1⅓ cups risotto rice
    15ml/1 tbsp fresh thyme leaves
    900ml/1½ pints/3¾ cups boiling pork
      or chicken stock
    salt and ground black pepper

1 Put the chops in a shallow dish and sprinkle the garlic over. To make the marinade, mix the lemon juice and soft light brown sugar together, and drizzle this over the chops.

2 Turn the chops to coat both sides with the lemon mixture, then cover the dish and leave them to marinate in the refrigerator while making the risotto.

5 Cook the chops when the risotto is half cooked. Melt the butter in a large, heavy frying pan. Remove the chops from the marinade, allowing the lemon juice to drip off, and fry them for 3–4 minutes on each side.

6 Divide the risotto among four plates and arrange the chops on top. Serve at once, garnished with fresh thyme.

LAVENDER AND THYME CHICKEN

HERE, LAVENDER FLOWERS ARE USED TO PERFUME AND FLAVOUR CHICKEN COOKED IN A LARGE CASSEROLE WITH RED WINE, ORANGE AND THYME. WHEN THE LID IS REMOVED AFTER COOKING, THE HEADY AROMA WILL ENTICE AS MUCH AS THE DELICIOUS FLAVOUR.

SERVES FOUR

INGREDIENTS

4 chicken portions
15ml/1 tbsp butter
15ml/1 tbsp olive oil
8 shallots
30ml/2 tbsp plain (all-purpose) flour
250ml/8fl oz/1 cup red wine
250ml/8fl oz/1 cup chicken stock
4 sprigs thyme
10ml/2 tsp thyme flowers, removed
  from the stalk
10ml/2 tsp lavender flowers
grated (shredded) rind and juice of
  1 orange
salt and ground black pepper
For the garnish
1 orange, divided into segments
12 lavender sprigs
20ml/4 tsp lavender flowers

1 Cut each chicken portion into two using a large, sharp knife.

2 Heat the butter and olive oil in a heavy pan and add the chicken pieces. Cook them for about 5 minutes, or until they are browned all over, then transfer to a large, flameproof casserole.

3 Add the shallots to the frying pan and cook for 2 minutes. Add to the chicken in the casserole.

4 Add the flour to the frying pan, and cook for 2 minutes, stirring continuously. Pour in enough of the wine and stock to make a thin sauce. Bring to the boil, stirring all the time, and season to taste.

5 Stir in the thyme sprigs, thyme and lavender flowers, orange rind and juice.

6 Pour the sauce over the chicken in the casserole, then cover and simmer for 30–40 minutes, or until the chicken is tender.

7 Remove the thyme sprigs before serving. Serve the stew garnished with orange segments, and fresh lavender sprigs and flowers.

MEDALLIONS OF VENISON WITH HERBY HORSERADISH DUMPLINGS

VENISON IS LEAN AND FULL-FLAVOURED AND IS ESPECIALLY DELICIOUS SERVED WITH THESE HORSERADISH AND HERB DUMPLINGS. THIS RECIPE MAKES A SPECTACULAR MAIN COURSE TO SERVE AT A DINNER PARTY AND IS ACTUALLY VERY EASY TO PREPARE.

SERVES FOUR

INGREDIENTS
- 600ml/1 pint/2½ cups venison stock
- 120ml/4fl oz/½ cup port
- 15ml/1 tbsp sunflower oil
- 4 medallions of venison, about 175g/6oz each
- chopped parsley, to garnish
- steamed baby vegetables, such as carrots, courgettes (zucchini) and turnips, to serve

For the dumplings
- 75g/3oz/⅔ cup self-raising (self-rising) flour
- 40g/1½oz beef suet
- 15ml/1 tbsp chopped fresh mixed herbs
- 5ml/1 tsp creamed horseradish
- 45–60ml/3–4 tbsp water
- salt and ground black pepper

1 To make the dumplings, mix together the flour, beef suet, mixed herbs and seasoning, and make a well in the middle. Add the creamed horseradish and water, then mix to make a soft but not sticky dough. Shape the dough into walnut-size balls and chill in the refrigerator for up to 1 hour.

2 Boil the venison stock in a pan until reduced by half. Add the port and continue boiling until reduced again by half, then pour the reduced stock into a large frying pan. Heat the stock until it is simmering and add the dumplings. Poach them gently for 5–10 minutes, or until risen and cooked through. Use a draining spoon to remove the dumplings from the pan.

3 Smear the oil over a non-stick griddle and heat until very hot. Add the venison medallions and cook them for 2–3 minutes on each side. Remove from the pan. Place them on warm serving plates and pour the sauce over. Serve with the dumplings and the baby vegetables, garnished with chopped parsley.

VEAL CHOPS WITH BASIL BUTTER

VEAL CHOPS FROM THE LOIN ARE AN EXPENSIVE CUT AND ARE BEST COOKED QUICKLY AND SIMPLY. THE FLAVOURS OF BASIL AND DIJON MUSTARD GO WELL WITH VEAL AND ARE SUPERB IN A MELTING BUTTER. NEW POTATOES AND A MIXED SALAD ARE PERFECT ACCOMPANIMENTS.

SERVES TWO

INGREDIENTS

  2 veal loin chops, 2.5cm/1in thick,
    about 225g/8oz each
  olive oil, for brushing
  salt and ground black pepper
  fresh basil sprigs, to garnish
For the basil butter
  25g/1oz/2 tbsp butter, softened
  15ml/1 tbsp Dijon mustard
  15ml/1 tbsp chopped fresh basil

1 To make the basil butter, cream the softened butter with the Dijon mustard and chopped fresh basil in a large mixing bowl, then season with plenty of freshly ground black pepper.

2 Brush both sides of each chop with olive oil and season with a little salt.

3 Cook the chops on a hot griddle or in a heavy frying pan for 7–10 minutes, basting with oil and turning once, until done to your liking. (Medium-rare meat will still be slightly soft when pressed, medium meat will be springy, and well-done firm.) Top each chop with half the basil butter and serve at once, garnished with basil.

HERB-CRUSTED RACK OF LAMB WITH PUY LENTILS

THIS ROAST IS QUICK AND EASY TO PREPARE, YET IMPRESSIVE WHEN SERVED: THE PERFECT CHOICE WHEN ENTERTAINING. BOILED OR STEAMED NEW POTATOES AND LIGHTLY COOKED BROCCOLI OR SUGAR SNAP PEAS ARE SUITABLE ACCOMPANIMENTS FOR THE LAMB. SERVE WITH A LIGHT RED WINE.

SERVES FOUR

INGREDIENTS
2 x 6-bone racks of lamb, chined
50g/2oz/1 cup fresh white
 breadcrumbs
2 large garlic cloves, crushed
90ml/6 tbsp chopped mixed fresh
 herbs, such as rosemary, thyme, flat
 leaf parsley and marjoram, plus
 extra sprigs to garnish
50g/2oz ¼ cup butter, melted
salt and ground black pepper
For the Puy lentils
1 red onion, chopped
30ml/2 tbsp olive oil
400g/14oz can Puy or green lentils,
 rinsed and drained
400g/14oz can chopped tomatoes
30ml/2 tbsp chopped fresh parsley

1 Preheat the oven to 220°C/425°F/ Gas 7. Trim any excess fat from the lamb, season and place in a roasting tin.

2 Mix together the breadcrumbs, garlic, chopped herbs and butter. Press the mixture on to the fat-sides of the lamb. Roast for 25 minutes. Cover with foil and stand for 5 minutes before carving.

3 Cook the onion in the olive oil until softened. Add the lentils and tomatoes and cook gently for 5 minutes, or until the lentils are piping hot. Stir in the parsley and season to taste.

4 Cut each rack of lamb in half and serve with the lentils and new potatoes. Garnish with herb sprigs.

ROAST VEAL WITH PARSLEY STUFFING

*COOKING THIS JOINT OF VEAL, WITH ITS FRAGRANT PARSLEY AND LEEK STUFFING, IN A ROASTING BAG
ENSURES THAT IT IS SUCCULENT AND FULL FLAVOURED WHEN SERVED.*

SERVES SIX

INGREDIENTS

25g/1oz/2 tbsp butter
15ml/1 tbsp sunflower oil
1 leek, finely chopped
1 celery stick, finely chopped
50g/2oz/1 cup fresh white
  breadcrumbs
50g/2oz/½ cup chopped fresh flat
  leaf parsley
900g/2lb boned loin of veal
salt and ground black pepper
gravy, sautéed potatoes, asparagus
  and mangetouts, to serve

1 Preheat the oven to 180°C/350°F/
Gas 4. Heat the butter and oil in a
frying pan until foaming. Cook the leek
and celery until they are just starting to
colour, then remove the pan from the
heat and stir in the breadcrumbs,
parsley and seasoning.

2 Lay the joint of veal out flat. Spread
the stuffing over the meat, then roll it
up carefully and tie the joint at regular
intervals to secure it in a neat shape.

VARIATION
Other mild herbs can be used in the
stuffing instead of parsley. Try tarragon,
chervil and chives, but avoid strong-
flavoured herbs, such as marjoram,
oregano and thyme, which tend to
overpower the delicate flavour of veal.

3 Place the veal in a roasting bag and
close the bag with an ovenproof tie,
then place it in a roasting pan. Roast
the veal for 1¼ hours.

4 Pierce the joint with a metal skewer
to check whether it is cooked: when
cooked the meat juices will run clear.
Leave to stand for 10–15 minutes, then
carve it into thick slices. Serve with a
light gravy, sautéed potatoes, asparagus
and mangetouts.

RABBIT AND LEMON GRASS RISOTTO

SCENTED LEMON GRASS IMPARTS A PLEASANT TANG TO THIS CREAMY RISOTTO. QUICKLY COOKED STRIPS OF TENDER RABBIT ADD A RICH FLAVOUR, WHILE FRESH THYME CONTRIBUTES FLAVOUR.

SERVES THREE TO FOUR

INGREDIENTS

225g/8oz rabbit meat, cut into strips
seasoned flour
50g/2oz/¼ cup butter
15ml/1 tbsp olive oil
45ml/3 tbsp dry sherry
1 onion, finely chopped
1 garlic clove, crushed
1 lemon grass stalk, peeled and very
　finely sliced
275g/10oz/1½ cups risotto rice,
　preferably carnaroli
1 litre/1¾ pints/4 cups simmering
　chicken stock
10ml/2 tsp chopped fresh thyme
45ml/3 tbsp double (heavy) cream
25g/1oz/⅓ cup freshly grated
　(shredded) Parmesan cheese
salt and ground black pepper

VARIATION
This recipe would also work well using chicken or turkey instead of the rabbit.

1 Coat the rabbit strips in the seasoned flour. Heat half the butter and olive oil in a frying pan and fry the rabbit quickly until evenly brown. Add the sherry, and allow to boil briefly to burn off the alcohol. Season with salt and pepper and set aside.

2 Heat the remaining olive oil and butter in a large pan. Fry the onion and garlic over a low heat for 4–5 minutes, or until the onion is soft. Add the sliced lemon grass and cook for a few more minutes.

3 Add the rice and stir to coat in the oil. Add a ladleful of stock and cook, stirring, until the liquid has been absorbed. Continue adding the stock gradually, stirring constantly. When the rice is almost cooked, stir in three-quarters of the meat, with the pan juices. Add the thyme and seasoning.

4 Continue cooking until the rice is tender but still has a "bite". Stir in the cream and Parmesan, remove from the heat and cover. Leave to rest before serving, garnished with rabbit strips.

HONEY-ROAST PORK WITH THYME AND ROSEMARY

LEAN PORK TENDERLOIN IS BAKED WITH A COVERING OF HONEY, MUSTARD, ROSEMARY AND THYME. THE FLAVOURS ARE ROUNDED OFF WITH A GLORIOUS RED ONION CONFIT.

SERVES FOUR

INGREDIENTS
  450g/1lb pork tenderloin
  30ml/2 tbsp set (crystallized) honey
  30ml/2 tbsp Dijon mustard
  5ml/1 tsp chopped fresh rosemary
  2.5ml/½ tsp chopped fresh thyme
  1.5ml/¼ tsp whole tropical
    peppercorns
  sprigs of fresh rosemary and thyme,
    to garnish
  Anna potatoes (see Cook's Tip) and
    cauliflower, to serve
For the red onion confit
  4 red onions
  350ml/12fl oz/1½ cups
    vegetable stock
  15ml/1 tbsp red wine vinegar
  15ml/1 tbsp caster (superfine) sugar
  1 garlic clove, crushed
  30ml/2 tbsp ruby port
  pinch of salt

1 Preheat the oven to 180°C/350°F/Gas 4. Trim off any visible fat from the pork. Put the honey, mustard, rosemary and thyme in a bowl and mix together.

2 Crush the peppercorns using a mortar and pestle. Spread the honey mixture over the pork and sprinkle with the crushed peppercorns. Place in a non-stick roasting pan and cook in the preheated oven for 35–45 minutes.

3 To make the red onion confit, slice the onions into rings and put them into a heavy pan.

4 Add the stock, vinegar, sugar and garlic to the pan. Bring to the boil, then reduce the heat. Cover and simmer for 15 minutes.

5 Uncover and pour in the port and continue to simmer the confit, stirring occasionally, until the onions are soft and the juices thick and syrupy. Season to taste with salt.

6 Slice the pork. Serve garnished with herbs and accompanied by the confit and vegetables.

COOK'S TIP
For Anna potatoes, peel and thinly slice potatoes. Arrange in layers in a dish. Season each layer and dot with butter. Cover with foil, and bake for 1 hour at 190°C/375°F/Gas 5.

SKEWERED LAMB <u>WITH</u> CORIANDER YOGURT

TENDER GRILLED OR BARBECUED LAMB IS MARINATED WITH THE AROMATIC FLAVOURS OF ONION, BAY, AND ROSEMARY, AND SERVED WITH A FRESH MINT AND CORIANDER YOGURT.

3 Mix together the onion, herbs, lemon rind and juice, sugar and oil, then season to taste.

4 Pour the marinade over the meat in the bowl and stir to ensure the meat is thoroughly covered. Cover with clear film and leave to marinate in the refrigerator for several hours.

5 Drain the meat and thread on to metal skewers. Cook under a hot grill (broiler), or on a barbecue, for about 10 minutes. Garnish with rosemary and serve with lemon wedges and the coriander yogurt (barbecue the lemon wedges as well, if you like).

SERVES FOUR

INGREDIENTS
    900g/2lb lean boneless lamb
    1 large onion, grated (shredded)
    3 bay leaves
    5 rosemary or thyme sprigs
    grated rind and juice of 1 lemon
    2.5ml/½ tsp caster (superfine) sugar
    75ml/2½fl oz/⅓ cup olive oil
    salt and ground black pepper
    sprigs of fresh rosemary, to garnish
    lemon wedges, to serve
For the coriander yogurt
    150ml/¼ pint/⅔ cup thick natural
        (plain) yogurt
    15ml/1 tbsp chopped fresh mint
    15ml/1 tbsp chopped fresh coriander
        (cilantro)
    10ml/2 tsp grated (shredded) onion

1 To make the coriander yogurt, mix together the natural yogurt, chopped fresh mint, chopped fresh coriander and grated onion. Transfer the mixture to a serving bowl.

2 To make the kebabs, cut the lamb into 2.5cm/1in cubes and put in a bowl.

COOK'S TIP
If possible, try to use real Greek (US strained plain) yogurt for the coriander yogurt in this recipe. Made from either sheep's or cow's milk, it is deliciously thick and creamy, and is also much less acidic than skimmed milk natural (plain) yogurt. American readers need to strain natural yogurt to thicken it up.

BEEF AND GRILLED SWEET POTATO SALAD WITH SHALLOT AND HERB DRESSING

THIS SALAD MAKES A GOOD MAIN DISH FOR A SUMMER BUFFET. IT HAS AN ABSOLUTELY DELICIOUS DRESSING OF MIXED HERBS AND DIJON MUSTARD, PERKED UP WITH A LITTLE GREEN CHILLI. SERVE WITH SOME PEPPERY SALAD LEAVES, SUCH AS WATERCRESS, MIZUNA OR ROCKET.

SERVES SIX TO EIGHT

INGREDIENTS
  800g/1¾lb fillet of beef
  5ml/1 tsp black peppercorns, crushed
  10ml/2 tsp chopped fresh thyme
  60ml/4 tbsp olive oil
  450g/1lb orange-fleshed sweet
    potato, peeled
  salt and ground black pepper
For the dressing
  1 garlic clove, chopped
  15g/½oz/½ cup flat leaf parsley
  30ml/2 tbsp chopped fresh
    coriander (cilantro)
  15ml/1 tbsp small salted
    capers, rinsed
  ½–1 fresh green chilli, seeded
    and chopped
  10ml/2 tsp Dijon mustard
  10–15ml/2–3 tsp white wine vinegar
  75ml/5 tbsp extra virgin olive oil
  2 shallots, finely chopped

1 Roll the beef in the peppercorns and thyme. Set aside to marinate. Heat the oven to 200°C/400°F/Gas 6.

2 Heat half the olive oil in a heavy frying pan. Add the marinated beef and brown it all over, turning frequently, to seal it. Place on a baking tray and cook in the preheated oven for 15–20 minutes.

3 Remove the beef from the oven, cover it with foil, then leave it to rest for 10–15 minutes.

4 Meanwhile, preheat the grill (broiler). Cut the sweet potatoes into 1cm/½in slices. Brush with the remaining oil, season to taste, and grill (broil) for 5–6 minutes on each side. Cut the sweet potato slices into strips and place them in a bowl.

5 Cut the beef into slices or strips and toss with the sweet potato, then set the bowl aside.

6 For the dressing, process the garlic, parsley, coriander, capers, chilli, mustard and 10ml/2 tsp of the vinegar in a food processor or blender until chopped. With the motor running, gradually pour in the oil to make a smooth dressing. Season the dressing with salt and pepper and add more vinegar, to taste. Stir in the shallots.

7 Toss the shallot and herb dressing into the sweet potatoes and beef and leave the salad to stand for up to 2 hours before serving.

LAMB WITH LAVENDER BALSAMIC MARINADE

FRAGRANT LAVENDER IS AN UNUSUAL FLAVOUR TO USE WITH MEAT, BUT ITS HEADY, SUMMERY SCENT WORKS WELL WITH GRILLED OR BARBECUED LAMB. IF YOU PREFER, ROSEMARY CAN TAKE ITS PLACE.

SERVES FOUR

INGREDIENTS

4 racks of lamb, with 3–4 cutlets
on each
1 shallot, finely chopped
45ml/3 tbsp chopped fresh lavender
florets, plus extra to garnish
15ml/1 tbsp balsamic vinegar
30ml/2 tbsp olive oil
15ml/1 tbsp lemon juice
salt and ground black pepper
handful of lavender sprigs

1 Place the racks of lamb in a large mixing bowl or wide dish and sprinkle over the chopped shallot.

2 Sprinkle the chopped fresh lavender over the racks of lamb.

3 Beat together the balsamic vinegar, olive oil and lemon juice and pour them over the lamb. Season well with salt and ground black pepper and then turn the meat to coat it evenly.

4 Scatter a few of the lavender sprigs over the grill (broiler) or on the coals of a medium-hot barbecue. Cook the lamb for about 15–20 minutes, turning once and basting with any remaining marinade.

5 Serve the lamb while it is still slightly pink in the centre, garnished with the remaining lavender.

LAMB STEAKS <u>WITH</u> MINT <u>AND</u> LEMON

USE THIS SIMPLE AND TRADITIONAL MARINADE TO MAKE THE MOST OF FINE-QUALITY LAMB LEG STEAKS. THE COMBINATION OF LEMON AND FRESH MINT GOES EXTREMELY WELL WITH THE FLAVOUR OF GRILLED OR BARBECUED LAMB.

SERVES FOUR

INGREDIENTS
  4 lamb steaks, about 225g/8oz each
  5ml/1 tsp finely chopped fresh mint
  fresh mint leaves, to garnish
For the marinade
  grated (shredded) rind and juice of
    ½ lemon
  1 garlic clove, crushed
  1 spring onion (scallion), finely chopped
  30ml/2 tbsp extra virgin olive oil
  salt and ground black pepper

1 Mix all the ingredients for the marinade and season to taste with salt and ground black pepper.

2 Place the lamb steaks in a shallow dish and add the marinade and mint, ensuring that all the meat is coated. Cover with clear film and leave the lamb to marinate in the refrigerator for several hours or overnight if possible.

3 Drain the lamb and cook under a medium-hot grill (broiler), or on a barbecue, for 10–15 minutes, or until just cooked, basting with marinade occasionally and turning once. Garnish with the fresh mint leaves.

Make vegetarian dishes even more tempting by adding herbs. Enrich chickpeas with coriander (cilantro), turmeric, chilli and creamy ground cashew nuts, or top grilled polenta with caramelized sweet onions. For entertaining, serve a roulade with a delicious filling of bell peppers, ricotta cheese, walnuts and basil, or serve a vegetable curry enlivened with lemon grass and Eastern spices. Here is a wealth of vegetarian ideas that is sure to please.

Vegetarian

RISOTTO <u>WITH</u> BASIL <u>AND</u> RICOTTA

THIS IS A WELL-FLAVOURED RISOTTO, WHICH BENEFITS FROM THE DISTINCTIVE PUNGENCY OF BASIL,
MELLOWED WITH SMOOTH RICOTTA.

SERVES THREE TO FOUR

INGREDIENTS

45ml/3 tbsp olive oil
1 onion, finely chopped
275g/10oz/1½ cups risotto rice
1 litre/1¾ pints/4 cups simmering
    vegetable stock
175g/6oz/¾ cup ricotta cheese
50g/2oz/generous 1 cup finely
    chopped fresh basil leaves, plus
    extra leaves to garnish
75g/3oz/1 cup freshly grated
    (shredded) Parmesan cheese
salt and ground black pepper

1 Heat the oil in a large pan or flameproof casserole and fry the chopped onion over a gentle heat, stirring frequently until it is soft.

2 Tip in the rice. Cook for a few minutes, stirring, until the rice is coated with oil and is slightly translucent.

3 Pour in about a quarter of the stock. Cook, stirring, until all the stock has been absorbed, then add another ladleful. Continue in this manner, adding more stock when the previous ladleful has been absorbed, for about 20 minutes, or until the rice is just tender.

4 Spoon the ricotta cheese into a bowl and break it up a little with a fork. Stir into the risotto along with the basil and Parmesan. Taste and adjust the seasoning, then cover and allow to stand for 2–3 minutes before serving, garnished with basil leaves.

ROSEMARY RISOTTO WITH BORLOTTI BEANS

THIS IS A CLASSIC RISOTTO WITH A SUBTLE AND COMPLEX TASTE, FROM THE HEADY FLAVOURS OF ROSEMARY TO THE SAVOURY BEANS AND THE FRUITY-SWEET TASTES OF MASCARPONE AND PARMESAN.

3 Heat the olive oil in a large pan and gently fry the onion and garlic for 6–8 minutes, or until very soft. Add the rice and cook over a medium heat for a few minutes, stirring constantly, until the grains are thoroughly coated in oil and are slightly translucent.

4 Pour in the wine. Cook over a medium heat for 2–3 minutes, stirring all the time, until the wine has been absorbed. Add the stock gradually, a ladleful at a time, waiting for each quantity to be absorbed before adding more, and continuing to stir.

5 When the rice is about three-quarters cooked, stir in the bean purée (paste). Continue to cook the risotto, adding any stock that remains, until it has reached a creamy consistency and the rice is tender but still has a bit of "bite".

6 Add the reserved beans, with the mascarpone, Parmesan and rosemary, then season to taste with salt and pepper. Stir thoroughly, then cover and leave to stand for about 5 minutes so that the risotto absorbs the flavours fully and the rice finishes cooking. Serve with extra Parmesan, if you like.

VARIATION
Fresh thyme or marjoram could be used for this risotto instead of rosemary, if preferred. One of the great virtues of risotto is that it lends itself well to a range of equally tasty variations. Experiment with different herbs to make your own speciality dish.

SERVES THREE TO FOUR

INGREDIENTS
  400g/14oz can borlotti beans
  30ml/2 tbsp olive oil
  1 onion, chopped
  2 garlic cloves, crushed
  275g/10oz/1½ cups risotto rice
  175ml/6fl oz/¾ cup dry white wine
  900ml–1 litre/1½–1¾ pints/
    3¾–4 cups simmering
    vegetable stock
  60ml/4 tbsp mascarpone cheese
  65g/2½oz/¾ cup freshly grated
    (shredded) Parmesan cheese,
    plus extra to serve (optional)
  5ml/1 tsp chopped fresh rosemary
  salt and ground black pepper

1 Drain the canned borlotti beans, rinse them well under plenty of cold water and drain again.

2 Purée about two-thirds of the beans fairly coarsely in a food processor or blender. Set the remainder aside.

FRESH HERB RISOTTO

HERE IS A RISOTTO TO CELEBRATE THE ABUNDANCE OF SUMMER HERBS. AN AROMATIC BLEND OF OREGANO, CHIVES, PARSLEY AND BASIL COMBINES WITH ARBORIO RICE TO MAKE A CREAMY AND SATISFYING MEAL.

3 Pour in the dry white wine and bring to the boil. Reduce the heat and cook for 10 minutes, or until all the wine has been absorbed.

4 Add the hot vegetable stock, a little at a time, waiting for each quantity to be absorbed before adding more, and stirring continuously. After 20–25 minutes the rice should be tender and creamy. Season well.

5 Add the herbs and wild rice; heat for 2 minutes, stirring frequently. Stir in two-thirds of the Parmesan and cook until melted. Serve sprinkled with the remaining Parmesan.

SERVES FOUR

INGREDIENTS

90g/3½oz/½ cup wild rice
15ml/1 tbsp butter
15ml/1 tbsp olive oil
1 small onion, finely chopped
450g/1lb/2¼ cups arborio rice
300ml/½ pint/1¼ cups dry white wine
1.2 litres/2 pints/5 cups simmering vegetable stock
45ml/3 tbsp chopped fresh oregano
45ml/3 tbsp chopped fresh chives
60ml/4 tbsp chopped fresh flat leaf parsley
60ml/4 tbsp chopped fresh basil
75g/3oz/1 cup freshly grated (shredded) Parmesan cheese
salt and ground black pepper

1 Cook the wild rice in boiling salted water according to the instructions on the packet.

2 Heat the butter and oil in a large, heavy pan. When the butter has melted, add the onion and cook for 3 minutes. Add the arborio rice and cook for 2 minutes, stirring to coat.

COOK'S TIPS
• Risotto rice is essential to achieve the correct creamy texture in this dish. Other types of rice simply will not do.
• Fresh herbs are also a must, but you can use tarragon, chervil, marjoram or thyme instead of the ones listed here, if you prefer.

GARLIC AND CHIVE RISOTTO WITH FRIZZLED ONIONS AND PARMESAN

GARLIC, ONIONS AND CHIVES BELONG TO THE ALLIUM FAMILY OF PLANTS. THE ONIONS ARE FIRST GENTLY COOKED IN BUTTER — AS IN ALL CLASSIC RISOTTOS — THEN GARLIC AND CHIVES ARE ADDED. THE RISOTTO IS TOPPED WITH A FINAL SPRINKLING OF DELICIOUS, CRISP FRIED ONIONS.

4 Continue cooking for 18–20 minutes, adding one or two ladlefuls of stock at a time, until the rice is swollen and tender outside, but still *al dente* on the inside. Keep the heat low and stir frequently. The finished risotto should be moist, but not like soup.

5 Separate the slices of yellow onion into rings while the risotto is cooking. Heat a shallow layer of oil in a frying pan. Cook the onion rings slowly at first until they are soft, then increase the heat and fry them briskly until they are brown and crisp. Drain them thoroughly on kitchen paper.

6 Beat the chopped chives, the remaining butter and half the Parmesan into the risotto until it looks creamy. Taste and add salt and ground black pepper, if necessary.

7 Serve the risotto in warmed bowls, topped with the crisp fried onions. Add more grated Parmesan to taste at the table.

SERVES FOUR

INGREDIENTS
75g/3oz/6 tbsp butter
15ml/1 tbsp olive oil, plus extra for shallow frying
1 onion, finely chopped
4 garlic cloves, finely chopped
350g/12oz/1⅔ cups risotto rice
150ml/¼ pint/⅔ cup dry white wine
pinch of saffron threads (about 12 threads)
about 1.2 litres/2 pints/5 cups simmering vegetable stock
1 large yellow onion, thinly sliced
15g/½oz chopped fresh chives
75g/3oz/1 cup freshly grated (shredded) Parmesan cheese, plus extra to taste
salt and ground black pepper

1 Melt half the butter with the oil in a large, deep frying pan or heavy pan. Add the onion with a pinch of salt and cook over a very low heat, stirring frequently, for 10–15 minutes, or until softened and just turning golden. Do not allow the onion to brown.

2 Add the garlic and rice and cook, stirring constantly, for 3–4 minutes, or until the rice is coated and looks translucent. Season with a little salt and ground black pepper.

3 Pour in the wine and stir in the saffron with a ladleful of hot stock. Cook slowly, stirring frequently, until all the liquid has been absorbed.

RICE WITH DILL AND BROAD BEANS

THIS IS A FAVOURITE RICE DISH IN IRAN, WHERE IT IS CALLED BAGHALI POLO. THE COMBINATION OF BROAD BEANS, DILL, WARM CINNAMON AND CUMIN WORKS VERY WELL. THE SAFFRON RICE ADDS A SPLASH OF BRIGHT COLOUR.

SERVES FOUR

INGREDIENTS

   275g/10oz/1½ cups basmati
     rice, soaked
   750ml/1¼ pints/3 cups water
   40g/1½oz/3 tbsp butter
   175g/6oz/1½ cups frozen baby broad
     (fava) beans, thawed and peeled
   90ml/6 tbsp finely chopped fresh
     dill, plus 1 fresh dill sprig,
     to garnish
   5ml/1 tsp ground cinnamon
   5ml/1 tsp ground cumin
   2–3 saffron threads, soaked in
     15ml/1 tbsp boiling water
   salt

1 Drain the rice, tip it into a pan and pour in the water. Add a little salt. Bring to the boil, then lower the heat and simmer very gently for 5 minutes. Drain, rinse well in warm water and then drain once again.

2 Melt the butter gently in a non-stick pan. Pour two-thirds of the melted butter into a small jug (pitcher) and set aside.

3 Spoon enough rice into the pan to cover the base. Add a quarter of the beans and a little dill. Spread over another layer of rice, then a layer of beans and dill. Repeat the layers until all the beans and dill have been used up, ending with a layer of rice. Cook over a gentle heat for 8 minutes until the rice and beans are nearly tender.

4 Pour the reserved melted butter over the rice. Sprinkle with the ground cinnamon and cumin. Cover the pan with a clean dish towel and a tight-fitting lid, lifting the corners of the cloth back over the lid. Cook over a low heat for 25–30 minutes.

5 Spoon about 45ml/3 tbsp of the cooked rice into the bowl of saffron water; mix well. Mound the remaining rice mixture on a large serving plate and spoon the saffron rice on one side to decorate. Serve at once, decorated with the sprig of dill.

ONION TART

THIS CLASSIC ONION TART, FLAVOURED WITH NUTMEG, COMES FROM ALSACE IN EASTERN FRANCE.
IT IS TRADITIONALLY SERVED IN SMALL SLICES AS A FIRST COURSE, BUT IT ALSO MAKES A DELICIOUS
WARM MAIN COURSE WHEN ACCOMPANIED BY A GREEN SALAD.

SERVES FOUR TO SIX

INGREDIENTS
    175g/6oz/1½ cups plain
        (all-purpose) flour
    75g/3oz/6 tbsp butter, chilled
    30–45ml/2–3 tbsp iced water
For the filling
    50g/2oz/¼ cup butter
    900g/2lb Spanish onions,
        sliced
    1 egg plus 2 egg yolks
    250ml/8fl oz/1 cup double
        (heavy) cream
    1.5ml/¼ tsp freshly grated
        (shredded) nutmeg
    salt and ground black pepper

1 Process the flour, a pinch of salt and the butter in a food processor until reduced to fine crumbs. Or, rub the fat into the flour using the fingertips. Add the iced water and process, or knead, briefly to form a dough. Gather into a ball and chill for 40 minutes.

2 Meanwhile, start the filling. Melt the butter in a large pan and add the onions and a pinch of salt. Turn them in the butter. Cover and cook very gently, stirring frequently, for 30–40 minutes. The onions should gradually turn golden yellow. Cool slightly.

VARIATIONS
There are endless variations on this classic tart: try adding chopped fresh herbs, such as thyme, or, for meat-eaters, 115g/4oz/⅔ cup chopped smoked pancetta.

3 Preheat the oven to 190°C/375°F/Gas 5. Roll out the dough thinly and use to line a 23–25cm/9–10in loose-based flan tin (quiche pan). Line with baking parchment and baking beans, then bake blind for 10 minutes.

4 Remove the paper and baking beans and bake for 4–5 minutes more, until the pastry is lightly cooked to a pale brown (blonde is quite a good description). Reduce the oven setting to 180°C/350°F/Gas 4.

5 Beat the egg, egg yolks and cream together. Season with salt, lots of black pepper and the grated nutmeg. Place half the onions in the pastry shell and add half the egg mixture. Add the remaining onions, then pour in as much of the remaining custard as you can.

6 Place on a baking sheet and bake on the middle shelf for 40–50 minutes, or until the custard is risen, browned and set in the centre. Serve warm rather than piping hot.

THAI VEGETABLE AND CORIANDER CURRY WITH LEMON GRASS JASMINE RICE

AN ARRAY OF THAI SEASONINGS GIVES THIS RICH CURRY ITS MARVELLOUS FLAVOUR. LEMON GRASS ADDS ITS DELICATE SCENT TO THE CURRY AND THE JASMINE RICE ACCOMPANIMENT.

SERVES FOUR

INGREDIENTS

10ml/2 tsp vegetable oil
400ml/14fl oz/1⅔ cups coconut milk
300ml/½ pint/1¼ cups good-quality
  vegetable stock
225g/8oz new potatoes, halved or
  quartered, if large
130g/4½oz baby corn cobs
5ml/1 tsp golden caster (superfine)
  sugar
185g/6½oz broccoli florets
1 red (bell) pepper, seeded and
  sliced lengthways
115g/4oz spinach, tough stalks
  removed and finely sliced
30ml/2 tbsp chopped fresh
  coriander (cilantro)
salt and ground black pepper
For the spice paste
1 red chilli, seeded and chopped
3 green chillies, seeded and chopped
1 lemon grass stalk, outer leaves
  removed and lower 5cm/2in
  finely chopped
2 shallots, chopped
finely grated (shredded) rind of
  1 lime
2 garlic cloves, chopped
5ml/1 tsp ground coriander
2.5ml/½ tsp ground cumin
1cm/½in fresh galangal, finely
  chopped or 2.5ml/½ tsp dried
  (optional)
45ml/3 tbsp chopped fresh coriander
  (cilantro)
For the rice
225g/8oz/generous 1 cup jasmine
  rice, rinsed
1 lemon grass stalk, outer leaves
  removed and cut into three pieces
6 cardamom pods, bruised

COOK'S TIP
Galangal is the pungent, aromatic root of an Oriental plant. It can usually be found, in either fresh or dried form, in good Oriental supermarkets.

1 Begin by making the spice paste. Place all the ingredients together in a food processor or blender and blend to a coarse paste.

2 Heat the oil in a large, heavy pan and fry the spice paste for 1–2 minutes, stirring constantly. Add the coconut milk and stock, and bring to the boil.

3 Reduce the heat, add the potatoes, and simmer for 15 minutes. Add the baby corn and seasoning, then cook for 2 minutes. Stir in the sugar, broccoli and red pepper, and cook for 2 minutes more, or until the vegetables are tender. Stir in the finely sliced spinach and 15ml/1 tbsp of the chopped fresh coriander. Cook for another 2 minutes.

VARIATION
Try substituting other vegetables for the ones used here. Mushrooms and carrots would both work well.

4 Meanwhile, prepare the rice. Tip the rinsed rice into a large pan and add the pieces of lemon grass stalk and the cardamom pods. Pour over 475ml/16fl oz/2 cups water.

5 Bring to the boil, then reduce the heat, cover the pan and allow to cook for 10–15 minutes, or until the water is absorbed and the rice is tender and slightly sticky. Season with salt, leave to stand for 10 minutes, then fluff up the rice with a fork.

6 Remove the spices and serve the rice with the curry, sprinkled with the remaining fresh coriander.

SESAME-SEED-COATED FALAFEL <u>WITH</u> TAHINI <u>AND</u> MINT YOGURT DIP

THESE SPICY PATTIES HAVE A CRUNCHY COATING OF SESAME SEEDS. SERVE WITH THE MINT-FLAVOURED TAHINI YOGURT DIP AND WARM PITTA BREAD AS A LIGHT LUNCH OR SUPPER DISH.

<u>SERVES FOUR</u>

INGREDIENTS
   250g/9oz/1⅓ cups dried chickpeas
   2 garlic cloves, crushed
   1 red chilli, seeded and finely sliced
   5ml/1 tsp ground coriander seeds
   5ml/1 tsp ground cumin
   15ml/1 tbsp chopped fresh mint
   15ml/1 tbsp chopped fresh parsley
   2 spring onions (scallions), finely
     chopped
   1 large egg, beaten
   sesame seeds, for coating
   sunflower oil, for frying
   salt and ground black pepper
For the tahini yogurt dip
   30ml/2 tbsp light tahini
   200g/7oz/scant 1 cup natural
     (plain) yogurt
   5ml/1 tsp cayenne pepper, plus extra
     for sprinkling
   15ml/1 tbsp chopped fresh mint
   1 spring onion (scallion),
     finely sliced

3 Combine the chickpeas with the garlic, chilli, ground spices, herbs, spring onions and seasoning, then mix in the egg. Place in a food processor and blend until the mixture forms a coarse paste. If the paste seems too soft, chill it for 30 minutes.

4 Form the chilled chickpea paste into 12 patties with your hands, then roll in the sesame seeds to coat thoroughly.

5 Heat enough oil to cover the base of a frying pan. Fry the falafel for 6 minutes, turning once. Serve with the yogurt dip.

1 Place the chickpeas in a bowl, cover with cold water and leave to soak overnight. Drain and rinse them, then place in a pan and cover with cold water. Bring to the boil and boil rapidly for 10 minutes, reduce the heat and simmer for 1½–2 hours. Drain.

2 To make the tahini yogurt dip, mix together the tahini, yogurt, cayenne pepper and mint in a small bowl. Sprinkle the spring onion and extra cayenne on top, and chill until required.

HERBY THAI TEMPEH CAKES <u>WITH</u> SWEET DIPPING SAUCE

MADE FROM SOYA BEANS, TEMPEH IS SIMILAR TO TOFU BUT HAS A NUTTIER TASTE. HERE, IT IS COMBINED WITH A FRAGRANT BLEND OF LEMON GRASS, CHILLIES AND GINGER AND FORMED INTO SMALL PATTIES.

MAKES EIGHT CAKES

INGREDIENTS
    1 lemon grass stalk, outer leaves
        removed and inside finely chopped
    2 garlic cloves, chopped
    2 spring onions (scallions), finely
        chopped
    2 shallots, roughly chopped
    2 fresh chillies, seeded and finely
        chopped
    2.5cm/1in piece fresh root ginger,
        finely chopped
    60ml/4 tbsp chopped fresh coriander,
        (cilantro) plus extra to garnish
    250g/9oz tempeh, thawed if
        frozen, sliced
    15ml/1 tbsp lime juice
    5ml/1 tsp caster (superfine) sugar
    45ml/3 tbsp plain (all-purpose) flour
    1 large egg, lightly beaten
    vegetable oil, for frying
    salt and ground black pepper
For the dipping sauce
    45ml/3 tbsp mirin
    45ml/3 tbsp white wine vinegar
    2 spring onions (scallions), finely
        sliced
    15ml/1 tbsp sugar
    2 fresh chillies, finely chopped
    30ml/2 tbsp chopped fresh
        coriander
    large pinch of salt

1 To make the sauce, mix all the ingredients in a bowl and set aside.

2 Place the lemon grass, garlic, spring onions, shallots, chillies, ginger and coriander in a food processor or blender; process the mixture to form a coarse paste.

3 Add the tempeh, lime juice and sugar to the processor or blender, then process until the ingredients are well combined. Add the seasoning, flour and beaten egg. Process again until the mixture forms a coarse, sticky paste.

4 Using one heaped serving-spoonful of the tempeh mixture at a time, form into rounds with your hands – the mixture will be quite sticky.

5 Heat enough oil to cover the base of a large frying pan. Fry the tempeh cakes in batches for 5–6 minutes, turning once, until they are golden. Drain on kitchen paper and serve warm with the dipping sauce, garnished with the reserved coriander.

COOK'S TIP
Mirin is a sweet, almost syrupy Japanese rice wine brewed specially for cooking purposes. Buy it from good Oriental grocers.

BAKED VEGETABLES <u>WITH</u> THYME

CRUNCHY GOLDEN BATTER SURROUNDS THIS ATTRACTIVE COMBINATION OF BRIGHT PEPPERS, ONION, AUBERGINE AND COURGETTES. FLAVOURED WITH THYME, THEY ARE BOTH DELICIOUS AND FILLING, AND, SERVED WITH SALAD, MAKE AN EXCELLENT LIGHT LUNCH.

SERVES SIX

INGREDIENTS
    1 small aubergine (eggplant),
        trimmed, halved and thickly sliced
    1 egg
    115g/4oz/1 cup plain (all-purpose)
        flour
    300ml/½ pint/1¼ cups milk
    30ml/2 tbsp fresh thyme leaves,
        or 10ml/2 tsp dried
    1 red onion
    2 large courgettes (zucchini)
    1 red (bell) pepper
    1 yellow (bell) pepper
    60–75ml/4–5 tbsp sunflower oil
    30ml/2 tbsp freshly grated
        (shredded) Parmesan cheese
    salt and ground black pepper
    fresh herbs, to garnish

1 Place the aubergine in a colander or sieve, sprinkle generously with salt, and leave for 10 minutes. Drain, rinse well and pat dry on kitchen paper.

2 Meanwhile, beat the egg in a bowl, then gradually beat in the flour and a little milk to make a smooth, thick paste. Gradually blend in the rest of the milk, add the thyme and seasoning to taste, and stir until smooth. Leave in a cool place until required. Preheat the oven to 220°C/425°F/Gas 7.

COOK'S TIP

It is essential to get the fat in the roasting pan really hot before adding the batter, which should sizzle slightly as it goes in. Use a pan that is not too deep.

3 Quarter the onion, slice the courgettes and seed and quarter the peppers. Put the oil in a roasting pan and heat in the oven. Add the vegetables, including the aubergines, toss in the oil to coat thoroughly and return to the oven for 20 minutes.

4 Whisk the batter, then pour it over the vegetables and return to the oven for 30 minutes. When puffed up and golden, reduce the heat to 190°C/375°F/ Gas 5 for 10–15 minutes, or until crisp around the edges. Sprinkle with Parmesan and herbs, and serve.

BAKED HERB CRÊPES

ADD FRESH HERBS TO MAKE CRÊPES SOMETHING SPECIAL, THEN FILL WITH SPINACH, PINE NUTS AND RICOTTA CHEESE FLAVOURED WITH BASIL. DELICIOUS SERVED WITH A GARLICKY TOMATO SAUCE.

SERVES FOUR

INGREDIENTS
 25g/1oz/½ cup chopped fresh herbs
 15ml/1 tbsp sunflower oil, plus extra
  for frying
 120ml/4fl oz/½ cup milk
 3 eggs
 25g/1oz/¼ cup plain (all-purpose)
  flour
 pinch of salt
 oil, for greasing
For the sauce
 30ml/2 tbsp olive oil
 1 small onion, chopped
 2 garlic cloves, crushed
 400g/14oz can chopped tomatoes
 pinch of soft light brown sugar
For the filling
 450g/1lb fresh spinach, cooked
  and drained
 175g/6oz/¾ cup ricotta cheese
 25g/1oz/¼ cup pine nuts, toasted
 5 sun-dried tomato halves in olive
  oil, drained and chopped
 30ml/2 tbsp chopped fresh basil
 salt, nutmeg and ground
  black pepper
 4 egg whites

3 To make the sauce, heat the oil in a small pan, add the onion and garlic and cook gently for 5 minutes. Add the tomatoes and sugar and cook for about 10 minutes, or until thickened. Purée in a blender, then sieve and set aside.

4 To make the filling, mix together the spinach with the ricotta, pine nuts, tomatoes and basil. Season with salt, nutmeg and pepper.

5 Preheat the oven to 190°C/375°F/ Gas 5. Whisk the egg whites until stiff. Fold one-third into the spinach mixture, then gently fold in the rest.

6 Place one crêpe at a time on a lightly oiled baking sheet, add a spoonful of filling and fold into quarters. Bake for 12 minutes until set. Reheat the sauce and serve with the crêpes.

1 To make the crêpes, place the herbs and oil in a food processor and blend until smooth. Add the milk, eggs, flour and salt and process again until smooth. Leave to rest for 30 minutes.

2 Heat a small, non-stick frying pan and add a small amount of oil. Add a ladleful of batter. Swirl around to cover the base. Cook for 2 minutes, turn and cook for 2 minutes. Make seven more crêpes.

FRITTATA WITH TOMATOES AND THYME

A FRITTATA IS AN ITALIAN OMELETTE THAT IS COOKED UNTIL FIRM ENOUGH TO BE CUT INTO WEDGES.
SUN-DRIED TOMATOES AND A HINT OF THYME GIVE THIS FRITTATA A DISTINCTIVE FLAVOUR.

SERVES THREE TO FOUR

INGREDIENTS

   6 sun-dried tomatoes
   60ml/4 tbsp olive oil
   1 small onion, finely chopped
   60ml/4 tbsp fresh thyme leaves
   6 eggs
   50g/2oz/⅔ cup freshly grated
    (shredded) Parmesan cheese
   salt and ground black pepper
   sprigs of thyme, to garnish
   shavings of Parmesan, to serve

1 Place the tomatoes in a small bowl and pour on enough hot water just to cover them. Leave to soak for about 15 minutes. Lift the tomatoes out of the water and pat dry on kitchen paper. Reserve the soaking water. Cut the tomatoes into thin strips.

2 Heat the oil in a large, non-stick frying pan. Stir in the chopped onion and cook for 5–6 minutes, or until softened and golden.

3 Stir in the sun-dried tomatoes and thyme, and cook over a moderate heat for a further 2–3 minutes, stirring from time to time. Season with salt and ground black pepper.

COOK'S TIP
If you find it difficult to slide the frittata on to a plate, simply place the pan under a hot grill to brown the top, protecting the handle if necessary.

4 Break the eggs into a bowl and beat lightly. Stir in 45ml/3 tbsp of the tomato soaking water and the Parmesan. Raise the heat under the pan. When the oil is sizzling, add the eggs. Mix quickly into the other ingredients, then stop stirring. Lower the heat to moderate and cook for 4–5 minutes, or until the base is golden and the top puffed.

5 Take a large plate, place it upside down over the pan and, holding it firmly with oven gloves, turn the pan and the frittata over on to it. Slide the frittata back into the pan, and continue cooking for 3–4 minutes, or until golden on the second side. Remove from the heat. Cut into wedges, garnish with thyme and serve with Parmesan.

GRILLED POLENTA WITH CARAMELIZED ONIONS, RADICCHIO AND THYME

SLICES OF GRILLED POLENTA ARE TASTY TOPPED WITH SLOWLY CARAMELIZED ONIONS FLAVOURED WITH GARLIC, THYME AND BUBBLING TALEGGIO CHEESE, IN THIS DISH FROM NORTHERN ITALY.

SERVES FOUR

INGREDIENTS

900ml/1½ pints/3¾ cups water
150g/5oz/1¼ cups polenta
  or corn meal
50g/2oz/⅔ cup freshly grated
  (shredded) Parmesan cheese
5ml/1 tsp chopped fresh thyme
90ml/6 tbsp olive oil
675g/1½lb onions, halved and sliced
2 garlic cloves, chopped
a few fresh thyme sprigs
5ml/1 tsp brown sugar
30ml/2 tbsp balsamic vinegar
2 heads radicchio, cut into thick
  slices or wedges
225g/8oz Taleggio cheese, sliced
salt and ground black pepper

1 In a large pan, bring the water to the boil and add 5ml/1 tsp salt. Adjust the heat so that it simmers. Stirring all the time, add the polenta or corn meal in a steady stream, then bring to the boil. Cook over a very low heat, stirring frequently, for 30–40 minutes, or until thick and smooth.

2 Beat in the Parmesan and chopped thyme, then turn out the mixture on to a work surface or tray. Spread evenly, then leave to cool and set.

3 Heat 30ml/2 tbsp of the oil in a frying pan over a moderate heat. Add the onions and stir to coat in the oil, then cover and cook over a very low heat for 15 minutes, stirring occasionally.

4 Add the garlic and a few thyme sprigs and cook, uncovered, for 10 minutes, or until light brown and very soft. Add the sugar, 15ml/1 tbsp of the vinegar and salt and pepper. Cook for another 10 minutes, or until soft and well-browned. Taste and add more vinegar and seasoning as necessary.

5 Heat the grill (broiler). Cut the polenta into thick slices and brush with a little of the remaining oil, then grill (broil) until crusty and lightly browned.

6 Turn the polenta slices and add the wedges of radicchio to the grill rack (broiler) or pan. Season the radicchio and brush with a little oil. Grill until the polenta and radicchio are browned. Drizzle a little balsamic vinegar over the radicchio.

7 Heap the onions on to the polenta. Scatter the cheese and a few sprigs of thyme over both polenta and radicchio. Grill until the cheese is bubbling. Season to taste with ground black pepper and serve immediately.

SUMMER HERB RICOTTA FLAN

SIMPLE TO MAKE AND INFUSED WITH AROMATIC BASIL, CHIVES AND OREGANO, THIS DELICATE FLAN MAKES A DELIGHTFUL LUNCH DISH, ACCOMPANIED BY AN OLIVE AND GARLIC TAPENADE.

SERVES FOUR

INGREDIENTS
  olive oil, for greasing and glazing
  800g/1¾lb/3½ cups ricotta cheese
  75g/3oz/1 cup finely grated
    (shredded) Parmesan cheese
  3 eggs, separated
  60ml/4 tbsp torn fresh basil leaves
  60ml/4 tbsp chopped fresh chives
  45ml/3 tbsp fresh oregano leaves
  2.5ml/½ tsp salt
  ground black pepper
  2.5ml/½ tsp paprika
  fresh herb leaves, to garnish
For the tapenade
  400g/14oz/3½ cups pitted black
    olives, rinsed and halved,
    reserving a few whole olives to
    garnish (optional)
  5 garlic cloves, crushed
  75ml/2½fl oz/⅓ cup olive oil

1 Preheat the oven to 180°C/350°F/ Gas 4 and then lightly grease a 23cm/ 9in springform cake tin (pan) with olive oil. Mix together the ricotta, Parmesan and egg yolks in a food processor. Add all the herbs, and the salt and pepper, and blend until smooth and creamy.

2 Whisk the egg whites in a large bowl until they form soft peaks. Gently fold the egg whites into the ricotta mixture, taking care not to knock out too much air. Spoon the ricotta mixture into the tin and smooth the top.

3 Bake for 1 hour 20 minutes, or until the flan has risen and the top is golden. Remove from the oven and brush lightly with olive oil, then sprinkle with paprika. Cool before removing from the tin.

4 Make the tapenade. Place the olives and garlic in a food processor or blender and process until finely chopped. Gradually add the olive oil and blend to a coarse paste, then transfer to a serving bowl. Garnish the flan with fresh herb leaves and serve with the tapenade.

RED ONION AND GOAT'S CHEESE PASTRIES

FRESH THYME ADDS A TASTY EDGE TO THE RED ONION IN THESE SCRUMPTIOUS PASTRIES. RING THE CHANGES BY SPREADING THE PASTRY BASE WITH PESTO OR TAPENADE BEFORE YOU ADD THE FILLING.

SERVES FOUR

INGREDIENTS
  15ml/1 tbsp olive oil
  450g/1lb red onions, sliced
  30ml/2 tbsp fresh thyme or 10ml/
    2 tsp dried
  15ml/1 tbsp balsamic vinegar
  425g/15oz packet ready-rolled puff
    pastry, thawed if frozen
  115g/4oz goat's cheese, cubed
  1 egg, beaten
  salt and ground black pepper
  fresh oregano sprigs, to garnish
    (optional)
  mixed green salad leaves, to serve

1 Heat the oil in a large, heavy frying pan, add the onions and fry over a gentle heat for 10 minutes, or until softened, stirring occasionally. Add the thyme, seasoning and vinegar, and cook for another 5 minutes. Remove the pan from the heat and leave to cool.

2 Preheat the oven to 220°C/425°F/ Gas 7. Unroll the puff pastry and, using a 15cm/6in plate as a guide, cut four rounds. Place the pastry rounds on a dampened baking sheet and, using the point of a knife, score a border, 2cm/¾in inside the edge of each round. (Do not cut through the pastry.)

3 Divide the onions among the pastry rounds and top with the goat's cheese. Brush the edge of each round with beaten egg.

4 Bake the pastries for 25–30 minutes, or until they are golden. Garnish with oregano sprigs, if you like, before serving with mixed salad leaves.

Let herbs bring diversity to your pizza and bread cooking. Add freshness to pizzas with a crisp rocket (arugula) topping, or an exotic touch to breads with combinations of herbs and spices. Mint imparts its unique taste, and olives and oregano give a full-bodied flavour to savoury breads. Here are recipes for every occasion, waiting to be enjoyed.

Pizzas and Breads

BRESAOLA AND ROCKET PIZZA

HERE IS A QUICK AND TASTY PIZZA SPREAD WITH PESTO — A MIXTURE OF GROUND BASIL, PARSLEY AND PINE NUTS — AND TOPPED WITH GARLIC, TOMATOES, WILD MUSHROOMS AND BRESAOLA. CRISP, PEPPERY ROCKET GIVES IT A FRESH FINISH.

SERVES FOUR

INGREDIENTS
    150g/5oz packet pizza base mix
    120ml/4fl oz/½ cup lukewarm water
    flour, for dusting
    225g/8oz/3¼ cups mixed
      wild mushrooms
    25g/1oz/2 tbsp butter
    2 garlic cloves, coarsely chopped
    60ml/4 tbsp pesto
    8 slices bresaola
    4 tomatoes, sliced
    75g/3oz/scant ⅓ cup full-fat
      cream cheese
    25g/1oz rocket (arugula)
    salt and ground black pepper

1 Preheat the oven to 200°C/400°F/ Gas 6. Tip the packet of pizza base mix into a large mixing bowl and pour in enough of the lukewarm water to mix to a soft, not sticky, dough.

2 Turn out the dough on to a lightly floured surface and knead for about 5 minutes, or until smooth and elastic. Divide the dough into two equal pieces, knead lightly to form two balls, then pat out the balls of dough into flat rounds.

COOK'S TIP

If you are in a hurry, buy two ready-made pizza bases instead of the pizza mix and bake for 10 minutes.

3 Roll out each piece of the pizza dough on a lightly floured surface to a 23cm/9in round and then transfer to baking sheets.

4 Slice the wild mushrooms. Melt the butter in a frying pan and cook the garlic for 2 minutes. Add the sliced mushrooms and cook them over a high heat for about 5 minutes, or until they have softened but are not overcooked. Season to taste with salt and ground black pepper.

5 Spread pesto on the pizza bases, leaving a 2cm/¾in border around the edge of each one. Arrange the bresaola and tomato slices around the rim of the pesto layer, then spoon the cooked garlic mushrooms into the centre.

6 Dot the cream cheese on top of the pizzas and then bake in the preheated oven for 15–18 minutes, or until the bases are crisp and the cheese has just melted. Top each pizza with a handful of the rocket leaves just before serving. Serve the pizzas at once.

ROCKET AND TOMATO PIZZA

GARLIC AND BASIL FLAVOUR A TOMATO SAUCE THAT BLENDS BEAUTIFULLY WITH CREAMY MOZZARELLA.
ROCKET, WITH ITS PRONOUNCED FLAVOUR, ADDS THE FINAL TOUCH.

SERVES TWO

INGREDIENTS
    10ml/2 tsp olive oil, plus extra
        for drizzling and greasing
    1 garlic clove, crushed
    150g/5oz canned chopped tomatoes
    2.5ml/½ tsp sugar
    30ml/2 tbsp torn fresh basil leaves
    2 tomatoes, seeded and chopped
    150g/5oz mozzarella cheese, sliced
    20g/¾oz rocket (arugula) leaves
    coarse salt and ground black pepper
For the pizza base
    225g/8oz/2 cups strong white bread
        flour, sifted, plus extra for dusting
    5ml/1 tsp salt
    2.5ml/½ tsp easy-blend (rapid-rise)
        dried yeast
    15ml/1 tbsp olive oil, plus extra
        for greasing

2 Cover the dough with the upturned bowl or a dish towel and leave to rest for about 5 minutes, then knead for a further 5 minutes, or until smooth and elastic. Place in a lightly oiled bowl and cover with clear film. Leave in a warm place for about 45 minutes, or until doubled in size.

3 Preheat the oven to 220°C/425°F/ Gas 7. To make the topping, heat the oil in a frying pan and fry the garlic for 1 minute. Add the canned tomatoes and sugar, and cook for 5–7 minutes, or until reduced and thickened. Stir in the basil and seasoning, then set aside.

1 To make the pizza base, place the flour, salt and easy-blend dried yeast in a large bowl. Make a well in the centre and add the oil and 150ml/¼ pint/⅔ cup warm water. Mix with a round-bladed knife to form a soft dough. Turn out on to a lightly floured work surface and knead for 5 minutes.

4 Knead the risen dough lightly, then roll out to form a rough 30cm/12in round. Place on a lightly oiled baking sheet and push up the edges of the dough to form a shallow, even rim.

5 Spoon the tomato mixture over the pizza base, then top with the chopped fresh tomatoes, and the mozzarella. Season, then drizzle with olive oil. Bake in the top of the oven for 10–12 minutes, or until crisp and golden. Scatter with rocket and serve.

RED ONION, GORGONZOLA AND SAGE PIZZAS

THE TOPPING ON THESE INDIVIDUAL PIZZAS COMBINES THE RICHNESS OF GORGONZOLA WITH THE EARTHY FLAVOURS OF SAGE AND SWEET RED ONIONS.

SERVES FOUR

INGREDIENTS
  30ml/2 tbsp garlic oil
  2 small red onions
  150g/5oz Gorgonzola piccante cheese
  2 garlic cloves
  10ml/2 tsp chopped fresh sage
  ground black pepper
For the pizza dough
  175g/6oz/1½ cups strong white bread
    flour, plus extra for dusting
  1.5ml/¼ tsp salt
  5ml/1 tsp easy-blend (rapid-rise)
    dried yeast
  120–150ml/4–5fl oz/½–⅔ cup
    lukewarm water
  15ml/1 tbsp olive oil

1 To make the dough, sift the flour and salt into a bowl. Stir in the yeast. Make a well in the centre of the ingredients. Pour in the water and oil and mix to a soft dough.

2 Knead the dough on a lightly floured surface for about 10 minutes until smooth and elastic, then place in a greased bowl and cover with clear film. Leave in a warm place to rise for about 1 hour, or until doubled in size.

3 Knock back (punch down) the dough, and knead again for 2–3 minutes. Preheat the oven to 220°C/425°F/Gas 7. Divide the dough into eight and roll out each one on a lightly floured surface to a small oval about 5mm/¼in thick. Place well apart on two greased baking sheets and prick with a fork. Brush the bases with 15ml/1 tbsp of the oil.

4 Slice the onions into thin wedges. Scatter the slices over the pizza bases. Remove the rind from the Gorgonzola. Cut the cheese into small cubes, then scatter it over the onions.

5 Cut the garlic lengthways into thin strips and sprinkle over, along with the sage. Drizzle the remaining oil on top and grind over plenty of black pepper. Bake for 10–15 minutes, or until crisp and golden. Serve immediately.

FETA, ROASTED GARLIC AND OREGANO PIZZA

THIS IS A PIZZA FOR GARLIC LOVERS! MASH DOWN THE CLOVES AS YOU EAT — THEY SHOULD BE SOFT AND WILL HAVE LOST THEIR PUNGENCY. FRESH OREGANO PROVIDES THE FINISHING TOUCH.

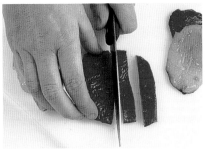

5 Place the peppers skin-side up on a baking sheet and grill (broil) evenly. Put in a covered bowl for 10 minutes. Peel off the skins. Cut the flesh into strips.

6 Put the tomatoes in a bowl and pour over boiling water. Leave for 30 seconds, then plunge into cold water. Peel, seed and roughly chop the flesh.

7 Divide the dough into four. Roll out each on flour to a 14cm/5½in circle.

8 Place on greased baking sheets, then push up the dough edges. Brush with half the oil and add the tomatoes, peppers, feta and garlic. Drizzle over the remaining oil and season. Bake for 15–20 minutes. Garnish with oregano.

SERVES FOUR

INGREDIENTS
 1 medium garlic bulb, unpeeled
 45ml/3 tbsp olive oil
 1 medium red bell pepper, quartered
  and seeded
 1 medium yellow bell pepper,
  quartered and seeded
 2 plum tomatoes
 175g/6oz feta cheese, crumbled
 ground black pepper
 15–30ml/1–2 tbsp chopped fresh
  oregano, to garnish
For the pizza dough
 175g/6oz/1½ cups strong white
  bread flour, plus extra for dusting
 1.5ml/¼ tsp salt
 5ml/1 tsp easy-blend (rapid-rise)
  dried yeast
 120–150ml/4–5fl oz/½–⅔ cup
  lukewarm water
 15ml/1 tbsp olive oil

1 To make the dough, sift the flour and salt into a bowl. Stir in the yeast. Make a well in the centre of the ingredients. Pour in the water and oil and mix to a soft dough.

2 Knead the dough on a lightly floured surface for about 10 minutes until smooth and elastic, then place in a greased bowl and cover with clear film. Leave in a warm place to rise for about 1 hour, or until doubled in size.

3 Knock back (punch down) the dough, and knead again for 2–3 minutes.

4 Preheat the oven to 220°C/425°F/ Gas 7. Break the garlic into cloves, discarding the outer papery leaves. Toss in 15ml/1 tbsp of the oil.

NEW POTATO, ROSEMARY AND GARLIC PIZZA

WAXY NEW POTATOES, SMOKED MOZZARELLA, ROSEMARY AND GARLIC MAKE THE FLAVOUR OF THIS PIZZA UNIQUE. FOR A DELICIOUS VARIATION, USE SAGE INSTEAD OF ROSEMARY.

SERVES TWO TO THREE

INGREDIENTS
   350g/12oz new potatoes
   45ml/3 tbsp olive oil
   2 garlic cloves, crushed
   1 pizza base, 25–30cm/10–12in
     diameter
   1 red onion, thinly sliced
   150g/5oz/1¼ cups grated (shredded)
     smoked mozzarella cheese
   10ml/2 tsp chopped fresh rosemary
   salt and ground black pepper
   30ml/2 tbsp freshly grated Parmesan,
     to garnish

1 Preheat the oven to 220°C/425°F/ Gas 7. Scrape the potatoes and cook in boiling salted water for 5 minutes. Drain well. When cool, peel and slice thinly.

2 Heat 30ml/2 tbsp of the oil in a frying pan. Add the sliced potatoes and garlic and fry for 5–8 minutes, or until tender.

3 Brush the pizza base with the remaining oil. Scatter over the onion, then arrange the potatoes on top.

4 Sprinkle over the mozzarella and rosemary. Grind over plenty of black pepper and bake for 15–20 minutes, or until crisp and golden. Remove from the oven and sprinkle over the Parmesan to serve.

TOMATO, FENNEL AND PARSLEY PIZZA

THIS PIZZA RELIES ON THE WINNING COMBINATION OF TOMATOES, FENNEL AND PARSLEY. THE FENNEL ADDS BOTH A CRISP TEXTURE AND A DISTINCTIVE FLAVOUR.

SERVES TWO TO THREE

INGREDIENTS
1 fennel bulb
45ml/3 tbsp garlic oil
1 pizza base, 25–30cm/10–12in
    diameter
30ml/2 tbsp chopped fresh flat leaf
    parsley
50g/2oz/½ cup grated (shredded)
    mozzarella cheese
50g/2oz/⅔ cup freshly grated
    (shredded) Parmesan cheese
salt and ground black pepper
For the tomato sauce
15ml/1 tbsp olive oil
1 onion, finely chopped
1 garlic clove, crushed
400g/14oz can chopped tomatoes
15ml/1 tbsp tomato purée (paste)
15ml/1 tbsp chopped fresh mixed
    herbs, such as parsley, thyme, basil
    and oregano
pinch of sugar
salt and ground black pepper

1 To make the tomato sauce, heat the oil in a pan and fry the onion and garlic until softened. Add the tomatoes, tomato purée (paste), herbs, sugar and seasoning. Simmer, stirring occasionally, until the tomatoes have reduced to a thick pulp.

2 Preheat the oven to 220°C/425°F/ Gas 7. Trim and quarter the fennel bulb lengthways. Remove the core and slice thinly.

3 Heat 30ml/2 tbsp of the oil in a frying pan and sauté the fennel for 4–5 minutes, or until just tender. Season.

4 Brush the pizza base with the remaining oil and spread over the tomato sauce. Spoon the fennel on top and scatter over the flat leaf parsley.

5 Mix together the mozzarella and Parmesan and sprinkle evenly over the top of the pizza. Bake for 15–20 minutes, or until crisp and golden. Serve immediately.

FRESH HERB PIZZA

WONDERFUL FRESH SUMMER HERBS COMBINE WITH CREAM AND GARLIC IN THIS HEAVENLY PIZZA.
SERVE WITH A CRISP GREEN SALAD WITH PLENTY OF DRESSING.

SERVES EIGHT

INGREDIENTS
   115g/4oz/4 cups mixed fresh herbs,
      such as parsley, basil and oregano
   3 garlic cloves, crushed
   120ml/4fl oz/½ cup double
      (heavy) cream
   1 pizza base, 25–30cm/10–12in
      diameter
   15ml/1 tbsp garlic oil
   115g/4oz/1 cup grated Pecorino
      cheese
   salt and ground black pepper

1 Preheat the oven to 220°C/425°F/
Gas 7. Chop the herbs, in a food
processor if you have one.

2 In a bowl mix together the herbs,
garlic, cream and seasoning.

3 Brush the pizza base with the garlic
oil, then spread over the herb mixture.

4 Sprinkle over the Pecorino. Bake for
15–20 minutes, or until crisp and
golden and the topping is still moist.
Cut into thin wedges and serve
immediately.

ITALIAN FLAT BREAD WITH ROSEMARY

ROSEMARY LEAVES ADD THEIR UNMISTAKABLE FLAVOUR TO THE TUSCAN VERSION OF AN ITALIAN FLAT BREAD. IT CAN BE ROLLED TO VARYING THICKNESSES TO GIVE EITHER A CRISP OR SOFT FINISH.

MAKES ONE LARGE LOAF

INGREDIENTS
  60ml/4 tbsp extra virgin olive oil,
    plus extra for greasing
  350g/12oz/3 cups unbleached white
    bread flour, plus extra for dusting
  2.5ml/½ tsp salt
  15g/½oz fresh yeast
  200ml/7fl oz/scant 1 cup
    lukewarm water
For the topping
  30ml/2 tbsp extra virgin olive oil
  30ml/2 tbsp fresh rosemary leaves
  coarse salt, for sprinkling

1 Lightly oil a baking sheet. Sift the flour and salt into a bowl and make a well in the centre. Cream the yeast with half the water. Add to the well with the remaining water and oil and mix to a soft dough. Turn out on to a lightly floured surface and knead for 10 minutes, until smooth and elastic.

2 Place the dough in a lightly oiled bowl, cover with a layer of lightly oiled clear film and leave to rise in a warm place for about 1 hour, or until it has doubled in bulk.

3 Knock back (punch down) the dough, turn out on to a lightly floured surface and knead gently. Roll to a 30 × 20cm/12 × 8in rectangle and place on the prepared baking sheet. Brush with some of the olive oil for the topping and cover with lightly oiled clear film.

4 Leave the dough to rise once again in a warm place for about 20 minutes. Brush with the remaining olive oil, prick all over with a fork and sprinkle with fresh rosemary leaves and coarse salt. Leave to rise again in a warm place for a further 15 minutes.

5 Meanwhile, preheat the oven to 200°C/400°F/Gas 6. Bake the loaf for 30 minutes, or until light golden. Transfer to a wire rack to cool slightly. Serve while still warm.

GARLIC AND HERB BREAD

THIS IRRESISTIBLE GARLIC BREAD INCLUDES PLENTY OF FRESH MIXED HERBS. YOU CAN VARY THE OVERALL FLAVOUR ACCORDING TO THE COMBINATION OF HERBS YOU CHOOSE.

SERVES THREE TO FOUR

INGREDIENTS
1 baguette or bloomer loaf
For the garlic and herb butter
115g/4oz/½ cup unsalted (sweet) butter, softened
5–6 large garlic cloves, finely chopped or crushed
30–45ml/2–3 tbsp chopped fresh herbs (such as parsley, chervil and a little tarragon)
15ml/1 tbsp chopped fresh chives
coarse salt and ground black pepper

1 Preheat the oven to 200ºC/400ºF/ Gas 6. Make the garlic and herb butter by beating the butter with the garlic, herbs, chives and seasoning.

VARIATIONS
• Use 105ml/7 tbsp extra virgin olive oil instead of the butter.
• Flavour the butter with garlic, a little chopped fresh chilli, grated (shredded) lime rind and chopped fresh coriander (cilantro).
• Add chopped, pitted black olives or sun-dried tomatoes to the butter with a little grated lemon rind.

2 Cut the bread into 1cm/½in thick diagonal slices, but be sure to leave them attached at the base so that the loaf stays intact.

3 Spread the garlic and herb butter between the slices evenly, being careful not to detach them, and then spread any remaining butter over the top of the loaf.

4 Wrap the loaf in foil and bake in the preheated oven for 20–25 minutes, until the butter is melted and the crust is golden and crisp. Cut the loaf into slices to serve.

COOK'S TIP
This loaf makes an excellent addition to a barbecue. If space permits, place the foil-wrapped loaf on the top of the barbecue and cook for about the same length of time as for oven baking. Turn the foil parcel over several times to ensure it cooks evenly.

RED ONION AND ROSEMARY FOCACCIA

THIS BREAD IS RICH IN OLIVE OIL AND IT HAS AN AROMATIC TOPPING OF RED ONION, FRESH ROSEMARY AND COARSE SALT.

2 Set the yeast aside in a warm, but not hot, place for 10 minutes, until it has turned frothy.

3 Add the yeast, the remaining water, 15ml/1 tbsp of the oil and the chopped rosemary to the flour. Mix all the ingredients together to form a dough, then gather the dough into a ball and knead on a floured work surface for about 5 minutes, until smooth and elastic. You may need to add a little extra flour if the dough is very sticky.

4 Place the dough in a lightly oiled bowl and slip it into a polythene bag or cover with oiled clear film and leave to rise. The length of time you leave it for depends on the temperature: leave it all day in a cool place, overnight in the refrigerator, or for 1–2 hours in a warm, but not hot, place.

5 Lightly oil a baking sheet. Knead the dough to form a flat loaf that is about 30cm/12in round or square. Place on the baking sheet, cover with oiled polythene or clear film and leave to rise again in a warm place for a further 40–60 minutes.

6 Preheat the oven to 220°C/425°F/ Gas 7. Toss the onion in 15ml/1 tbsp of the oil and scatter over the loaf with the rosemary sprigs and a scattering of coarse salt. Bake for 15–20 minutes until golden brown.

SERVES FOUR TO FIVE

INGREDIENTS
- 450g/1lb/4 cups strong white bread flour, plus extra for dusting
- 5ml/1 tsp salt
- 7g/¼oz fresh yeast or generous 5ml/1 tsp dried yeast
- 2.5ml/½ tsp light muscovado (molasses) sugar
- 250ml/8fl oz/1 cup lukewarm water
- 60ml/4 tbsp extra virgin olive oil, plus extra for greasing
- 5ml/1 tsp very finely chopped fresh rosemary, plus 6–8 small sprigs
- 1 red onion, thinly sliced
- coarse salt

1 Sift the flour and salt into a bowl. Set aside. Cream the fresh yeast with the sugar, and gradually stir in half the water. If using dried yeast, stir the sugar into the water and sprinkle the dried yeast over.

ONION, THYME AND OLIVE BREAD

THIS BREAD IS DELICIOUSLY FLAVOURED WITH BLACK OLIVES, ONION AND THYME, AND IS GOOD FOR SANDWICHES OR CUT INTO THICK SLICES AND DIPPED IN OLIVE OIL. IT IS ALSO EXCELLENT TOASTED, MAKING A WONDERFUL BASE FOR BRUSCHETTA OR DELICIOUS CROÛTONS FOR TOSSING INTO SALAD.

MAKES ONE LARGE OR
TWO SMALL LOAVES

INGREDIENTS
  350g/12oz/3 cups unbleached
    strong white bread flour, plus
    extra for dusting
  115g/4oz/1 cup corn meal, plus a
    little extra
  rounded 5ml/1 tsp salt
  15g/½oz fresh yeast or 10ml/2 tsp
    dried yeast
  5ml/1 tsp muscovado (molasses)
    sugar
  warm water
  15ml/1 tbsp chopped fresh thyme
  30ml/2 tbsp olive oil, plus extra
    for greasing
  1 red onion, finely chopped
  75g/3oz/1 cup freshly grated
    (shredded) Parmesan cheese
  90g/3½oz/scant 1 cup pitted black
    olives, halved

1 Mix the flour, corn meal and salt in a warmed bowl. If using fresh yeast, cream it with the sugar and gradually stir in 120ml/4fl oz/½ cup of the warm water. If using dried yeast, stir the sugar into the water and sprinkle the dried yeast over the surface. Leave in a warm place for 10 minutes, or until frothy.

COOK'S TIP
The best type of Parmesan is Parmigiano reggiano, which is made in the Reggio Emilia area of Italy. It will keep for several weeks in the refrigerator, wrapped in foil.

2 Make a well in the centre of the dry ingredients and pour in the yeast liquid and a further 150ml/¼ pint/⅔ cup of warm water.

3 Add the chopped thyme and 15ml/ 1 tbsp of the olive oil and mix thoroughly with a wooden spoon, gradually drawing in the dry ingredients until they are fully incorporated. Add a dash more warm water, if necessary, to make a soft, but not sticky, dough.

4 Knead the dough on a lightly floured work surface for 5 minutes, or until it is smooth and elastic.

5 Place in a clean, lightly oiled bowl and then place in a plastic bag or cover with oiled clear film. Set aside to rise in a warm, but not hot, place for 1–2 hours, or until well risen.

6 Meanwhile, heat the remaining olive oil in a large, heavy frying pan. Add the chopped onion and cook over a fairly gentle heat, stirring occasionally, for about 8 minutes, or until the onion has turned soft and golden, but is not at all browned. Set aside to cool.

VARIATION
If you prefer, shape the dough into a loaf, roll in corn meal and place in a lightly oiled loaf tin (pan). Leave to rise, as in step 9, until risen well above the rim of the tin. Bake for 35–40 minutes, or until it sounds hollow when turned out and tapped on the base.

7 Brush a baking sheet with olive oil. Turn out the risen dough on to a floured work surface. Gently knead in the cooked onions, followed by the freshly grated Parmesan cheese and, finally, the halved black olives.

8 Shape the dough into one or two oval loaves. Sprinkle the extra corn meal on to the work surface and roll the bread in it, then place the loaf or loaves on the prepared baking sheet.

9 Make several criss-cross lines across the top of the loaf or loaves. Slip the baking sheet into the plastic bag, or cover with a layer of oiled clear film and leave to rise once again in a warm place for about 1 hour, or until well risen. Preheat the oven to 200°C/400°F/Gas 6.

10 Bake the loaf or loaves for 30–35 minutes, or until the bread sounds hollow when tapped on the base. Leave to cool on a wire rack.

POPPY-SEEDED BLOOMER

THIS SATISFYING WHITE BREAD HAS A CRUNCHY, POPPY-SEED TOPPING. IT IS MADE BY A SLOWER RISING METHOD AND WITH LESS YEAST THAN USUAL. THIS PRODUCES A LONGER-KEEPING LOAF WITH A FULLER FLAVOUR. THE DOUGH TAKES ABOUT 8 HOURS TO RISE.

MAKES ONE LOAF

INGREDIENTS
  oil, for greasing
  675g/1½lb/6 cups unbleached strong
    white bread flour, plus extra for dusting
  10ml/2 tsp salt
  15g/½oz fresh yeast
  430ml/15fl oz/1⅞ cups water
For the topping
  2.5ml/½ tsp salt
  30ml/2 tbsp water
  poppy seeds, for sprinkling

1 Lightly grease a baking sheet. Sift the flour and salt together into a large bowl and make a well in the centre.

2 Mix the yeast and 150ml/¼ pint/ ⅔ cup of the water in a bowl. Mix in the remaining water and add to the centre of the flour. Mix it in, gradually incorporating the surrounding flour, until the mixture forms a firm dough.

3 Turn out on to a lightly floured surface and knead the dough very well, for at least 10 minutes, or until smooth and elastic.

4 Place the dough in a lightly oiled bowl, cover with lightly oiled clear film and leave to rise, at cool room temperature, about 15–18°C/60–65°F, for 5–6 hours, or until doubled in bulk.

5 Knock back (punch down) the dough, turn out on to a lightly floured surface and knead it thoroughly and quite hard for about 5 minutes. Return the dough to the bowl, and re-cover. Leave to rise, at cool room temperature, for a further 2 hours or slightly longer.

6 Knock back again and repeat the thorough kneading. Leave the dough to rest for 5 minutes, then roll out on a lightly floured surface into a rectangle 2.5cm/1in thick. Roll the dough up from one long side and shape it into a square-ended thick baton shape, about 33 × 13cm/13 × 5in.

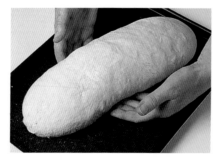

7 Place it seam-side up on a baking sheet, cover and leave to rest for 15 minutes. Turn over. Plump up by tucking the dough under the sides and ends. Using a sharp knife, cut six diagonal slashes on the top.

8 Leave to rest, covered, in a warm place, for 10 minutes. Meanwhile, preheat the oven to 230°C/450°F/Gas 8.

9 Mix the salt and water together and brush this glaze over the bread. Sprinkle with poppy seeds.

10 Spray the oven with water. Bake the bread immediately for 20 minutes, then reduce the oven temperature to 200°C/ 400°F/Gas 6; bake for 25 minutes more, or until golden. Transfer to a wire rack to cool.

VARIATION
For a more rustic loaf, replace up to half the flour with wholemeal (whole-wheat) bread flour.

COOK'S TIPS
• The traditional cracked, crusty appearance of this loaf is difficult to achieve in a domestic oven. However, you can get a similar result by spraying the oven with water before baking.
• If the underneath of the loaf is not very crusty at the end of baking, turn the loaf over on the baking sheet, switch off the heat and leave in the oven for a further 5–10 minutes.

SAFFRON FOCACCIA <u>WITH</u> ROSEMARY TOPPING

A DAZZLING YELLOW BREAD WITH A DISTINCTIVE FLAVOUR, THIS SAFFRON FOCACCIA IS TOPPED WITH GARLIC, ONION, ROSEMARY AND OLIVES. IT MAKES A TASTY SNACK OR ACCOMPANIMENT.

MAKES ONE LOAF

INGREDIENTS
    pinch of saffron threads
    150ml/¼ pint/⅔ cup boiling water
    225g/8oz/2 cups plain (all-purpose)
       flour, plus extra for dusting
    2.5ml/½ tsp salt
    5ml/1 tsp easy-blend (rapid-rise)
       dried yeast
    15ml/1 tbsp olive oil, plus extra
       for greasing
For the topping
    2 garlic cloves, sliced
    1 red onion, cut into thin wedges
    fresh rosemary sprigs
    12 black olives, pitted and
       coarsely chopped
    15ml/1 tbsp olive oil

1 In a jug, infuse (steep) the saffron in the boiling water. Leave until lukewarm.

2 Place the flour, salt, yeast and oil in a food processor. Turn on, gradually add the saffron liquid until the dough forms a ball. Alternatively, put the dry ingredients into a bowl, make a well in the centre and pour in the liquids. Gradually mix in.

3 Transfer the dough on to a lightly floured work surface and knead for 10–15 minutes, or until smooth and elastic. Place in a bowl, cover and leave in a warm place for 30–40 minutes, or until the dough has doubled in bulk. Lightly grease a baking sheet and set aside.

4 Knock back (punch down) the risen dough on a lightly floured surface and roll out into an oval shape about 1cm/½in thick. Place on the prepared baking sheet and then leave to rise in a warm place for 20–30 minutes.

5 Preheat the oven to 200°C/400°F/Gas 6. Use your fingers to press small indentations in the dough.

6 Cover the dough with the garlic, onion, rosemary and olives, brush lightly with the olive oil, and bake the loaf in the oven for about 25 minutes, or until it sounds hollow when tapped underneath.

7 Transfer the cooked loaf to a wire rack to cool. Serve the focaccia in slices or wedges.

SYRIAN ONION BREAD WITH MINT AND SPICES

FRESH MINT CONTRASTS WITH GROUND CUMIN AND CORIANDER SEEDS AND ONION TO TOP THESE SAVOURY BREADS FROM SYRIA. THEY MAKE AN EXCELLENT ACCOMPANIMENT FOR SOUPS OR SALADS.

MAKES EIGHT BREADS

INGREDIENTS
450g/1lb/4 cups unbleached strong white bread flour, plus extra for dusting
5ml/1 tsp salt
20g/¾oz fresh yeast
280ml/9fl oz/scant 1¼ cups lukewarm water
oil, for greasing
For the topping
60ml/4 tbsp finely chopped onion
5ml/1 tsp ground cumin
10ml/2 tsp ground coriander seeds
10ml/2 tsp chopped fresh mint
30ml/2 tbsp olive oil

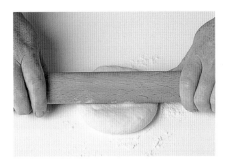

4 Knock back (punch down) the dough and turn out on to a lightly floured surface. Divide into eight equal pieces and roll into 13–15cm/5–6in rounds. Make them slightly concave. Prick all over and space well apart on the baking sheets. Cover with lightly oiled clear film and leave to rise for 15–20 minutes.

5 Meanwhile, preheat the oven to 200°C/400°F/Gas 6. Mix the chopped onion, ground cumin, ground coriander and chopped mint in a bowl. Brush the breads with the olive oil for the topping, sprinkle evenly with the spicy onion mixture and bake for 15–20 minutes. Serve the onion breads warm.

1 Lightly flour two baking sheets. Sift the flour and salt together into a large bowl and make a well in the centre. Cream the yeast with a little of the water, then mix in the remainder.

2 Add the yeast mixture to the centre of the flour and mix to a firm dough. Turn out on to a lightly floured surface and knead for 8–10 minutes, or until smooth and elastic.

3 Place in a lightly oiled bowl, cover with lightly oiled clear film and leave to rise, in a warm place, for about 1 hour, or until doubled in size.

COOK'S TIP
If you haven't any fresh mint to hand, then add 15ml/1 tbsp dried mint. Use the freeze-dried variety if you can as it has much more flavour.

POPPY-SEEDED BLOOMER

THIS SATISFYING WHITE BREAD HAS A CRUNCHY, POPPY-SEED TOPPING. IT IS MADE BY A SLOWER RISING METHOD AND WITH LESS YEAST THAN USUAL. THIS PRODUCES A LONGER-KEEPING LOAF WITH A FULLER FLAVOUR. THE DOUGH TAKES ABOUT 8 HOURS TO RISE.

MAKES ONE LOAF

INGREDIENTS
    oil, for greasing
    675g/1½lb/6 cups unbleached strong
        white bread flour, plus extra for dusting
    10ml/2 tsp salt
    15g/½oz fresh yeast
    430ml/15fl oz/1⅞ cups water
For the topping
    2.5ml/½ tsp salt
    30ml/2 tbsp water
    poppy seeds, for sprinkling

1 Lightly grease a baking sheet. Sift the flour and salt together into a large bowl and make a well in the centre.

2 Mix the yeast and 150ml/¼ pint/ ⅔ cup of the water in a bowl. Mix in the remaining water and add to the centre of the flour. Mix it in, gradually incorporating the surrounding flour, until the mixture forms a firm dough.

3 Turn out on to a lightly floured surface and knead the dough very well, for at least 10 minutes, or until smooth and elastic.

4 Place the dough in a lightly oiled bowl, cover with lightly oiled clear film and leave to rise, at cool room temperature, about 15–18°C/60–65°F, for 5–6 hours, or until doubled in bulk.

5 Knock back (punch down) the dough, turn out on to a lightly floured surface and knead it thoroughly and quite hard for about 5 minutes. Return the dough to the bowl, and re-cover. Leave to rise, at cool room temperature, for a further 2 hours or slightly longer.

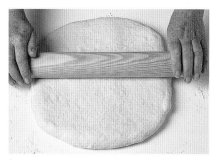

6 Knock back again and repeat the thorough kneading. Leave the dough to rest for 5 minutes, then roll out on a lightly floured surface into a rectangle 2.5cm/1in thick. Roll the dough up from one long side and shape it into a square-ended thick baton shape, about 33 × 13cm/13 × 5in.

7 Place it seam-side up on a baking sheet, cover and leave to rest for 15 minutes. Turn over. Plump up by tucking the dough under the sides and ends. Using a sharp knife, cut six diagonal slashes on the top.

8 Leave to rest, covered, in a warm place, for 10 minutes. Meanwhile, preheat the oven to 230°C/450°F/Gas 8.

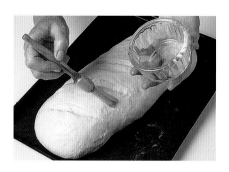

9 Mix the salt and water together and brush this glaze over the bread. Sprinkle with poppy seeds.

10 Spray the oven with water. Bake the bread immediately for 20 minutes, then reduce the oven temperature to 200°C/ 400°F/Gas 6; bake for 25 minutes more, or until golden. Transfer to a wire rack to cool.

VARIATION
For a more rustic loaf, replace up to half the flour with wholemeal (whole-wheat) bread flour.

COOK'S TIPS
• The traditional cracked, crusty appearance of this loaf is difficult to achieve in a domestic oven. However, you can get a similar result by spraying the oven with water before baking.
• If the underneath of the loaf is not very crusty at the end of baking, turn the loaf over on the baking sheet, switch off the heat and leave in the oven for a further 5–10 minutes.

WARM HERBY BREAD

This mouth-watering, Italian-style bread, flavoured with basil, rosemary, olive oil and sun-dried tomatoes, is absolutely delicious served warm with fresh salads and sliced salami or prosciutto. The olive oil not only lends a delicious flavour to the bread, but also helps it to keep fresh for longer.

3 As the mixture becomes stiffer, bring it together with your hands. Mix to a soft but not sticky dough, adding a little extra water if needed.

4 Turn the dough out on to a lightly floured surface and knead for 5 minutes until smooth and elastic. Put back into the bowl, cover loosely with oiled clear film and then put in a warm place for 30–40 minutes, or until doubled in size.

5 Knead again until smooth and elastic, then cut into three pieces. Shape each into an oval loaf about 18cm/7in long, and arrange on oiled baking sheets. Slash the top of each loaf with a knife in a criss-cross pattern.

MAKES THREE LOAVES

INGREDIENTS
  20g/¾oz fresh yeast or 15ml/1 tbsp
    dried yeast
  5ml/1 tsp caster (superfine) sugar
  900ml/1½ pints/3¾ cups warm water
  1.3kg/3lb/12 cups strong white bread
    flour, plus extra for dusting
  15ml/1 tbsp salt
  75ml/5 tbsp mixed fresh chopped
    basil and rosemary leaves
  50g/2oz/1 cup drained sun-dried
    tomatoes, roughly chopped
  150ml/¼ pint/⅔ cup extra virgin olive
    oil, plus extra for greasing and brushing
To finish
  15ml/1 tbsp rosemary leaves
  sea salt flakes

1 Cream the fresh yeast with the sugar, and gradually stir in 150ml/¼ pint/⅔ cup warm water. If you are using dried yeast, put the sugar into a small bowl, pour on the same amount of warm water, then sprinkle the yeast over the top. Leave the mixture in a warm place for 10–15 minutes, or until it has reached a frothy consistency.

2 Put the flour, salt, chopped basil and rosemary leaves, and chopped sun-dried tomatoes into a large mixing bowl. Add the olive oil together with the frothy yeast mixture, then gradually mix in the remaining warm water with a spoon.

6 Loosely cover and leave in a warm place for 15–20 minutes, or until well risen. Preheat the oven to 220°C/425°F/ Gas 7. Brush the loaves with a little olive oil and sprinkle with rosemary leaves and salt flakes. Cook for about 25 minutes, or until golden brown. The bases should sound hollow when they are tapped.

SAFFRON AND BASIL BREADSTICKS

THESE TASTY BREADSTICKS HAVE THE DELICATE AROMA AND FLAVOUR OF SAFFRON, AS WELL AS ITS RICH YELLOW COLOUR. THEY ARE IDEAL AS AN ACCOMPANIMENT TO SOUPS OR SALADS OR AS A SNACK.

MAKES THIRTY-TWO

INGREDIENTS
  generous pinch of saffron strands
  30ml/2 tbsp hot water
  450g/1lb/4 cups strong white bread
    flour, plus extra for dusting
  5ml/1 tsp salt
  10ml/2 tsp easy-blend (rapid-rise)
    dried yeast
  300ml/½ pint/1¼ cups lukewarm water
  45ml/3 tbsp olive oil, plus extra
    for greasing
  45ml/3 tbsp chopped fresh basil

1 In a small bowl, infuse (steep) the saffron strands in the hot water for 10 minutes.

2 Sift the flour and salt into a large mixing bowl. Stir in the yeast, then make a well in the centre of the dry ingredients. Pour in the lukewarm water and the saffron liquid and start to mix together a little.

3 Add the oil and basil and continue to mix to form a soft dough, then transfer to a lightly floured surface and knead for about 10 minutes, or until the dough is smooth and elastic.

4 Place in a greased bowl, cover with clear film and leave to rise in a warm place for about 1 hour, or until the dough has doubled in bulk.

5 Knock back (punch down) the dough and transfer it to a lightly floured surface. Knead it for 2–3 minutes.

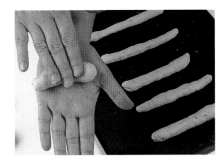

6 Preheat the oven to 220°C/425°F/Gas 7. Lightly grease two baking sheets and set aside. Divide the dough into 32 even pieces and shape into long sticks. Place them well apart on the prepared baking sheets, then leave them for a further 15–20 minutes, or until they become puffy. Bake in the oven for about 15 minutes, or until crisp and golden. Transfer to a wire rack to cool. Serve warm or cold.

SOUR RYE BREAD <u>WITH</u> CARAWAY SEEDS

AROMATIC CARAWAY SEEDS TOP THIS EAST EUROPEAN BREAD. IT USES A SOURDOUGH "STARTER", WHICH NEEDS TO BE MADE A DAY OR TWO IN ADVANCE.

<u>MAKES TWO LOAVES</u>

INGREDIENTS
    450g/1lb/4 cups rye flour
    450g/1lb/4 cups strong white bread
    flour, plus extra for dusting
    15ml/1 tbsp salt
    7g/¼oz sachet easy-blend (rapid-rise)
    dried yeast
    25g/1oz/2 tbsp butter, softened, plus
    extra for greasing
    600ml/1 pint/2½ cups warm water
    15ml/1 tbsp caraway seeds
For the sourdough starter
    60ml/4 tbsp rye flour
    45ml/3 tbsp warm milk

1 For the starter, mix the rye flour and milk in a bowl. Cover with clear film. Leave in a warm place for 1–2 days.

2 Sift together both types of flour and the salt into a large mixing bowl. Stir in the easy-blend dried yeast. Make a well in the centre of the dry ingredients and add the butter, warm water and sourdough starter. Mix well with a wooden spoon until you have formed a soft dough.

3 Turn out the dough on to a lightly floured surface and knead for about 10 minutes, or until smooth and elastic. Put in a clean bowl, cover with greased clear film and leave to rise in a warm place for 1 hour, or until doubled in size.

4 Knead for 1 minute, then divide the dough in half. Shape each piece into a round 15cm/6in across. Transfer to two greased baking sheets. Cover with greased clear film and leave the loaves to rise for 30 minutes.

5 Preheat the oven to 200°C/400°F/ Gas 6. Brush the loaves with water, then sprinkle with caraway seeds.

6 Bake for 35–40 minutes, or until the loaves are browned and sound hollow when tapped on the bottom. Cool on a wire rack.

COOK'S TIP
Sour rye bread keeps fresh for up to a week. This recipe can also be made without yeast, but the resulting bread will be much denser.

WELSH CLAY-POT LOAVES WITH HERBS

THESE BREADS ARE FLAVOURED WITH CHIVES, PARSLEY, SAGE AND GARLIC, AND TOPPED WITH FENNEL SEEDS. YOU CAN USE ANY SELECTION OF YOUR FAVOURITE HERBS. FOR EVEN MORE FLAVOUR, TRY ADDING A LITTLE GRATED RAW ONION AND GRATED CHEESE TO THE DOUGH.

MAKES TWO LOAVES

INGREDIENTS
  50g/2oz/¼ cup butter, melted, plus
    extra for greasing
  115g/4oz/1 cup wholemeal (whole-
    wheat) bread flour
  350g/12oz/3 cups unbleached strong
    white bread flour, plus extra for dusting
  7.5ml/1½ tsp salt
  15g/½oz fresh yeast
  150ml/¼ pint/⅔ cup lukewarm milk
  120ml/4fl oz/½ cup lukewarm water
  15ml/1 tbsp chopped fresh chives
  15ml/1 tbsp chopped fresh parsley
  5ml/1 tsp chopped fresh sage
  1 garlic clove, crushed
  oil, for greasing
  beaten egg, for glazing
  fennel seeds, for sprinkling (optional)

1 Lightly grease two clean 14cm/5½in-diameter, 12cm/4½in-high clay flower pots. Sift the flours and salt together into a large bowl and make a well in the centre.

2 Blend the yeast with a little of the milk until smooth, then stir in the remaining milk. Pour the yeast liquid into the centre of the flour and sprinkle over a little of the flour from around the edge. Cover the bowl and leave in a warm place for 15 minutes.

3 Add the water, melted butter, herbs and garlic to the flour mixture and blend together to form a dough. Turn out on to a lightly floured surface and knead for about 10 minutes, or until the dough is smooth and elastic.

4 Place in a lightly oiled bowl, cover with lightly oiled clear film and leave to rise, in a warm place, for 1¼–1½ hours, or until doubled in bulk.

5 Turn the dough out on to a lightly floured surface and knock back (punch down). Divide in two. Shape and fit into the flower pots. It should about half fill the pots. Cover with oiled clear film and leave to rise for 30–45 minutes in a warm place, or until the dough is 2.5cm/1in from the top of the pots.

6 Meanwhile, preheat the oven to 200°C/400°F/Gas 6. Brush the tops with beaten egg and sprinkle with fennel seeds, if using. Bake for 35–40 minutes, or until golden. Turn out on to a wire rack to cool.

OLIVE AND OREGANO BREAD

THIS TASTY ITALIAN BREAD IS HIGHLY FLAVOURED WITH OREGANO, PARSLEY AND OLIVES AND IS AN EXCELLENT ACCOMPANIMENT TO ALL SALADS. SERVE WARM TO ENJOY THE FLAVOURS AT THEIR BEST.

MAKES ONE LOAF

INGREDIENTS
   7g/¼oz fresh yeast or 5ml/1 tsp
      dried yeast
   pinch of sugar
   300ml/½ pint/1¼ cups warm water
   15ml/1 tbsp olive oil, plus extra
      for greasing
   1 onion, chopped
   450g/1lb/4 cups strong white bread
      flour, plus extra for dusting
   5ml/1 tsp salt
   1.5ml/¼ tsp ground black pepper
   50g/2oz/½ cup pitted black olives,
      roughly chopped
   15ml/1 tbsp black olive paste
   15ml/1 tbsp chopped fresh oregano
   15ml/1 tbsp chopped fresh parsley

1 Cream the fresh yeast with the sugar, and then gradually stir in half the warm water. If you are using dried yeast, put half the warm water in a jug (pitcher) and then sprinkle the yeast on top.

2 Add the sugar, stir well and leave the mixture to stand for 10 minutes, or until it is frothy.

3 Heat the oil in a frying pan and fry the onion until golden brown, stirring occasionally. Remove the pan from the heat and set aside.

4 Sift the flour into a mixing bowl with the salt and pepper. Make a well in the centre. Add the yeast mixture, the fried onions (with the oil), the olives, olive paste, oregano, parsley and remaining water. Gradually incorporate the flour, and mix to a soft dough, adding a little extra water if necessary.

5 Turn the dough out on to a lightly floured surface and knead for 5 minutes, or until smooth and elastic.

6 Place in a mixing bowl, cover with a damp dish towel and leave to rise in a warm place for about 2 hours until the dough has doubled in bulk. Lightly grease a baking sheet and set aside.

7 Turn the dough out on to a lightly floured surface and knead again for a few minutes. Shape into a 20cm/8in flat round and place on the prepared baking sheet.

8 Using a sharp knife, make criss-cross cuts over the top of the dough. Cover and leave in a warm place for 30 minutes, or until well risen. Preheat the oven to 220°C/425°F/Gas 7.

9 Dust the loaf with a little flour. Bake in the oven for 10 minutes then lower the oven temperature to 200°C/400°F/Gas 6. Bake for a further 20 minutes, or until the loaf sounds hollow when it is tapped underneath. Transfer to a wire rack to cool. Serve the bread warm or cold in slices or wedges.

Bring the delightful tastes of herbs to desserts and cakes. The delicate scent of rose petals transforms apples or a subtle cream to accompany shortcakes. Lavender flowers perfume cakes, a meringue and biscuits (cookies). Herbs add depth to the flavours of cakes and puddings, and a tasty crunch is added to cakes and scones with sunflower and poppy seeds. This chapter holds many tasty treats in store.

Desserts
and Cakes

LEMON GRASS SKEWERS WITH BAY LEAVES

GRILLED FRUITS MAKE A FINE FINALE TO A BARBECUE, WHETHER THEY ARE COOKED OVER THE COALS OR UNDER A HOT GRILL. THE LEMON GRASS SKEWERS GIVE THE FRUIT A SUBTLE LEMON TANG THAT IS COMPLEMENTED BY THE FLAVOUR OF THE BAY LEAVES. ALMOST ANY SOFT FRUITS CAN BE SUBSTITUTED.

SERVES FOUR

INGREDIENTS

  4 long fresh lemon grass stalks
  1 mango, peeled, stoned (pitted) and
    cut into chunks
  1 papaya, peeled, seeded and cut
    into chunks
  1 star fruit, cut into chunks
  8 fresh bay leaves
  oil, for greasing
  a little nutmeg
  60ml/4 tbsp maple syrup
  50g/2oz/¼ cup demerara (raw) sugar
For the lime cheese
  150g/5oz/⅔ cup curd (farmer's)
    cheese or low-fat soft cheese
  120ml/4fl oz/½ cup double
    (heavy) cream
  grated (shredded) rind and juice
    of ½ lime
  30ml/2 tbsp icing (confectioners')
    sugar

1 Prepare the barbecue or preheat the grill (broiler). Cut the top of each lemon grass stalk into a point with a sharp knife. Discard the outer leaves, then use the back of the knife to bruise the length of each stalk to release the oils.

2 Thread each lemon grass stalk, skewer-style, with a selection of the fruit pieces and two bay leaves.

3 Support a piece of foil on a baking sheet and roll up the edges to make a rim. Grease the foil, lay the kebabs on top and grate a little nutmeg over each. Drizzle the maple syrup over and dust liberally with the demerara sugar. Grill (broil) or cook on a barbecue or 5 minutes, until the kebabs are lightly charred.

4 Meanwhile, make the lime cheese. Mix together the cheese, cream, grated lime rind and juice, and icing sugar in a bowl. Serve at once with the lightly charred fruit kebabs.

COOK'S TIP
Only fresh lemon grass will work as skewers. It is now possible to buy lemon grass stalks in jars.

GOOSEBERRY AND ELDERFLOWER FOOL

ELDERFLOWERS AND GOOSEBERRIES ARE A MATCH MADE IN HEAVEN, EACH BRINGING OUT THE FLAVOUR OF THE OTHER. SERVE WITH AMARETTI OR OTHER DESSERT BISCUITS FOR DIPPING.

SERVES SIX

INGREDIENTS

   450g/1lb/4 cups gooseberries,
     trimmed
   30ml/2 tbsp water
   50–75g/2–3oz/¼–⅓ cup caster
     (superfine) sugar
   30ml/2 tbsp elderflower cordial
   400g/14oz carton ready-made
     custard sauce
   300ml/½ pint/1¼ cups double
     (heavy) cream
   crushed amaretti, to decorate
   amaretti, to serve

1 Put the gooseberries and water in a pan. Cover and cook for 5–6 minutes.

2 Add the sugar and elderflower cordial to the gooseberries, then stir vigorously or mash until the fruit forms a pulp.

3 Remove the pan from the heat, spoon the gooseberry pulp into a bowl and set aside to cool.

4 Stir the custard into the fruit. Whip the cream to form soft peaks, then fold it into the mixture and chill.

5 Serve in dessert glasses, decorated with crushed amaretti, and accompanied by amaretti.

APPLE AND ROSE-PETAL SNOW

THIS IS A LOVELY, LIGHT AND REFRESHING DESSERT, WHICH IS IDEAL TO MAKE WHEN THE ORCHARDS ARE GROANING WITH APPLES. THE ROSE PETALS GIVE A DELICATE FRAGRANCE BUT OTHER EDIBLE PETALS SUCH AS HONEYSUCKLE, LAVENDER AND GERANIUM COULD ALSO BE USED.

SERVES FOUR

INGREDIENTS
  2 large cooking apples
  150ml/¼ pint/⅔ cup thick
    apple juice
  30ml/2 tbsp rose water
  2 egg whites
  75g/3oz/6 tbsp caster (superfine) sugar
  a few rose petals from an
    unsprayed rose
  crystallized rose petals, to decorate
  crisp biscuits (cookies) or brandy
    snaps, to serve

VARIATION
Make an Apple and Rose-petal Fool. Fold 150ml¼ pint/⅔ cup each custard and whipped cream into the apple purée.

1 Peel and chop the apples and cook them with the apple juice until they are soft. Sieve, add the rose water and leave to cool.

2 Whisk the egg whites until they form stiff peaks, then gently whisk in the caster sugar.

3 Gently fold together the apple and rose water purée and the egg whites. Stir in most of the rose petals.

4 Spoon the snow into four glasses and chill. Decorate with the crystallized rose petals and serve with some crisp biscuits or brandy snaps.

BANANAS <u>WITH</u> LIME <u>AND</u> CARDAMOM SAUCE

AROMATIC CARDAMOM AND FRESH LIME GIVE AN EXOTIC HINT TO THE FLAKED ALMONDS IN THIS DELICIOUS SAUCE FOR POURING OVER BANANAS.

SERVES FOUR

INGREDIENTS

6 small bananas
50g/2oz/¼ cup butter
50g/2oz/½ cup flaked (sliced) almonds
seeds from 4 cardamom
  pods, crushed
thinly pared rind and juice
  of 2 limes
50g/2oz/¼ cup light muscovado
  (molasses) sugar
30ml/2 tbsp dark rum
vanilla ice cream, to serve

VARIATIONS

If you prefer not to use alcohol in your cooking, replace the rum with a fruit juice of your choice, such as orange or even pineapple juice. The sauce is equally good poured over folded crêpes.

1 Peel the bananas and cut them in half lengthways. Heat half the butter in a large frying pan. Add half the bananas, and cook until the undersides are golden. Turn carefully, using a fish slice (spatula). Cook until golden.

2 As they cook, transfer the bananas to a heatproof serving dish. Cook the remaining bananas in the same way.

3 Melt the remaining butter, then add the almonds and cardamom seeds. Cook, stirring until golden.

4 Stir in the lime rind and juice, then the sugar. Cook, stirring, until the mixture is smooth, bubbling and slightly reduced. Stir in the rum. Pour the sauce over the bananas and serve immediately, with vanilla ice cream.

GARDEN FLOWER PAVLOVA

PAVLOVA MUST BE ONE OF THE MOST LAVISH DESSERTS. HERE IT IS PERFUMED WITH LAVENDER SUGAR, FILLED WITH FRESH PEACHES AND CREAM, AND DECORATED WITH SUGARED FLOWERS. IT MAKES AN ENCHANTING SUMMER TREAT.

SERVES EIGHT

INGREDIENTS
   5 large egg whites
   250g/9oz/1¼ cups lavender sugar
   5ml/1 tsp cornflour (cornstarch)
   5ml/1 tsp white wine vinegar
   sugared flowers, to decorate
For the filling
   300ml/½ pint/1¼ cups double
     (heavy) cream
   2 ripe peaches

COOK'S TIP
To make lavender sugar, mix 15ml/1 tbsp dried culinary lavender with 1kg/2¼lb/ 5 cups caster (superfine) sugar. Store in an airtight container. Shake regularly.

1 Preheat the oven to 110°C/225°F/ Gas ¼. Line two baking sheets with baking parchment and draw a 23cm/9in circle on one and a 16cm/6¼in circle on the second.

2 Put the egg whites in a large bowl and whisk until they form stiff but moist-looking peaks. Gradually whisk in the sugar, a spoonful at a time, and continue whisking for 2 minutes until the meringue is thick and glossy.

3 Mix the cornflour and vinegar together and fold into the meringue mixture. Using two dessertspoons, drop spoonfuls of meringue over the smaller circle. Make the larger circle in the same way, and level the centre slightly.

4 Cook for 1¼ hours, or until pale golden. (Swap the positions of the baking sheets during cooking so that the layers cook to an even colour.) The meringues should come away from the paper easily; test by peeling away an edge of the paper but leave the meringues on the paper to cool.

5 To serve, remove the paper and put the larger meringue on a large, flat serving plate. Softly whip the cream, and spoon over the meringue. Halve, stone and slice the peaches and arrange on the cream. Place the second meringue on top of the peaches. Chill. When ready to serve, decorate with a selection of crystallized flowers and serve immediately.

CURD TARTS WITH LEMON AND COINTREAU

LEMON EMPHASIZES THE ORANGE AND COINTREAU FILLING, AND A LITTLE NUTMEG ADDS A WARM AND SPICY TOUCH TO THESE TRADITIONAL ENGLISH TARTS. EXCELLENT SERVED WITH HOME-MADE CUSTARD.

SERVES SIX

INGREDIENTS

175g/6oz/1½ cups plain (all-purpose) flour, plus extra for dusting
40g/1½oz/3 tbsp block margarine, diced
40g/1½oz/3 tbsp white vegetable fat (shortening), diced
30ml/2 tbsp caster (superfine) sugar
1 egg yolk
2.5ml/½ tsp ground nutmeg
orange segments and thinly pared orange rind, to decorate

For the filling

25g/1oz/2 tbsp butter, melted
50g/2oz/¼ cup caster (superfine) sugar
1 egg
175g/6oz/¾ cup curd (farmer's) cheese
30ml/2 tbsp double (heavy) cream
50g/2oz/¼ cup currants
15ml/1 tbsp grated (shredded) lemon rind
15ml/1 tbsp grated (shredded) orange rind
15ml/1 tbsp Cointreau

1 Start by making the pastry. Sift the flour into a large mixing bowl and rub in the margarine and vegetable fat until the mixture resembles fine breadcrumbs. Stir in the sugar and egg yolk and then add enough cold water to make a firm dough.

2 Wrap the pastry in clear film and chill for 30 minutes. Preheat the oven to 190°C/375°F/Gas 5.

COOK'S TIPS

• Curd cheese is a soft, unripened cheese with a milky, tangy flavour. If it is not available, cottage cheese can be used instead, although it will not have the same tang. Process in a food processor or press through a sieve, then use as curd cheese.

• To make a large tart, use the pastry to line an 18cm/7in flan tin (quiche pan). Spoon in the filling and bake at the same temperature for 45–55 minutes.

3 Roll out the dough on a lightly floured surface and use it to line six 10cm/4in fluted flan tins (tart pans).

4 To make the filling, combine the melted butter, sugar, egg, curd cheese, cream, currants, grated lemon and orange rinds and Cointreau in a bowl. Mix well. Spoon the mixture into the pastry cases and smooth out, sprinkle over the nutmeg and bake for 30–35 minutes. Serve decorated with orange segments and the pared orange rind.

WALNUT SHORTBREAD WITH SPICED APPLE SLICES

SOFT, CARAMELIZED APPLES WITH GINGER, CINNAMON AND NUTMEG MAKE A PERFECT ACCOMPANIMENT FOR WALNUT SHORTBREAD. SERVE WARM WITH YOGURT OR ICE CREAM.

SERVES FOUR

INGREDIENTS
  25g/1oz/2 tbsp unsalted (sweet)
    butter
  4 dessert apples, thinly sliced
  30ml/2 tbsp soft light brown sugar
  10ml/2 tsp ground ginger
  5ml/1 tsp ground cinnamon
  2.5ml/½ tsp ground nutmeg
For the walnut shortbread
  75g/3oz/⅔ cup wholemeal (whole-
    wheat) flour
  75g/3oz/⅔ cup unbleached plain (all-
    purpose) flour, plus extra for
    dusting
  25g/1oz/¼ cup oatmeal
  5ml/1 tsp baking powder
  1.5ml/¼ tsp salt
  50g/2oz/¼ cup golden caster
    (superfine) sugar
  115g/4oz/½ cup unsalted (sweet)
    butter, plus extra for greasing
  40g/1½oz/¼ cup walnuts, finely
    chopped
  15ml/1 tbsp milk, plus extra
    for brushing
  demerara (raw) sugar, for sprinkling

1 Preheat the oven to 180°C/350°F/
Gas 4. Grease one or two baking sheets.

2 To make the walnut shortbread, sift
together the flours, adding any bran left
in the sieve, and mix with the oatmeal,
baking powder, salt and sugar. Rub in
the butter with your fingers until the
mixture resembles fine breadcrumbs.

3 Add the chopped walnuts, then stir in
enough of the milk to form a soft dough.

4 Gently knead the dough on a floured
work surface. Form into a round, then
roll out to a 5mm/¼in thickness. Using
a 7.5cm/3in fluted cutter, stamp out
eight rounds – you may have some
dough left over.

5 Place the shortbread rounds on the
prepared baking sheets. Brush the tops
with milk and sprinkle with sugar. Bake
for 12–15 minutes, or until golden, then
transfer to a wire rack and leave to cool.

6 To prepare the apples, melt the butter
in a heavy frying pan. Add the apple
slices and cook for 3–4 minutes over a
gentle heat until softened.

7 Increase the heat to medium, add the
sugar and spices, and stir well. Cook
for a few minutes, stirring frequently,
until the sauce turns golden brown
and caramelizes. Serve warm, with
the shortbread.

DATE, FIG AND ORANGE PUDDING

THE FULL AND RICH FLAVOUR OF FIGS AND DATES IS HIGHLIGHTED BY ZESTY ORANGE IN THIS WARM AND COMFORTING PUDDING. IDEAL TO SERVE ON COLD, WINTRY DAYS.

2 Leave the fruit mixture to cool, then transfer to a food processor or blender and process until smooth. Press the mixture through a sieve to remove the fig seeds, if you wish.

3 Cream the butter and sugar until pale and fluffy, then beat in the fig purée. Beat in the eggs, then fold in the flours and mix until combined.

4 Grease a 1.5 litre/2½ pint/6¼ cup pudding basin, and pour in the golden syrup, if using. Tilt the bowl to cover the inside with a layer of syrup. Spoon in the pudding mixture. Cover the top with greaseproof (waxed) paper, with a pleat down the centre, and then with pleated foil, and tie down with string.

5 Place the bowl in a large pan and pour in enough water to come halfway up the sides of the bowl. Cover with a tight-fitting lid and steam for 2 hours. Check the water occasionally and top up if necessary.

6 Turn the pudding out and decorate with the reserved orange rind. Serve piping hot.

SERVES SIX

INGREDIENTS
 juice and grated (shredded) rind
  of 2 oranges
 115g/4oz/⅔ cup pitted, chopped,
  ready-to-eat dried dates
 115g/4oz/⅔ cup chopped ready-to-eat
  dried figs
 30ml/2 tbsp orange liqueur (optional)
 175g/6oz/¾ cup unsalted (sweet)
  butter, plus extra for greasing
 175g/6oz/¾ cup soft light brown sugar
 3 eggs
 75g/3oz/⅔ cup self-raising (self-rising)
  wholemeal (whole-wheat) flour
 115g/4oz/1 cup unbleached self-
  raising (self-rising) flour
 30ml/2 tbsp golden (light corn)
  syrup (optional)

1 Reserve a few strips of orange rind for the decoration and put the rest in a pan with the orange juice. Add the dates and figs, and orange liqueur, if using. Cook, covered, over a gentle heat for 8–10 minutes, or until soft.

SOUFFLÉED RICE PUDDING WITH NUTMEG

*VANILLA AND NUTMEG ADD THEIR DELICATE FLAVOURS TO THIS CREAMY SOUFFLÉED RICE PUDDING.
IT IS EQUALLY DELICIOUS SERVED COLD.*

SERVES FOUR

INGREDIENTS
  65g/2½oz/⅓ cup short grain
    pudding rice
  45ml/3 tbsp clear honey
  750ml/1¼ pints/3 cups milk
  1 vanilla pod (bean) or 2.5ml/½ tsp
    vanilla essence (extract)
  butter, for greasing
  2 egg whites
  5ml/1 tsp freshly grated
    (shredded) nutmeg
  wafer biscuits (cookies),
    to serve (optional)

1 Place the rice, honey and milk in a heavy or non-stick pan, and bring the milk to just below boiling point, watching it closely to prevent it from boiling over. Add the vanilla pod, if using.

2 Reduce the heat to the lowest setting and cover the pan. Leave to cook for 1–1¼ hours, stirring occasionally to prevent sticking, until most of the liquid has been absorbed.

3 Remove the vanilla pod or, if using vanilla essence, add this to the rice mixture now. Preheat the oven to 220°C/425°F/Gas 7. Grease a 1 litre/ 1¾ pint/4 cup baking dish with butter.

COOK'S TIP
This pudding is especially delicious topped with a stewed, dried-fruit salad, although a fresh summer-fruit compote would also work well.

4 Place the egg whites in a large grease-free bowl and whisk them until they hold soft peaks. Using either a large metal spoon or a fish slice (spatula), fold the egg whites evenly into the rice and milk mixture. Tip into the baking dish.

5 Sprinkle with grated nutmeg and then bake in the oven for 15–20 minutes, or until the rice pudding has risen well and the surface is golden brown. Serve the rice pudding hot, with wafer biscuits, if you like.

LAVENDER CAKE

BAKE A SUMMER-SCENTED CAKE THAT IS REMINISCENT OF THOSE DISTANT ELIZABETHAN TIMES WHEN LAVENDER WAS AN EXTREMELY POPULAR CULINARY HERB, NOT JUST FOR ITS EVOCATIVE FRAGRANCE BUT FOR ITS DISTINCTIVE FLAVOUR, TOO.

SERVES EIGHT

INGREDIENTS
  175g/6oz/¾ cup unsalted (sweet)
    butter, plus extra for greasing
  175g/6oz/scant 1 cup caster
    (superfine) sugar
  3 eggs, lightly beaten
  175g/6oz/1⅔ cups self-raising (self-
    rising) flour, sifted, plus extra
  30ml/2 tbsp fresh lavender florets
  2.5ml/½ tsp vanilla essence (extract)
  30ml/2 tbsp milk
  50g/2oz/½ cup icing (confectioners')
    sugar, sifted
  2.5ml/½ tsp water
  a few fresh lavender florets

1 Preheat the oven to 180°C/350°F/ Gas 4. Lightly grease and flour a ring tin (pan) or a deep 20cm/8in round, loose-based cake tin (pan).

2 Cream the butter and sugar together thoroughly until the mixture is light and fluffy.

3 Add the beaten egg gradually, beating thoroughly between each separate addition, until the mixture has become thick and glossy.

4 Gently fold in the flour, together with the lavender florets, vanilla essence and milk.

5 Spoon the mixture into the tin and bake for 1 hour. Leave to stand for 5 minutes, then turn out on to a wire rack to cool.

6 Mix the icing sugar with the water until smooth. Pour the icing over the cake and decorate with a few fresh lavender florets.

VARIATION
For a pretty colour contrast, add a little orange food colouring to the icing before pouring over the cake.

GREEK YOGURT AND FIG CAKE

BAKED FRESH FIGS, THICKLY SLICED, MAKE A DELECTABLE TOPPING FOR A FEATHERLIGHT SPONGE.
FIGS THAT ARE A BIT ON THE FIRM SIDE WORK BEST FOR THIS PARTICULAR RECIPE.

SERVES SIX TO EIGHT

INGREDIENTS

  6 firm fresh figs, thickly sliced
  45ml/3 tbsp clear honey, plus extra
    for glazing
  200g/7oz/scant 1 cup butter,
    softened, plus extra for greasing
  175g/6oz/scant 1 cup caster
    (superfine) sugar
  grated (shredded) rind of 1 lemon
  grated (shredded) rind of 1 orange
  4 eggs, separated
  225g/8oz/2 cups plain (all-purpose)
    flour
  5ml/1 tsp baking powder
  5ml/1 tsp bicarbonate of soda
    (baking soda)
  250ml/8fl oz/1 cup Greek
    (US strained plain) yogurt

1 Preheat the oven to 180°C/350°F/ Gas 4. Grease a 23cm/9in cake tin (pan) and line the base of it with baking parchment.

2 Arrange the figs over the base of the tin and drizzle over the honey.

3 In a large mixing bowl, cream the butter and caster sugar with the lemon and orange rinds until the mixture is pale and fluffy, then gradually beat in the egg yolks.

4 Sift the dry ingredients together in a separate bowl. Add a little to the creamed mixture, beat well, then beat in a spoonful of Greek yogurt. Repeat this process until all the dry ingredients and Greek yogurt have been incorporated into the creamed mixture.

5 Whisk the egg whites in a grease-free bowl until they form stiff peaks. Stir half the whites into the cake mixture to slacken it slightly, then fold in the rest. Pour the mixture over the figs in the base of the cake tin.

6 Bake in the preheated oven for 1¼ hours, or until golden and a skewer inserted in the centre of the cake comes out clean.

7 Turn the cake out on to a wire rack, peel off the lining paper and cool. Drizzle the figs with a little extra honey before serving.

RICH LEMON POPPY-SEED CAKE

THE CLASSIC COMBINATION OF POPPY SEEDS AND LEMON IS USED FOR THIS LIGHT CAKE, WHICH HAS A DELICIOUS LEMON CURD AND FROMAGE FRAIS FILLING.

SERVES EIGHT

INGREDIENTS

350g/12oz/1½ cups unsalted (sweet) butter, plus extra for greasing
350g/12oz/1¾ cups golden caster (superfine) sugar
45ml/3 tbsp poppy seeds
20ml/4 tsp finely grated (shredded) lemon rind
70ml/4½ tbsp luxury lemon curd
6 eggs, separated
120ml/4fl oz/½ cup semi-skimmed (low-fat) milk
350g/12oz/3 cups unbleached self-raising (self-rising) flour, plus extra for dusting
icing (confectioners') sugar, to decorate

For the filling
150g/5oz/½ cup luxury lemon curd
150ml/¼ pint/⅔ cup fromage frais

1 Butter and lightly flour two 23cm/9in springform cake tins (pans). Preheat the oven to 180°C/350°F/Gas 4.

2 Cream the butter and sugar until light and fluffy. Add the poppy seeds, lemon rind, lemon curd and egg yolks and beat well, then add the milk and mix well. Fold in the flour until combined.

3 Whisk the egg whites using a hand-held electric mixer until they form soft peaks. Carefully fold the egg whites into the cake mixture until just combined. Divide between the prepared tins.

4 Bake for 40–45 minutes, or until a skewer inserted into the centre of the cakes comes out clean and the tops are golden.

5 Leave the cakes to cool in the tins for 5 minutes, then remove from the tins and leave to cool completely on wire racks.

VARIATION
Replace the lemon curd and fromage frais filling with a lemon syrup. Boil 45ml/3 tbsp lemon juice, 15ml/1 tbsp lemon rind and 30ml/2 tbsp caster sugar for 3 minutes until syrupy and glossy. Make a single cake using half the ingredients. Pour the syrup over the warm cake and leave to cool.

6 To finish, spread one cake with the lemon curd and spoon the fromage frais evenly over the lemon curd. Put the second cake on top, press down gently, then dust the top with icing sugar before serving.

DATE AND WALNUT SPICE CAKE

NUTMEG, MIXED SPICE AND WALNUTS FLAVOUR THIS SCRUMPTIOUS CAKE, AND DATES MAKE IT DELICIOUSLY MOIST. IT GOES VERY WELL WITH MORNING COFFEE.

SERVES EIGHT

INGREDIENTS

115g/4oz/½ cup unsalted (sweet) butter, plus extra for greasing
175g/6oz/1½ cups unbleached self-raising (self-rising) flour, plus extra for dusting
175g/6oz/¾ cup soft dark brown sugar
2 eggs
5ml/1 tsp bicarbonate of soda (baking soda)
2.5ml/½ tsp freshly grated (shredded) nutmeg
5ml/1 tsp mixed spice
pinch of salt
175ml/6fl oz/¾ cup buttermilk
50g/2oz/⅓ cup ready-to-eat pitted dates, chopped
25g/1oz/¼ cup chopped walnuts
For the topping
60ml/4 tbsp clear honey
45ml/3 tbsp fresh orange juice
15ml/1 tbsp coarsely grated (shredded) orange rind, plus extra to decorate

1 Grease and lightly flour a 23cm/9in springform cake tin (pan). Preheat the oven to 180°C/350°F/Gas 4.

2 Cream together the butter and sugar until the mixture is fluffy and creamy. Add the eggs, one at a time, and then beat well to combine.

3 Sift together the flour, bicarbonate of soda, nutmeg, mixed spice and salt. Gradually add this to the creamed mixture, alternating with the buttermilk. Add the chopped dates and walnuts, and stir well.

4 Spoon the mixture into the prepared cake tin and level the top. Bake for 50 minutes, or until a skewer inserted into the centre comes out clean. Leave to cool for 5 minutes, then turn out on to a wire rack to cool completely.

5 To make the topping, heat the clear honey, orange juice and rind in a small, heavy pan. Bring to the boil and boil rapidly for 3 minutes, without stirring, until syrupy.

6 Make small holes over the top of the warm cake using the skewer, and then pour over the hot syrup. Decorate with the orange rind.

COOK'S TIP
To make a quite acceptable buttermilk substitute, simply mix 15ml/1 tbsp lemon juice with 250ml/8fl oz/1 cup semi-skimmed (low-fat) milk.

SWEET PEAR AND CARDAMOM SPONGE

SCENTED CARDAMOM SEEDS COMPLEMENT DESSERT PEARS IN THIS MOIST SPONGE. IT MAKES A DELICIOUS DESSERT SERVED WITH A DOLLOP OF WHIPPED CREAM OR ICE CREAM.

SERVES FOUR

INGREDIENTS
  115g/4oz/½ cup butter, softened,
    plus extra for greasing
  115g/4oz/1 cup self-raising (self-
    rising) flour, plus extra for dusting
  5 pears
  10 green cardamom pods
  5ml/1 tsp baking powder
  115g/4oz/generous ½ cup caster
    (superfine) sugar
  3 egg yolks
  30–45ml/2–3 tbsp warm water

1 Preheat the oven to 190ºC/375ºF/Gas 5. Line the base of a 20cm/8in-diameter cake tin (pan) with greaseproof (waxed) paper and then butter and lightly flour the sides.

2 Peel the pears, cut them in half and remove the cores. Lay the fruit cut-side up in a circle in the bottom of the tin.

COOK'S TIP
Choose very sweet dessert pears, like Comice or Williams. They need to be completely ripe and very juicy.

3 Remove the cardamom seeds from the pods and crush the seeds lightly using a mortar and pestle.

4 Sift together the flour and baking powder. Add the sugar, the crushed cardamom seeds, butter, egg yolks and 30ml/2 tbsp of the water. Beat with an electric or hand whisk until creamy. The mixture should fall off a spoon; if it does not, add a little more water.

5 Place the mixture on top of the pears and level with a knife. Bake the cake for 45–60 minutes, or until firm.

6 Turn the cake out on to a wire rack and peel off the greaseproof paper. Cool before serving.

LEMON AND WALNUT CAKE

DON'T STINT ON THE LEMON RIND — IT GIVES THIS CAKE A WONDERFUL ZESTY TANG THAT BLENDS PERFECTLY WITH THE WARM FLAVOUR OF THE WALNUTS.

4 Scrape the mixture into a bowl and fold in the remaining flour, with the walnut pieces.

5 Grate (shred) the rind from three lemons and thinly pare the rind from the fourth (reserve for the decoration). Squeeze the juice from two lemons, then stir the grated lemon rind and juice into the cake mixture.

6 Spoon the mixture into the prepared tin. Bake for 50–60 minutes, or until a fine skewer inserted in the centre of the cake comes out clean. Cool on a wire rack. Decorate the cake with the pared lemon rind.

COOK'S TIPS
• If the dried dates are very hard, soften them in boiling water for 10 minutes before draining and using.
• Make sure that you buy plain dried dates and not the kind that are chopped and coated with sugar.
• Look out for packets of walnut pieces in supermarkets, as they are usually much less expensive than either shelled walnuts or walnut halves.

SERVES EIGHT TO TEN

INGREDIENTS
    1 large banana, about 150g/5oz
    225g/8oz/1 cup butter, plus extra
        for greasing
    150g/5oz/1 cup dried, pitted
        dates, chopped
    5 small (US medium) eggs
    300g/11oz/scant 3 cups wholemeal
        (whole-wheat) flour, or half
        wholemeal and half plain (all-
        purpose) white flour
    75g/3oz/¾ cup walnut pieces
    4 large lemons

1 Preheat the oven to 180°C/350°F/ Gas 4. Grease a deep 20cm/8in spring-form cake tin (pan). Line the base of the tin with baking parchment.

2 Peel and chop the banana. Process with the butter and dates in a food processor or blender.

3 Add one egg and 15ml/1 tbsp of the flour to the creamed mixture. Process briefly to mix, then add the remaining eggs one at a time, each with a further 15ml/1 tbsp flour.

POPPY-SEED ROLL

THIS SWEET YEAST BAKE WITH ITS SPIRAL FILLING OF DRIED FRUITS, POPPY SEEDS AND LEMON IS A WONDERFUL EXAMPLE OF TRADITIONAL POLISH COOKING. IT MAKES AN UNUSUAL PASTRY TO SERVE WITH AFTERNOON TEA.

SERVES TWELVE

INGREDIENTS

   450g/1lb/4 cups plain (all-purpose)
     flour, plus extra for dusting
   pinch of salt
   30ml/2 tbsp caster (superfine) sugar
   10ml/2 tsp easy-blend (rapid-rise)
     dried yeast
   175ml/6fl oz/¾ cup milk
   finely grated (shredded) rind of 1 lemon
   50g/2oz/¼ cup butter
For the filling and glaze
   50g/2oz/¼ cup butter
   115g/4oz/⅔ cup poppy seeds
   50ml/2fl oz/¼ cup set (crystallized)
     honey
   65g/2½oz/½ cup raisins
   65g/2½oz/scant ½ cup finely
     chopped candied orange peel
   50g/2oz/½ cup ground almonds
   1 egg yolk
   50g/2oz/¼ cup caster (superfine) sugar
   oil, for greasing
   15ml/1 tbsp milk
   60ml/4 tbsp apricot jam
   15ml/1 tbsp lemon juice
   15ml/1 tbsp rum or brandy
   25g/1oz/¼ cup toasted flaked
     (sliced) almonds

1 Sift the flour, salt and sugar into a bowl. Stir in the easy-blend dried yeast. Make a well in the centre.

2 Heat the milk and lemon rind in a pan with the butter, until melted. Cool a little, then add to the dry ingredients and mix to a dough.

3 Knead the dough on a lightly floured surface for 10 minutes, until smooth and elastic. Put the dough in a clean bowl, cover and leave in a warm place to rise for 45–50 minutes, or until doubled in size.

4 For the filling, melt the butter in a pan. Reserve 15ml/1 tbsp of the poppy seeds, then process the rest in a food processor.

5 Add the processed poppy seeds to the pan with the honey, raisins and candied orange peel. Cook gently for 5 minutes. Stir in the ground almonds, then leave to cool.

6 Whisk the egg yolk and sugar together in a bowl until pale, then fold into the poppy seed mixture. Roll out the dough on a lightly floured surface to form a rectangle that measures 30 × 35cm/ 12 × 14in. Spread the filling to within 2.5cm/1in of the edges.

7 Roll both ends towards the centre. Place on a baking sheet, cover with oiled clear film and leave to rise for 30 minutes. Preheat the oven to 190°C/375°F/Gas 5.

8 Brush with the milk, then sprinkle with the reserved poppy seeds. Bake for 30 minutes, until golden brown.

9 Heat the jam and lemon juice gently until bubbling. Sieve, then stir in the rum or brandy. Brush over the roll while still warm and scatter with almonds.

LAVENDER SCONES

LEND AN UNUSUAL BUT DELICIOUS LAVENDER PERFUME TO YOUR SCONES — ITS FRAGRANCE MARRIES WELL WITH THE SWEETNESS OF SUMMER SOFT FRUIT AND MAKES FOR AN ELEGANT TEA-TIME TREAT. THE LAVENDER'S SCENTED QUALITY GIVES THE WELL-KNOWN TEA SCONE A FLAVOUR, WHICH NOWADAYS CAN SEEM PLEASANTLY UNUSUAL AND SURPRISING.

MAKES TWELVE

INGREDIENTS
225g/8oz/2 cups plain (all-purpose) flour, plus extra for dusting
15ml/1 tbsp baking powder
50g/2oz/¼ cup butter
50g/2oz/¼ cup sugar
10ml/2 tsp fresh lavender florets or 5ml/1 tsp dried culinary lavender, roughly chopped
about 150ml/¼ pint/⅔ cup milk
plum jam and clotted cream, to serve

1 Preheat the oven to 220°C/425°F/ Gas 7. Sift the flour and baking powder together. Rub the butter into the flour mixture until it resembles fine breadcrumbs.

2 Stir in the sugar and chopped lavender, reserving a pinch to sprinkle on the top of the scones (US biscuits) before baking them. Add enough milk so that the mixture forms a soft, sticky dough. Bind the dough together and then turn it out on to a floured surface.

3 Shape the dough into a round, gently patting down the top to give a 2.5cm/ 1in depth. Using a floured cutter, stamp out 12 scones.

4 Place the scones on a baking sheet. Brush the tops with a little milk and sprinkle over the reserved lavender.

5 Bake the scones for 10–12 minutes, or until golden. Serve warm with plum jam and clotted cream.

RASPBERRY AND ROSE-PETAL SHORTCAKES

ROSE-WATER-SCENTED CREAM AND FRESH RASPBERRIES FORM THE FILLING FOR THIS DELECTABLE AND LUXURIOUS DESSERT. ALTHOUGH THEY LOOK IMPRESSIVE, THESE SHORTCAKES ARE EASY TO MAKE AND WOULD BE AN EXCELLENT CHOICE FOR A DINNER PARTY.

MAKES SIX

INGREDIENTS
 115g/4oz/½ cup unsalted (sweet)
  butter, softened
 50g/2oz/¼ cup caster (superfine)
  sugar
 ½ vanilla pod (bean), split and
  seeds reserved
 115g/4oz/1 cup plain (all-purpose)
  flour, plus extra for dusting
 50g/2oz/⅓ cup semolina
For the filling
 300ml/½ pint/1¼ cups double
  (heavy) cream
 15ml/1 tbsp icing (confectioners')
  sugar, plus extra for dusting
 2.5ml/½ tsp rose water
 450g/1lb/2⅔ cups raspberries
For the decoration
 12 miniature roses, unsprayed
 6 mint sprigs
 1 egg white, beaten
 caster (superfine) sugar, for dusting

1 Cream the butter, sugar and vanilla seeds together in a bowl until the mixture is pale and fluffy. Sift the flour and semolina together, then gradually work the dry ingredients into the creamed mixture to make a biscuit (cookie) dough.

VARIATIONS
Other soft, red summer berries, such as mulberries, loganberries and tayberries, would be equally good in this dessert. You might also like to use different shapes of cutter for the shortcakes, such as flowers and hearts.

2 Gently knead the dough on a lightly floured surface until smooth. Roll out quite thinly and prick all over with a fork. Using a 7.5cm/3in fluted cutter, cut out 12 rounds. Place these on a baking sheet and then chill in the refrigerator for 30 minutes.

3 Meanwhile, make the filling. Whisk the double cream with the icing sugar until soft peaks form. Gently fold the rose water into the mixture and then chill until required.

4 Preheat the oven to 180°C/350°F/ Gas 4. Paint the roses and mint sprigs with the beaten egg white. Dust with sugar; place on a wire rack to dry.

5 Bake the shortcakes in the preheated oven for 15 minutes, or until they are lightly golden. Lift them off the baking sheet with a metal fish slice (spatula) and transfer to a wire rack to cool.

6 To assemble the shortcakes, spoon the rose-water cream on to half the shortcakes. Arrange a layer of raspberries on top of the cream, then top with a second shortcake.

7 Dust the filled shortcakes with icing sugar. Decorate with the frosted roses and mint sprigs.

COOK'S TIPS
• For best results, serve the shortcakes as soon as possible after assembling them. Otherwise, they are likely to turn soggy from the raspberries' liquid.
• If necessary, ground rice can be substituted for the semolina used for making the shortcakes.
• For the best-flavoured shortcakes, always use butter and not margarine.

SUNFLOWER SULTANA SCONES

THESE FRUITY SCONES HAVE A TASTY SUNFLOWER-SEED TOPPING. THEY MAKE A TEMPTING TEA-TIME TREAT SPREAD WITH BUTTER AND JAM.

MAKES TEN TO TWELVE

INGREDIENTS

> oil, for greasing
> 225g/8oz/2 cups self-raising (self-raising) flour, plus extra for dusting
> 5ml/1 tsp baking powder
> 25g/1oz/2 tbsp butter
> 30ml/2 tbsp golden caster (superfine) sugar
> 50g/2oz/⅓ cup sultanas (golden raisins)
> 30ml/2 tbsp sunflower seeds
> 150g/5oz/⅔ cup natural (plain) yogurt
> about 30–45ml/2–3 tbsp skimmed (low-fat) milk
> butter and jam, to serve (optional)

1 Preheat the oven to 230ºC/450ºF/Gas 8. Lightly oil a baking sheet. Sift the flour and baking powder into a bowl and rub in the butter.

2 Stir in the sugar, sultanas and half the sunflower seeds, then mix in the yogurt, with just enough milk to make a fairly soft, but not sticky dough.

3 Roll out on a lightly floured surface to a thickness of about 2cm/¾in. Cut into 6cm/2½in rounds with a biscuit (cookie) cutter and lift on to the baking sheet.

4 Brush the scones (US biscuits) with milk and then sprinkle with the reserved sunflower seeds. Bake in the preheated oven for 10–12 minutes, or until they are well risen and golden brown.

5 Cool the scones on a wire rack. Serve them split and spread with butter and jam, if you like.

LAVENDER HEART COOKIES

IN FOLKLORE, LAVENDER HAS ALWAYS BEEN LINKED WITH LOVE, AS HAS FOOD. SO MAKE SOME OF THESE HEART-SHAPED COOKIES AND SERVE THEM TO YOUR LOVED ONE ON VALENTINE'S DAY, OR ON ANY OTHER ROMANTIC ANNIVERSARY.

MAKES SIXTEEN TO EIGHTEEN

INGREDIENTS
   115g/4oz/½ cup unsalted (sweet)
     butter, softened
   50g/2oz/¼ cup caster (superfine)
     sugar
   175g/6oz/1½ cups plain (all-purpose)
     flour, plus extra for dusting
   30ml/2 tbsp fresh lavender florets or
     15ml/1 tbsp dried culinary lavender,
     roughly chopped
   25g/1oz/¼ cup icing (confectioners')
     sugar, for sprinkling

1 Cream the butter and sugar together until light and fluffy.

2 Mix together the flour and lavender, and add to the creamed mixture. Bring the mixture together in a soft ball. Cover and chill for 15 minutes.

3 Preheat the oven to 200°C/400°F/ Gas 6. Roll out the mixture on a lightly floured surface and stamp out about 18 biscuits (cookies), using a 5cm/2in heart-shaped cutter.

4 Place the biscuits on a heavy baking sheet and bake for about 10 minutes until they are golden.

5 Leave the biscuits to stand for about 5 minutes to firm up, then, using a palette knife (metal spatula), transfer them carefully from the baking sheet on to a wire rack to cool completely.

6 Sprinkle with icing sugar. You can store the biscuits in an airtight container for up to 1 week.

COOK'S TIPS
• Metal cutters make cutting easier, but remember to ensure that they are completely dry before putting them away, or they will turn rusty.
• Biscuits such as these can be made in advance and frozen very successfully, as long as they are well wrapped.

Summer flowers — rose geranium, elderflowers, rose petals and lavender — bring their subtle flavours to ices and sorbets. Or, discover the unusual tastes that bay and rosemary bring to sweet iced desserts. Add an exotic touch with lemon grass, or a taste of India with cardamoms. As coolers in summer or for refreshers in winter, here are some new and exciting ideas for you to enjoy.

Ices and Sorbets

STRAWBERRY AND LAVENDER SORBET

DELICATELY PERFUMED WITH JUST A HINT OF LAVENDER, THIS DELIGHTFUL, PASTEL PINK SORBET IS PERFECT FOR A SPECIAL-OCCASION DINNER.

SERVES SIX

INGREDIENTS

   150g/5oz/¾ cup caster (superfine)
     sugar
   300ml/½ pint/1¼ cups water
   6 fresh lavender flowers
   500g/1¼lb/5 cups strawberries,
     hulled
   1 egg white
   lavender flowers, to decorate

1 Put the sugar and measured water into a pan and bring to the boil, stirring constantly until the sugar has completely dissolved.

2 Take the pan off the heat, add the lavender flowers and leave to infuse (steep) for 1 hour. If time permits, chill the syrup before using.

3 Purée the strawberries in a food processor or in batches in a blender, then press the purée (paste) through a large sieve into a bowl.

4 By hand: Spoon the purée into a plastic tub or similar freezerproof container, strain in the lavender syrup and freeze for 4 hours, or until the mixture is mushy.
Using an ice cream maker: Pour the strawberry purée into the bowl of an ice cream maker and strain in the lavender syrup. Churn for 20 minutes, or until the mixture is thick.

5 Whisk the egg white until it has just turned frothy.
By hand: Scoop the sorbet from the tub into a food processor, process it until smooth, then add the egg white. Spoon the sorbet back into the tub and freeze for 4 hours, or until firm.
Using an ice cream maker: Add the egg white to the ice cream maker and continue to churn until the sorbet is firm enough to scoop.

6 Serve the sorbet in scoops, decorated with lavender flowers.

COOK'S TIP
The size of the lavender flowers may vary; if they are very small you may need to use eight instead of six. To double check, taste a little of the cooled lavender syrup. If you think the flavour is a little mild, add 2–3 more flowers, reheat and cool again before using.

KULFI WITH CARDAMOM

THIS FAMOUS INDIAN ICE CREAM IS TRADITIONALLY MADE BY SLOWLY BOILING MILK UNTIL IT HAS REDUCED TO ABOUT ONE-THIRD OF THE ORIGINAL QUANTITY. CARDAMOMS ARE SIMMERED WITH THE MILK SO THAT IT IS INFUSED WITH THEIR DELICATE, SPICY FLAVOUR.

SERVES FOUR

INGREDIENTS
    1.5 litres/2½ pints/6¼ cups full-fat
      (whole) milk
    3 cardamom pods
    25g/1oz/2 tbsp caster (superfine)
      sugar
    50g/2oz/⅓ cup pistachio
      nuts, skinned
    a few pink rose petals from an
      unsprayed rose, to decorate

1 Pour the milk into a large pan. Bring to the boil, lower the heat and simmer gently for 1 hour, stirring occasionally.

2 Put the cardamom pods in a mortar and crush them with a pestle. Add the pods and the seeds to the hot milk in the pan and continue to simmer the milk for 1–1½ hours, or until the volume of milk has reduced to about 475ml/16fl oz/2 cups.

3 Strain the flavoured milk into a jug (pitcher) or bowl, stir in the caster sugar and then leave to cool.

4 Grind half the skinned pistachio nuts to a smooth powder in a blender, nut grinder or cleaned coffee grinder. Cut the remaining nuts into thin slivers and set them aside for the decoration. Stir the ground pistachio nuts into the milk mixture.

5 Pour the milk mixture into four kulfi moulds. Freeze overnight until the kulfi is firm.

6 To unmould the kulfi, half-fill a plastic container or bowl with very hot water, stand the moulds in the water and count to ten. Immediately lift out the moulds and invert them on a baking sheet.

7 Transfer the ice creams to a platter or individual plates, cut a cross in the top of each and strew the sliced pistachios and rose petals around. Serve at once.

COOK'S TIPS
• Stay in the kitchen while the milk is simmering, so that you can control the heat to keep the milk gently bubbling without boiling over.
• If you don't have any kulfi moulds, use lolly moulds without the tops or even disposable plastic cups. If the ices won't turn out, dip a cloth in very hot water, wring it out and place it on the tops of the moulds, or plunge the moulds back into hot water for a few seconds.

ROSEMARY ICE CREAM

FRESH ROSEMARY HAS A LOVELY FRAGRANCE THAT WORKS AS WELL IN SWEET DISHES AS IT DOES IN SAVOURY. SERVE THIS ICE CREAM AS AN ACCOMPANIMENT TO SOFT FRUIT OR PLUM COMPOTE, OR ON ITS OWN, WITH AMARETTI OR RATAFIA BISCUITS.

2 Remove the rosemary sprigs from the milk, then return the pan to the heat and bring the milk almost to the boil. Pour it over the egg yolk mixture in the bowl, stirring well.

3 Return the mixture to the pan and cook it over a very gentle heat, stirring constantly until the custard thickens. Do not let it boil or the mixture may curdle.

4 Strain the custard through a sieve into a bowl. Cover the surface closely with greaseproof (waxed) paper and leave to cool. Chill until very cold, then stir in the crème fraîche.

5 By hand: Pour the mixture into a freezerproof container. Freeze for about 6 hours, beating twice using a fork, a whisk or a food processor to break up the ice crystals. Freeze until firm.
Using an ice cream maker: Churn the mixture in an ice cream maker until it is thick, then scrape it into a tub or similar freezerproof container. Freeze until ready to serve.

6 Transfer the ice cream to the refrigerator 30 minutes before serving so that it softens. Scoop into dessert dishes, sprinkle lightly with demerara sugar and decorate with rosemary sprigs and herb flowers. Offer amaretti or ratafia biscuits, if you like.

COOK'S TIP
A mixture of rosemary, lavender and chive flowers would look very attractive for the decoration.

SERVES SIX

INGREDIENTS
300ml/½ pint/1¼ cups milk
4 large fresh rosemary sprigs
3 egg yolks
75g/3oz/6 tbsp caster (superfine) sugar
10ml/2 tsp cornflour (cornstarch)
400ml/14fl oz/1⅔ cups crème fraîche
about 15ml/1 tbsp demerara (raw) sugar
fresh rosemary sprigs and herb flowers, to decorate
amaretti or ratafia biscuits (almond macaroons), to serve (optional)

1 Put the milk and rosemary sprigs in a heavy pan. Bring almost to the boil, then remove from the heat and leave to infuse (steep) for 20 minutes. Whisk the egg yolks in a bowl with the sugar and cornflour.

LAVENDER AND HONEY ICE CREAM

HONEY AND LAVENDER MAKE A MEMORABLE PARTNERSHIP IN THIS OLD-FASHIONED ICE CREAM. SERVE SCOOPED INTO GLASSES OR SET IN LITTLE MOULDS AND TOP WITH LIGHTLY WHIPPED CREAM.

SERVES SIX TO EIGHT

INGREDIENTS
   90ml/6 tbsp clear honey
   4 egg yolks
   10ml/2 tsp cornflour (cornstarch)
   8 lavender spikes, plus extra,
    to decorate
   450ml/¾ pint/scant 2 cups milk
   450ml/¾ pint/scant 2 cups whipping
    cream
   dessert biscuits (cookies), to serve

1 Put the honey in a bowl together with the egg yolks and cornflour. Pull the lavender flowers from the spikes and add them to the mixture in the bowl with a little of the milk. Whisk lightly to combine the ingredients.

2 Pour the remaining milk into a heavy pan and bring it to the boil. Pour it over the egg yolk mixture in the bowl, stirring well with a wooden spoon as you pour.

3 Return the custard mixture to the pan and cook it very gently, stirring constantly with the wooden spoon until the mixture thickens. Do not let it boil or it may curdle.

4 Pour the custard into a bowl, cover the surface closely with greaseproof (waxed) paper. Cool, then chill.

5 By hand: Whip the cream until it is thickened but still falls from the whisk, and stir into the custard. Transfer to a freezerproof container. Freeze for about 6 hours, beating twice using a fork, a whisk or a food processor to break up the ice crystals. Freeze until firm.
Using an ice cream maker: Stir the cream into the custard, then churn the mixture in an ice cream maker until it holds its shape. Transfer to a tub or similar freezerproof container and freeze until ready to serve.

6 Transfer the ice cream to the refrigerator 30 minutes before serving, so that it softens slightly. Scoop into small dishes, decorate with lavender flowers and serve with dessert biscuits.

LEMON AND CARDAMOM ICE CREAM

*THE CLASSIC PARTNERSHIP OF LEMON AND CARDAMOM GIVES THIS RICH ICE CREAM A LOVELY TANG.
IT IS PERFECT AFTER A SPICY MAIN COURSE.*

SERVES SIX

INGREDIENTS

15ml/1 tbsp cardamom pods
4 egg yolks
115g/4oz/generous ½ cup caster
  (superfine) sugar
10ml/2 tsp cornflour (cornstarch)
finely grated (shredded) rind and
  juice of 3 lemons
300ml/½ pint/1¼ cups milk
300ml/½ pint/1¼ cups whipping
  cream
fresh lemon balm sprigs and
  icing (confectioners') sugar,
  to decorate (optional)

1 Put the cardamom pods in a mortar
and crush them with a pestle to release
the seeds. Pick out and discard the
shells, then grind the seeds to break
them up slightly.

2 Put the yolks, sugar, cornflour, lemon
rind and juice in a bowl. Add the
cardamom seeds and whisk.

3 Bring the milk to the boil in a heavy
pan, then pour it over the egg yolk and
cardamom mixture in the bowl, stirring.

4 Return the mixture to the pan and
cook over a very gentle heat, stirring
constantly with a wooden spoon until
the custard thickens. Do not allow it to
boil or it may start to curdle.

5 Pour the custard into a bowl, cover
the surface with greaseproof (waxed)
paper and leave to cool. Chill in the
refrigerator until it is very cold.

6 By hand: Whip the cream until it has
thickened but still falls from the whisk,
and then stir into the custard. Transfer
to a freezerproof container. Freeze for
about 6 hours, beating twice, either
using a fork or whisk or in a food
processor, to break up the ice crystals.
Freeze until firm.

Using an ice cream maker: Whisk the
cream lightly into the chilled custard,
then churn the mixture in an ice cream
maker until it holds its shape. Transfer
to a plastic tub or similar freezerproof
container and freeze the ice cream
until needed.

7 Transfer the ice cream to the
refrigerator 30 minutes before serving.
Scoop into glasses. Decorate with the
sprigs of lemon balm, dusted with icing
sugar, if you like.

CASHEW AND ORANGE FLOWER ICE CREAM

A CASHEW-NUT CREAM FORMS THE BASIS OF THIS DELICIOUS ICE CREAM, DELICATELY PERFUMED WITH ORANGE FLOWER WATER AND ORANGE RIND. IT EVOKES IMAGES OF ALL KINDS OF DESSERTS THAT ARE POPULAR IN THE MIDDLE EAST.

SERVES FOUR TO SIX

INGREDIENTS

4 egg yolks
75g/3oz/6 tbsp caster (superfine) sugar
5ml/1 tsp cornflour (cornstarch)
300ml/½ pint/1¼ cups semi-skimmed (low-fat) milk
150g/5oz/scant 1 cup cashew nuts
300ml/½ pint/1¼ cups whipping cream
15ml/1 tbsp orange flower water
grated (shredded) rind of ½ orange, plus curls of thinly pared orange rind, to decorate

1 Whisk the egg yolks, sugar and cornflour in a bowl until the mixture is thick and foamy. Pour the milk into a heavy pan, bring it to the boil, then gradually whisk it into the yolk mixture.

2 Return the mixture to the pan and cook over a gentle heat, stirring constantly until the custard thickens and is smooth. Do not let it boil or it may curdle. Pour it back into the bowl. Leave to cool, then chill.

COOK'S TIPS
• For a more intense flavour, roast the cashew nuts under the grill (broiler) or dry-fry before chopping them.
• To curl the thinly pared orange rind, wrap each strip in turn around a cocktail stick and leave it for a minute or two.

3 Very finely chop the cashew nuts. Heat the cream in a small pan. When it boils, stir in the nuts. Leave to cool.

4 Stir the orange flower water and grated orange rind into the chilled custard. Process the nut cream in a food processor or blender until it forms a fine paste, then stir it into the orange custard mixture.

5 By hand: Pour the mixture into a freezerproof container and freeze for 6 hours, beating twice with a fork, a whisk or an electric mixer to break up the ice crystals.
Using an ice cream maker: Churn the mixture until it is firm enough to scoop.

6 Scoop the ice cream into dishes and decorate with orange rind curls.

ROSE GERANIUM MARQUISE

THIS DESSERT MAKES A GOOD CHOICE FOR A DINNER PARTY AS IT CAN BE MADE IN ADVANCE. ROSE GERANIUM LEAVES GIVE THE ICE CREAM A DELICATE, SCENTED FLAVOUR IN THIS ELEGANT DESSERT.

SERVES EIGHT

INGREDIENTS
    225g/8oz/generous 1 cup caster
        (superfine) sugar
    400ml/14fl oz/1⅔ cups water
    24 fresh rose geranium leaves
    45ml/3 tbsp lemon juice
    250g/9oz/generous 1 cup mascarpone
        cheese
    300ml/½ pint/1¼ cups double
        (heavy) or whipping cream
    200g/7oz savoiardi or sponge
        finger biscuits (cookies)
    90g/3½oz/generous ½ cup almonds,
        finely chopped and toasted
    geranium flowers and icing
        (confectioners') sugar,
        to decorate

1 Put the sugar and water in a heavy pan and heat gently, stirring occasionally, until the sugar has dissolved completely.

2 Add the rose geranium leaves to the pan and cook gently for 2 minutes. Leave to cool.

COOK'S TIP
If you cannot get savoiardi biscuits, use ordinary sponge finger biscuits instead. These tend to be smaller, though, so you will need to adjust the size of the rectangle accordingly.

3 Strain the cooled geranium syrup into a measuring jug (pitcher) and then stir in the lemon juice.

4 Put the mascarpone in a bowl and beat it until it has softened. Gradually beat in 150ml/¼ pint/⅔ cup of the syrup mixture.

5 Whip the cream until it forms peaks, then fold it into the mascarpone and syrup mixture. At this stage the mixture should hold its shape. If necessary, whip the mixture a little more.

6 Spoon a little of the mixture on to a flat, freezerproof serving plate and spread it out with a palette knife (metal spatula) to a 21 × 12cm/8½ × 4½in rectangle.

7 Pour the remaining geranium syrup into a shallow bowl. Dip a savoiardi or sponge finger biscuit into the syrup until it is moist but not disintegrating. Place on to the rectangle. Repeat with a third of the biscuits to cover the rectangle completely.

8 Spread another thin layer of the cream mixture over the biscuits. Set aside 15ml/1 tbsp of the nuts for the topping. Scatter half the remainder over the cream.

9 Make another two layers of the syrup-steeped biscuits, sandwiching them with more of the cream mixture and the remaining nuts, but leaving enough cream mixture to coat the dessert completely.

10 Spread the remaining cream mixture over the top and sides of the cake until it is evenly coated. Sprinkle with the reserved nuts. Freeze it for at least 5 hours or overnight.

11 Transfer the marquise to the refrigerator for 30 minutes before serving, so that it softens slightly. Scatter with geranium flowers, dust with icing sugar, and serve in slices.

VARIATION
If you prefer, use other kinds of nuts instead of the almonds used here. Macadamia nuts and walnuts would both work well.

LYCHEE AND ELDERFLOWER SORBET

THE MUSCAT FLAVOUR OF ELDERFLOWERS IS WONDERFUL WITH SCENTED LYCHEES. SERVE THIS SOPHISTICATED SORBET AFTER A RICH MAIN COURSE.

<u>SERVES FOUR</u>

INGREDIENTS
175g/6oz/scant 1 cup caster (superfine) sugar
400ml/14fl oz/1⅔ cups water
500g/1¼lb fresh lychees, peeled and pitted
15ml/1 tbsp elderflower cordial
dessert biscuits (cookies), to serve

COOK'S TIPS
• Switch the freezer to the coldest setting before making the sorbet – the faster the mixture freezes, the smaller the ice crystals and the better the texture.
• Use a metal freezerproof container for best results.

1 Place the sugar and water in a pan and heat gently until the sugar has dissolved. Increase the heat and boil for 5 minutes, then add the lychees. Lower the heat and simmer for 7 minutes. Remove from the heat and allow to cool.

2 Purée the fruit and syrup in a food processor or blender, then press as much as you can through a sieve into a bowl.

3 By hand: Stir the elderflower cordial into the purée (paste), pour into a freezerproof container. Freeze for 2 hours, or until crystals form around the edge. Process briefly in a food processor or blender to break up the crystals. Repeat twice, then freeze until firm.
Using an ice cream maker: Pour the elderflower cordial and the purée into an ice cream maker. Churn until the sorbet is firm enough to scoop.

4 Transfer to the refrigerator for 10 minutes to soften. Serve with biscuits.

COCONUT <u>AND</u> LEMON GRASS ICE CREAM <u>WITH</u> LIME SYRUP

LEMON GRASS, A VERSATILE FLAVOURING WHICH IS WIDELY USED IN ASIAN COOKERY, MELDS WITH LIME TO ADD AN EXOTIC FRAGRANCE TO ICE CREAM. IF YOU CANNOT GET FRESH LEMON GRASS STALKS, USE THE DRIED STALKS THAT COME IN JARS.

2 Whisk the egg yolks in a bowl with the sugar and cornflour until smooth. Gradually pour the coconut and lemon grass milk over the mixture, whisking well. Return the mixture to the pan and heat very gently, stirring until the custard starts to thicken. Do not let it boil or it may curdle.

3 Remove the custard from the heat and strain it into a clean bowl. Cover with a circle of dampened greaseproof (waxed) paper to prevent a skin forming. Leave to cool.

4 By hand: Whip the cream until it has thickened but still falls from the whisk, and stir into the custard with the lime rind. Transfer the mixture to a freezerproof container and freeze for 2 hours. Remove from the freezer and beat using a fork, a whisk or a food processor to break up the ice crystals. Freeze for another 2 hours then beat the mixture again.
Using an ice cream maker: Stir the cream and lime rind into the cooled custard. Churn.

5 Spoon the mixture into five or six dariole moulds. Freeze for at least 3 hours.

6 Meanwhile, make the lime syrup. Heat the sugar and water in a small, heavy pan until the sugar dissolves. Bring to the boil and allow to boil for 5 minutes without stirring. Reduce the heat, add the thinly sliced lime and the lime juice and simmer the syrup gently for 5 minutes more. Leave to cool.

7 To serve, loosen the edges of the dariole moulds with a knife. Dip them in very hot water for 2 seconds then turn out the ice creams on to dessert plates. Serve with the lime syrup and the lime slices spooned around.

SERVES FIVE TO SIX

INGREDIENTS
    4 lemon grass stalks
    400ml/14fl oz/1⅔ cups coconut milk
    3 egg yolks
    90g/3½oz/½ cup caster (superfine) sugar
    10ml/2 tsp cornflour (cornstarch)
    150ml/¼ pint/⅔ cup whipping cream
    finely grated (shredded) rind of 1 lime
    lime slices, to decorate
For the lime syrup
    75g/3oz/6 tbsp caster (superfine) sugar
    75ml/5 tbsp water
    1 lime, very thinly sliced, plus
        30ml/2 tbsp lime juice

1 Cut the lemon grass stalks in half lengthways and bruise the stalks by tapping them with a rolling pin. Put them in a heavy pan, add the coconut milk and bring to just below boiling point. Remove from the heat and leave to infuse (steep) for 30 minutes, then remove the lemon grass.

BAY AND RATAFIA SLICE

THE WARM BUT DELICATE FLAVOUR OF BAY LEAVES COMBINES PARTICULARLY WELL WITH ALMOND FLAVOURS. SERVE THIS SUMPTUOUS SLICE WITH FRESH APRICOTS, PLUMS, PEACHES OR SOFT FRUITS. AN EXCELLENT DINNER-PARTY DESSERT THAT CAN BE MADE IN ADVANCE.

SERVES SIX

INGREDIENTS
    300ml/½ pint/1¼ cups milk
    4 fresh bay leaves
    4 egg yolks
    75g/3oz/6 tbsp caster (superfine)
      sugar
    10ml/2 tsp cornflour (cornstarch)
    150g/5oz ratafia (almond macaroons)
      or macaroon biscuits (cookies)
    300ml/½ pint/1¼ cups whipping
      cream

1 Put the milk in a pan, add the bay leaves and bring slowly to the boil. Remove from the heat and infuse (steep) for 30 minutes. Meanwhile, whisk the egg yolks in a bowl with the sugar and cornflour.

2 Strain the milk over the egg yolk mixture and stir well. Return to the pan and cook over a gentle heat, stirring constantly until the custard thickens. Do not let it boil or it may curdle. Transfer the custard to a bowl, cover closely with greaseproof (waxed) paper and leave to cool completely. Chill until very cold.

3 Crush the biscuits in a strong plastic bag, using a rolling pin.

4 By hand: Whip the cream until it has thickened but still falls from the whisk, and stir into the custard. Transfer to a freezerproof container. Freeze for about 4 hours, beating twice using a fork, a hand whisk or a food processor to break up the ice crystals. Stir in 50g/2oz of the crushed biscuits and freeze for a further 2 hours.
Using an ice cream maker: Add the cream to the custard and churn until it is very thick. Scrape it into a bowl and add 50g/2oz of the crushed biscuits. Return to the ice cream maker and churn for 2 minutes more.

5 Working quickly, spoon the ice cream on to a sheet of greaseproof paper, packing it into a log shape, about 5cm/2in thick and 25cm/10in long.

6 Bring the greaseproof paper up around the ice cream to pack it together tightly and give it a good shape. Support on a baking sheet and freeze for at least 3 hours or overnight.

7 Spread the remaining crushed biscuits on a sheet of greaseproof paper. Unwrap the ice cream log and roll it quickly in the crumbs until coated. Return to the freezer until needed. Serve in slices.

COOK'S TIP
If the ice cream is not firm enough to roll, freeze for a couple of hours more.

GOOSEBERRY AND ELDERFLOWER SORBET

A CLASSIC COMBINATION THAT MAKES A REALLY REFRESHING SORBET. MAKE IT IN SUMMER, AS A STUNNING FINALE TO AN AL FRESCO MEAL, OR SAVE IT FOR SERVING AFTER A HEARTY WINTER STEW.

SERVES SIX

INGREDIENTS
- 150g/5oz/¾ cup caster (superfine) sugar
- 175ml/6fl oz/¾ cup water
- 10 elderflower heads
- 500g/1¼lb/5 cups gooseberries
- 200ml/7fl oz/scant 1 cup apple juice
- dash of green food colouring (optional)
- a little beaten egg white and caster (superfine) sugar, to decorate the glasses
- elderflowers, to decorate

1 Put 30ml/2 tbsp of the sugar in a pan with 30ml/2 tbsp of the water. Set aside. Mix the remaining sugar and water in a separate, heavy pan. Heat them gently, stirring occasionally, until dissolved. Bring to the boil and boil for 1 minute, without stirring, to make a syrup.

2 Remove from the heat and add the elderflower heads, pressing them into the syrup with a wooden spoon. Leave to infuse (steep) for about 1 hour.

3 Strain the elderflower syrup through a sieve placed over a bowl. Set the syrup aside. Add the gooseberries to the pan containing the reserved sugar and water. Cover and cook very gently for about 5 minutes until the gooseberries have softened and the juices have started to run.

COOK'S TIP
Elderflowers can only be picked for a very short time. At other times, use 90ml/6 tbsp elderflower cordial.

4 Tip the mixture into a food processor and add the apple juice. Process until smooth, then press the purée (paste) through a sieve into a bowl. Leave to cool. Stir in the elderflower syrup, with a dash of green food colouring, if you like. Chill until very cold.

5 By hand: Pour into a freezerproof container. Freeze for 2 hours, or until crystals start to form around the edges. Process briefly in a food processor or blender to break up the crystals. Repeat twice more, then freeze until firm.
Using an ice cream maker: Churn the mixture until it holds its shape. Scrape it into a freezer container and freeze for several hours or overnight, until firm.

6 To decorate the glasses, put a little egg white in a bowl. Spread out the caster sugar on a plate. Dip the rim of each glass in the egg white, then into the sugar. Allow to dry for a few minutes. Soften the sorbet in the refrigerator and serve, decorated with elderflowers.

ROSE-PETAL SORBET DECORATED WITH SUGARED ROSE PETALS

THIS SORBET MAKES A WONDERFUL END TO A SUMMER MEAL WITH ITS FABULOUS FLAVOUR OF ROSES. REMEMBER TO USE THE MOST SCENTED VARIETY YOU CAN FIND IN THE GARDEN. PICK FRESH BLOOMS WHICH ARE NEWLY OPENED, IDEALLY IN THE LATE MORNING, BEFORE THE HEAT OF THE DAY EVAPORATES THE ESSENTIAL OILS.

SERVES FOUR TO SIX

INGREDIENTS
  115g/4oz/generous ½ cup caster (superfine) sugar
  300ml/½ pint/1¼ cups boiling water
  petals of 3 large, scented red or deep-pink roses from an unsprayed rose, white ends of petals removed
  juice of 2 lemons
  300ml/½ pint/1¼ cups rosé wine
  whole crystallized roses or rose petals, to decorate

1 Place the sugar in a bowl and add the boiling water. Stir until the sugar has completely dissolved. Add the rose petals and leave to cool completely.

COOK'S TIPS
• If the sorbet is too hard, transfer it to the refrigerator for about 30 minutes before you are ready to serve.
• For a stunning presentation idea, scoop the sorbet into a rose ice bowl. The bowl and sorbet can be left in the freezer until they are needed.

2 Blend the mixture in a food processor, then strain through a sieve. Add the lemon juice and wine.

3 By hand: Pour into a freezerproof container. Freeze for several hours, or until ice crystals form around the edges. Whisk or use a food processor to break up the crystals. Re-freeze until frozen around the edges. Repeat the whisking and freezing process once or twice more, until the sorbet is pale and smooth. Freeze until firm.
Using an ice cream maker: Churn until firm with a good texture.

4 Serve in scoops, decorated with crystallized roses or rose petals.

VARIATION
If you prefer, a yellow version of this dish can be made using yellow rose petals and white wine instead of rosé.

LEMON SORBET

THIS IS PROBABLY THE MOST CLASSIC SORBET OF ALL MADE WITH FRESH, JUICY LEMONS. REFRESHINGLY TANGY AND YET DELICIOUSLY SMOOTH, IT QUITE LITERALLY MELTS IN THE MOUTH.

SERVES SIX

INGREDIENTS
  200g/7oz/1 cup caster (superfine) sugar
  300ml/½ pint/1¼ cups water
  4 lemons, well scrubbed
  1 egg white
  sugared lemon rind, to decorate

1 Put the sugar and water into a pan and bring to the boil, stirring occasionally until the sugar dissolves.

2 Pare the rind thinly from two lemons so that it falls straight into the pan. Simmer for 2 minutes without stirring, then take the pan off the heat. Leave to cool, then chill.

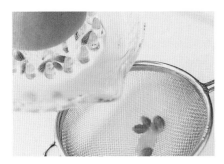

3 Squeeze the juice from all the lemons and add it to the syrup.
By hand: Strain the syrup into a shallow freezerproof container, reserving the rind. Freeze the mixture for 4 hours until it is mushy.
Using an ice cream maker: Strain the syrup and lemon juice, and churn the mixture until thick.

4 By hand: Scoop the sorbet into a food processor and beat it until smooth. Lightly whisk the egg white with a fork until it is just frothy. Spoon the sorbet back into the tub, beat in the egg white and return the mixture to the freezer for 4 hours.
Using an ice cream maker: Add the egg white to the mixture and continue to churn for 10–15 minutes, or until firm enough to scoop.

5 Scoop into bowls or glasses and decorate with sugared lemon rind.

COOK'S TIP
Cut the top off a lemon and retain as a lid. Squeeze the juice out of the larger portion. Remove any membrane and use the shell as a container. Scoop sorbet into the shell, top with the lid and add lemon leaves or small bay leaves. Allow one lemon for each person.

VARIATION
Sorbet can be made from any citrus fruit. As a guide you will need 300ml/½ pint/ 1¼ cups fresh fruit juice and the pared rind of half the squeezed fruit. Use 4 oranges or 2 oranges and 2 lemons, or, for a grapefruit sorbet, use the rind of 1 ruby grapefruit and the juice of 2. For lime sorbet, combine the rind of 3 limes with the juice of 6.

MINT ICE CREAM

THIS REFRESHING AND INVIGORATING FRESH MINT ICE CREAM WILL BE DELICIOUSLY COOLING ON A HOT SUMMER'S DAY.

SERVES EIGHT

INGREDIENTS

    8 egg yolks
    75g/3oz/6 tbsp caster (superfine) sugar
    600ml/1 pint/2½ cups single (light)
    cream
    1 vanilla pod (bean)
    60ml/4 tbsp chopped fresh mint
    mint sprigs, to decorate

1 Beat the egg yolks and sugar until pale and light. Transfer to a small pan.

2 In a separate pan, bring the cream to the boil with the vanilla pod.

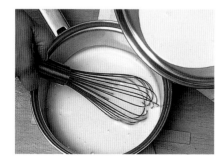

3 Remove the vanilla pod and pour on to the egg mixture, whisking briskly.

4 Continue whisking to ensure the eggs are mixed into the cream, then gently heat the mixture until the custard thickens enough to coat the back of a wooden spoon. Leave to cool.

5 By hand: Stir in the mint, then transfer to a freezerproof container. Freeze until the mixture is mushy then beat using a fork, a whisk or a food processor to break up the ice crystals. Freeze for another 3 hours, or until it is softly frozen, then whisk again. Finally, freeze until the ice cream is firm (this will take at least 6 hours).

Using an ice cream maker: Stir in the mint and churn in an ice cream maker until firm.

6 Transfer to the refrigerator for 20 minutes before serving, so that it will soften a little. Decorate with mint sprigs.

CLASSIC VANILLA ICE CREAM

NOTHING BEATS THE CREAMY SIMPLICITY OF TRUE VANILLA ICE CREAM. VANILLA PODS ARE EXPENSIVE, BUT WELL WORTH BUYING FOR THE SUPERB FLAVOUR THEY IMPART.

SERVES FOUR

INGREDIENTS

1 vanilla pod (bean)
300ml/½ pint/1¼ cups semi-skimmed (low-fat) milk
4 egg yolks
75g/3oz/6 tbsp caster (superfine) sugar
5ml/1 tsp cornflour (cornstarch)
300ml/½ pint/1¼ cups double (heavy) cream

3 Whisk the egg yolks, sugar and cornflour in a bowl until the mixture is thick and foamy. Gradually pour on the hot milk, whisking constantly. Return the mixture to the pan and cook over a gentle heat, stirring all the time.

4 When the custard thickens and is smooth, pour it back into the bowl. Cool it, then chill.

5 By hand: Whip the cream until it has thickened. Fold it into the custard, and pour into a plastic tub or freezerproof container. Freeze for 6 hours, or until firm enough to scoop, beating twice with a fork, or in a food processor.
Using an ice cream maker: Stir the cream into the custard and churn the mixture until thick.

6 Scoop the ice cream into dishes, bowls or bought cones.

1 Using a small knife, slit the vanilla pod lengthways. Pour the milk into a heavy pan, add the vanilla pod and bring to the boil. Remove from the heat and leave for 15 minutes to allow the flavours to infuse (steep).

2 Lift the vanilla pod up. Holding it over the pan, scrape the black seeds out of the pod with a small knife so that they fall back into the milk. Set the vanilla pod aside and bring the milk back to the boil.

COOK'S TIP
Don't throw the vanilla pod away after use. Instead, rinse it in cold water, dry and store in the sugar jar. After a week or so the sugar will take on the wonderful aroma and flavour of the vanilla and will be delicious sprinkled over summer fruits. Use it to sweeten whipped cream, custard, biscuits (cookies) and shortbread.

CINNAMON <u>AND</u> COFFEE PARFAIT

THIS FRENCH-STYLE ICE CREAM IS FLECKED WITH CINNAMON AND MIXED WITH JUST A HINT OF COFFEE. AS IT IS MADE WITH A BOILING SUGAR SYRUP IT DOESN'T REQUIRE BEATING DURING FREEZING, SO CAN BE POURED STRAIGHT INTO FREEZERPROOF SERVING DISHES.

SERVES SIX

INGREDIENTS
 15ml/1 tbsp instant coffee granules
 30ml/2 tbsp boiling water
 7.5ml/1½ tsp ground cinnamon
 4 egg yolks
 115g/4oz/generous ½ cup granulated
  sugar
 120ml/4fl oz/½ cup cold water
 300ml/½ pint/1¼ cups double
  (heavy) cream, lightly whipped
 200g/7oz/scant 1 cup crème fraîche
 extra ground cinnamon, to decorate

1 Spoon the coffee into a heatproof bowl, stir in the boiling water until dissolved, then stir in the cinnamon. Put the egg yolks in a large, heatproof bowl and whisk them lightly until frothy. Bring a medium pan of water to the boil and lower the heat so that it simmers gently.

2 Put the sugar in a small pan, add the cold water and heat gently, stirring occasionally, until the sugar has completely dissolved.

3 Increase the heat and boil for 4–5 minutes without stirring until the syrup registers 115°C/239°F on a sugar thermometer. Alternatively, test by dropping a little of the syrup into a cup of cold water. Pour the water away. If the syrup can be moulded to a soft ball, it is ready.

4 Put the bowl of egg yolks over the pan of simmering water and whisk in the sugar syrup. Whisk until the mixture is very thick and then remove from the heat. Continue whisking until it is cool.

5 Whisk the coffee and cinnamon into the yolk mixture, then fold in the cream and crème fraîche. Pour into a tub or individual freezerproof glass dishes. Freeze for 4 hours, or until firm. If frozen in a tub, scoop into bowls and decorate with a dusting of cinnamon.

COOK'S TIP
Test the syrup regularly. When it is nearly ready the syrup will fall slowly from the spoon. If the syrup fails to form a ball when tested in cold water, boil it for a few minutes more; if the syrup forms strands that snap it is overdone and you must start again.

GINGERED SEMI-FREDDO

THIS ICE CREAM IS LUXURIOUSLY CREAMY AND GENEROUSLY SPECKLED WITH CHOPPED STEM GINGER.
SEMI-FREDDO IS AN ITALIAN SEMI-FROZEN ICE CREAM THAT IS NEVER BEATEN DURING FREEZING. IT
WILL STAY SOFT WHEN FROZEN.

SERVES SIX

INGREDIENTS
- 4 egg yolks
- 115g/4oz/generous ½ cup caster (superfine) sugar
- 120ml/4fl oz/½ cup cold water
- 300ml/½ pint/1¼ cups double (heavy) cream
- 115g/4oz/⅔ cup drained stem (crystallized) ginger, finely chopped, plus extra slices, to decorate
- 45ml/3 tbsp whisky (optional)

1 Put the egg yolks in a large, heatproof bowl and whisk until frothy. Bring a pan of water to the boil and simmer gently.

2 Mix the sugar and measured cold water in a pan and heat gently, stirring occasionally, until the sugar has completely dissolved.

3 Increase the heat and boil for 4–5 minutes without stirring until the syrup registers 115°C/239°F on a sugar thermometer. Alternatively, test by dropping a little of the syrup into a cup of cold water. Pour the water away. You should be able to mould the syrup into a ball.

4 Put the bowl of egg yolks over the pan of simmering water and whisk in the sugar syrup. Continue whisking until the mixture is very thick. Remove from the heat and whisk until cool.

5 Whip the cream and lightly fold it into the yolk mixture, with the chopped ginger and whisky, if using. Pour into a plastic tub or similar freezerproof container and freeze for 1 hour.

6 Stir the semi-freddo to bring any ginger that has sunk to the bottom of the tub to the top, then return to the freezer for 5–6 hours, or until firm. Scoop into dishes or chocolate cases (see Cook's Tip). Decorate with slices of ginger.

COOK'S TIP
Semi-freddo looks wonderful in chocolate cases, made by spreading melted chocolate over squares of non-stick baking paper and then draping them over upturned tumblers. Peel the paper off when the chocolate has set and turn the cases the right way up before filling.

CHOCOLATE DOUBLE MINT

FULL OF BODY AND FLAVOUR, THIS CREAMY, SMOOTH ICE CREAM COMBINES THE SOPHISTICATION OF DARK CHOCOLATE WITH THE SATISFYING COOLNESS OF FRESH CHOPPED MINT. CRUSHED PEPPERMINTS PROVIDE EXTRA CRUNCH.

SERVES FOUR

INGREDIENTS
  4 egg yolks
  75g/3oz/6 tbsp caster (superfine)
    sugar
  5ml/1 tsp cornflour (cornstarch)
  300ml/½ pint/1¼ cups semi-skimmed
    (low-fat) milk
  200g/7oz dark (bittersweet)
    chocolate, broken into squares
  40g/1½oz/¼ cup peppermints
  60ml/4 tbsp chopped fresh mint
  300ml/½ pint/1¼ cups whipping
    cream
  sprigs of fresh mint dusted with icing
    (confectioners') sugar, to decorate

1 Put the egg yolks, sugar and cornflour in a bowl and whisk until thick and foamy. Pour the milk into a heavy pan, bring to the boil, then gradually whisk into the yolk mixture.

2 Scrape the mixture back into the pan and cook over a gentle heat, stirring constantly until the custard thickens and is smooth. Scrape it back into the bowl, add the chocolate, a little at a time, and stir until melted. Cool, then chill.

COOK'S TIP
If you freeze the ice cream in a tub, don't beat it in a food processor when breaking up the ice crystals or the crunchy texture of the crushed peppermints will be lost.

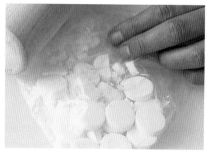

3 Put the peppermints in a strong plastic bag and crush them with a rolling pin. Stir them into the custard with the chopped mint.

4 By hand: Whip the cream until it has thickened, but is still soft enough to fall from a spoon. Fold it into the custard, scrape the mixture into a plastic tub or similar freezerproof container and freeze for 6–7 hours, beating once or twice with a fork or electric whisk to break up the ice crystals.
Using an ice cream maker: Mix the custard and cream together and churn the mixture until firm enough to scoop.

5 Serve the ice cream in scoops and then decorate with mint sprigs dusted with sifted icing sugar.

MAPLE AND WALNUT MERINGUE GATEAU

RICH WALNUTS AND SWEET MAPLE SYRUP ARE GREAT PARTNERS AND GO PARTICULARLY WELL WITH PALE-GOLDEN MERINGUE. THIS ICED DESSERT IS A FEAST FOR ALL MERINGUE LOVERS.

SERVES TEN TO TWELVE

INGREDIENTS
4 egg whites
200g/7oz/scant 1 cup light muscovado (molasses) sugar
150g/5oz/1¼ cups walnut pieces
600ml/1 pint/2½ cups double (heavy) cream
150ml/¼ pint/⅔ cup maple syrup, plus extra, to serve

1 Preheat the oven to 140°C/275°F/ Gas 1. Draw three 23cm/9in circles on separate sheets of non-stick baking parchment. Invert the sheets on three baking sheets. Whisk the egg whites in a grease-free bowl until stiff.

2 Whisk in the sugar, about 15ml/1 tbsp at a time, whisking well after each addition until the meringue is stiff and glossy. Spread to within 1cm/½in of the edge of each marked circle. Bake for about 1 hour or until crisp, swapping the baking sheets around halfway through cooking. Leave to cool.

3 Set aside 45ml/3 tbsp of the walnuts. Finely chop the remainder. Whip the cream with the maple syrup until it forms soft peaks. Fold in the chopped walnuts. Use about a third of the mixture to sandwich the meringues together on a flat, freezerproof serving plate.

4 Using a palette knife (metal spatula), spread the remaining cream mixture over the top and sides of the gâteau. Sprinkle with the reserved walnuts and freeze overnight.

5 Transfer the gâteau to the refrigerator about 1 hour before serving so that the cream filling softens slightly. Drizzle over the top a little of the extra maple syrup, just before serving. Serve in slices.

INDEX